CCNA Security
Lab Manual
Version 2

Cisco Networking Academy

Cisco Press

800 East 96th Street

Indianapolis, Indiana 46240 USA

CCNA Security Lab Manual Version 2
Cisco Networking Academy

Copyright© 2016 Cisco Systems, Inc.

Published by:
Cisco Press
800 East 96th Street
Indianapolis, IN 46240 USA

Printed in the United States of America

2   17

Library of Congress Control Number: 2015953182

ISBN-13: 978-1-58713-350-3

ISBN-10: 1-58713-350-4

Instructor's Answer Key

ISBN-13: 978-0-13-439960-7

ISBN-10: 0-13-439960-9

Warning and Disclaimer

Trademark Acknowledgments

This book is part of the Cisco Networking Academy" series from Cisco Press. The products in this series support and complement the Cisco Networking Academy curriculum. If you are using this book outside the Networking Academy, theo you are not preparing with a Cisco trained and authorized Networking Academy provider.

For more information on the Cisco Networking Academy or to locate a Networking Academy, please visit www.cisoo.com/edu.

CISCO

Feedback Information

At Cisco Press, our goal is to create in-depth technical books of the highest quality and value. Each book is crafted with care and precision, undergoing rigorous development that involves the unique expertise of members from the professional technical community.

Readers' feedback is a natural continuation of this process. If you have any comments regarding how we could improve the quality of this book, or otherwise alter it to better suit your needs, you can contact us through email at feedback@ciscopress.com. Please make sure to include the book title and ISBN in your message.

We greatly appreciate your assistance.

Publisher	Paul Boger
Associate Publisher	Dave Dusthimer
Business Operations Manager, Cisco Press	Jan Cornelssen
Executive Editor	Mary Beth Ray
Managing Editor	Sandra Schroeder
Project Editor	Mandie Frank
Editorial Assistant	Vanessa Evans
Cover Designer	Mark Shirar
Proofreader	Laura Hernandez

CISCO

Americas Headquarters
Cisco Systems, Inc.
San Jose, CA

Asia Pacific Headquarters
Cisco Systems (USA) Pte. Ltd.
Singapore

Europe Headquarters
Cisco Systems International BV
Amsterdam, The Netherlands

Cisco has more than 200 offices worldwide. Addresses, phone numbers, and fax numbers are listed on the Cisco Website at **www.cisco.com/go/offices.**

CCDE, CCENT, Cisco Eos, Cisco HealthPresence, the Cisco logo, Cisco Lumin, Cisco Nexus, Cisco StadiumVision, Cisco TelePresence, Cisco WebEx, DCE, and Welcome to the Human Network are trademarks; Changing the Way We Work, Live, Play, and Learn and Cisco Store are service marks; and Access Registrar, Aironet, AsyncOS, Bringing the Meeting To You, Catalyst, CCDA, CCDP, CCIE, CCIP, CCNA, CCNP, CCSP, CCVP, Cisco, the Cisco Certified Internetwork Expert logo, Cisco IOS, Cisco Press, Cisco Systems, Cisco Systems Capital, the Cisco Systems logo, Cisco Unity, Collaboration Without Limitation, EtherFast, EtherSwitch, Event Center, Fast Step, Follow Me Browsing, FormShare, GigaDrive, HomeLink, Internet Quotient, IOS, iPhone, iQuick Study, IronPort, the IronPort logo, LightStream, Linksys, MediaTone, MeetingPlace, MeetingPlace Chime Sound, MGX, Networkers, Networking Academy, Network Registrar, PCNow, PIX, PowerPanels, ProConnect, ScriptShare, SenderBase, SMARTnet, Spectrum Expert, StackWise, The Fastest Way to Increase Your Internet Quotient, TransPath, WebEx, and the WebEx logo are registered trademarks of Cisco Systems, Inc. and/or its affiliates in the United States and certain other countries.

All other trademarks mentioned in this document or website are the property of their respective owners. The use of the word partner does not imply a partnership relationship between Cisco and any other company. (0812R)

Contents

Chapter 1: Modern Network Security Threats

Lab 1.2.4.12 - Social Engineering...1
Lab 1.4.1.1 - Researching Network Attacks and Security Audit Tools.............................3

Chapter 2: Securing Network Devices

Lab 2.6.1.2 - Securing the Router for Administrative Access....................................7

Chapter 3: Authentication, Authorization, and Accounting

Lab 3.6.1.1 - Securing Administrative Access Using AAA and RADIUS.........................45

Chapter 4: Implementing Firewall Technologies

Lab 4.4.1.2 - Configuring Zone-Based Policy Firewalls 65

Chapter 5: Implementing Intrusion Prevention

Lab 5.4.1.1 - Configure an Intrusion Prevention System (IPS)...................................78

Chapter 6: Securing the Local Area Network

Lab 6.3.1.1 - Securing Layer 2 Switches...99

Chapter 7: Cryptographic Systems

Lab 7.5.1.2 - Exploring Encryption Methods...122

Chapter 8: Implementing Virtual Private Networks

Lab 8.4.1.3 - Configure Site-to-Site VPN using CLI..127

Chapter 9: Implementing the Cisco Adaptive Security Appliance

Lab 9.3.1.2 - Configure ASA Basic Settings and Firewall Using CLI............................143

Chapter 10: Advanced Cisco Adaptive Security Appliance

Lab A 10.1.4.8 - Configure ASA Basic Settings and Firewall Using ASDM 169
Lab B 10.2.1.9 - Configure a Site-to-Site IPsec VPN Using ISR CLI and ASA ASDM...........208
Lab C 10.3.1.1 - Configure Clientless Remote Access SSL VPNs Using ASDM................231
Lab D 10.3.1.2 - Configure AnyConnect Remote Access SSL VPN Using ASDM...............254

Chapter 11: Managing a Secure Network

Lab 11.3.1.2 - CCNA Security Comprehensive Lab 283

About This Lab Manual

This is the only authorized Lab Manual for the Cisco Networking Academy CCNA Security version 2 course.

The Cisco Networking Academy course on CCNA Security is a hands-on, career-oriented e-learning solution with an emphasis on practical experience to help you develop specialized security skills to expand your CCENT-level skill set and advance your career. The curriculum helps prepare students for entry-level security career opportunities and the Implementing Cisco IOS Network Security (IINS) certification exam (210-260) leading to the Cisco CCNA Security certification.

The CCNA Security Lab Manual provides you with all 15 labs from the course designed as hands-on practice to develop critical thinking and complex problem-solving skills needed to prepare for entry-level security specialist careers.

Through procedural, skills integration challenges, troubleshooting, and model building labs, this CCNA Security course aims to develop your in-depth understanding of network security principles as well as the tools and configurations used.

Command Syntax Conventions

The conventions used to present command syntax in this book are the same conventions used in the IOS Command Reference. The Command Reference describes these conventions as follows:

- **Boldface** indicates commands and keywords that are entered literally as shown. In actual configuration examples and output (not general command syntax), boldface indicates commands that are manually input by the user (such as a show command).
- *Italic* indicates arguments for which you supply actual values.
- Vertical bars (|) separate alternative, mutually exclusive elements.
- Square brackets ([ ]) indicate an optional element.
- Braces ({ }) indicate a required choice.
- Braces within brackets ([{ }]) indicate a required choice within an optional element

Chapter 1: Modern Network Security Threats

Lab 1.2.4.12 – Social Engineering

Objective

In this lab, you will research examples of social engineering and identify ways to recognize and prevent it.

Resources

- Computer with Internet Access

Step 1:   Research Social Engineering Examples

Social engineering, as it relates to information security, is used to describe the techniques used by a person (or persons) who manipulate people in order to access or compromise information about an organization or its computer systems. A social engineer is usually difficult to identify and may claim to be a new employee, a repair person, or a researcher. The social engineer might even offer credentials to support that identity. By gaining trust and asking questions, he or she may be able to piece together enough information to infiltrate an organization's network.

Use any Internet browser to research incidents of social engineering. Summarize three examples found in your research.

_____

_____

_____

Step 2:   Recognize the Signs of Social Engineering

Social engineers are nothing more than thieves and spies. Instead of hacking their way into your network via the Internet, they attempt to gain access by relying on a person's desire to be accommodating. Although not specific to network security, the scenario below illustrates how an unsuspecting person can unwittingly give away confidential information.

"The cafe was relatively quiet as I, dressed in a suit, sat at an empty table. I placed my briefcase on the table and waited for a suitable victim. Soon, just such a victim arrived with a friend and sat at the table next to mine. She placed her bag on the seat beside her, pulling the seat close and keeping her hand on the bag at all times.

After a few minutes, her friend left to find a restroom. The mark [target] was alone, so I gave Alex and Jess the signal. Playing a couple, Alex and Jess asked the mark if she would take a picture of them both. She was happy to do so. She removed her hand from her bag to take the camera and snap a picture of the "happy couple" and, while distracted, I reached over, took her bag, and locked it inside my briefcase. My victim had yet to notice her purse was missing as Alex and Jess left the café. Alex then went to a nearby parking garage.

It didn't take long for her to realize her bag was gone. She began to panic, looking around frantically. This was exactly what we were hoping for so, I asked her if she needed help.

She asked me if I had seen anything. I told her I hadn't but convinced her to sit down and think about what was in the bag. A phone. Make-up. A little cash. And her credit cards. Bingo!

I asked who she banked with and then told her that I worked for that bank. What a stroke of luck! I reassured her that everything would be fine, but she would need to cancel her credit card right away. I called the "help-desk" number, which was actually Alex, and handed my phone to her.

Alex was in a van in the parking garage. On the dashboard, a CD player was playing office noises. He assured the mark that her card could easily be canceled but, to verify her identity, she needed to enter her PIN on the keypad of the phone she was using. My phone and my keypad.

When we had her PIN, I left. If we were real thieves, we would have had access to her account via ATM withdrawals and PIN purchases. Fortunately for her, it was just a TV show."

"Hacking VS Social Engineering -by Christopher Hadnagy http://www.hackersgarage.com/hacking-vs-social-engineering.html

Remember: "Those who build walls think differently than those who seek to go over, under, around, or through them." Paul Wilson - The Real Hustle

Research ways to recognize social engineering. Describe three examples found in your research.

_____

_____

_____

Step 3:   Research Ways to Prevent Social Engineering

Does your company or school have procedures in place to help to prevent social engineering?

_____

If so, what are some of those procedures?

_____

_____

_____

_____

_____

Use the Internet to research procedures that other organizations use to prevent social engineers from gaining access to confidential information. List your findings.

_____

_____

_____

_____

_____

_____

_____

Lab 1.4.1.1 – Researching Network Attacks and Security Audit Tools/Attack Tools

Objectives

Part 1: Researching Network Attacks
- Research network attacks that have occurred.
- Select a network attack and develop a report for presentation to the class.

Part 2: Researching Network Security Audit Tools and Attack Tools
- Research network security audit tools.
- Select a tool and develop a report for presentation to the class.

Background / Scenario

Attackers have developed many tools over the years to attack and compromise networks. These attacks take many forms, but in most cases, they seek to obtain sensitive information, destroy resources, or deny legitimate users access to resources. When network resources are inaccessible, worker productivity can suffer, and business income may be lost.

To understand how to defend a network against attacks, an administrator must identify network vulnerabilities. Specialized security audit software, developed by equipment and software manufacturers, can be used to help identify potential weaknesses. These same tools used by individuals to attack networks can also be used by network professionals to test the ability of a network to mitigate an attack. After the vulnerabilities are discovered, steps can be taken to help protect the network.

This lab provides a structured research project that is divided into two parts: Researching Network Attacks and Researching Security Audit Tools. Inform your instructor about which network attack(s) and network security audit tool(s) you have chosen to research. This will ensure that a variety of network attacks and vulnerability tools are reported on by the members of the class.

In Part 1, research network attacks that have actually occurred. Select one of these attacks and describe how the attack was perpetrated and the extent of the network outage or damage. Next, investigate how the attack could have been mitigated, or what mitigation techniques might have been implemented to prevent future attacks. Finally, prepare a report based on the form included in this lab.

In Part 2, research network security audit tools and attack tools. Investigate one that can be used to identify host or network device vulnerabilities. Create a one-page summary of the tool based on the form included within this lab. Prepare a short (5–10 minute) presentation to give to the class.

You may work in teams of two, with one person reporting on the network attack and the other reporting on the tools. All team members deliver a short overview of their findings. You can use live demonstrations or PowerPoint, to summarize your findings.

Required Resources

- Computer with Internet access for research
- Presentation computer with PowerPoint or other presentation software installed
- Video projector and screen for demonstrations and presentations

Part 1: Researching Network Attacks

In Part 1 of this lab, you will research real network attacks and select one on which to report. Fill in the form below based on your findings.

Step 1: Research various network attacks.

List some of the attacks you identified in your search.

_____

_____

_____

_____

Step 2: Fill in the following form for the network attack selected.

Name of attack:	
Type of attack:	
Dates of attacks:	
Computers / Organizations affected:	
How it works and what it did:	

Mitigation options:
References and info links:
Presentation support graphics (include PowerPoint filename or web links):

Part 2: Researching Network Security Audit Tools and Attack Tools

In Part 2 of this lab, research network security audit tools and attack tools. Investigate one that can be used to identify host or network device vulnerabilities. Fill in the report below based on your findings.

Step 1: Research various network security audit tools and attack tools.

List some of the tools that you identified in your search.

_____

_____

_____

_____

_____

_____

_____

Step 2: Fill in the following form for the network security audit tool/attack tool selected.

Name of tool:	
Developer:	
Type of tool (character-based or GUI):	
Used on (network device or computer host):	
Cost:	
Description of key features and capabilities of product or tool:	

References and info links:

Reflection

1. What is the impact of network attacks on the operation of an organization? What are some key steps organizations can take to help protect their networks and resources?

    _____

    _____

    _____

    _____

    _____

    _____

2. Have you actually worked for an organization or know of one where the network was compromised? If so, what was the impact on the organization and what did it do about it?

    _____

    _____

    _____

    _____

    _____

    _____

3. What steps can you take to protect your own PC or laptop computer?

    _____

    _____

    _____

    _____

    _____

Chapter 2: Securing Network Devices

Lab 2.6.1.2 – Securing the Router for Administrative Access

Topology

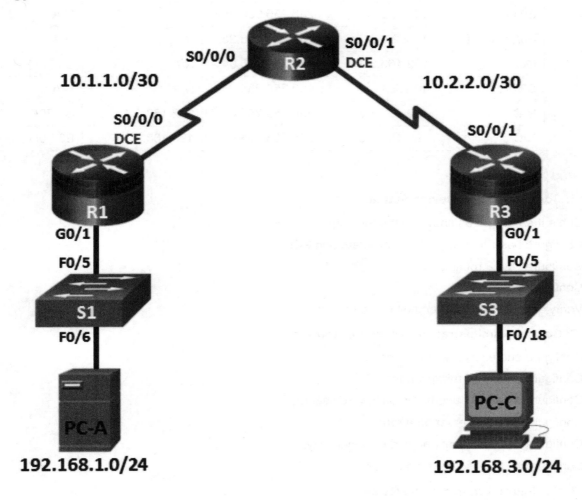

Note: ISR G1 devices use FastEthernet interfaces instead of GigabitEthernet Interfaces.

IP Addressing Table

Device	Interface	IP Address	Subnet Mask	Default Gateway	Switch Port
R1	G0/1	192.168.1.1	255.255.255.0	N/A	S1 F0/5
	S0/0/0 (DCE)	10.1.1.1	255.255.255.252	N/A	N/A
R2	S0/0/0	10.1.1.2	255.255.255.252	N/A	N/A
	S0/0/1 (DCE)	10.2.2.2	255.255.255.252	N/A	N/A
R3	G0/1	192.168.3.1	255.255.255.0	N/A	S3 F0/5
	S0/0/1	10.2.2.1	255.255.255.252	N/A	N/A
PC-A	NIC	192.168.1.3	255.255.255.0	192.168.1.1	S1 F0/6
PC-C	NIC	192.168.3.3	255.255.255.0	192.168.3.1	S3 F0/18

Objectives

Part 1: Configure Basic Device Settings

- Cable the network as shown in the topology.
- Configure basic IP addressing for routers and PCs.
- Configure OSPF routing.
- Configure PC hosts.
- Verify connectivity between hosts and routers.

Part 2: Control Administrative Access for Routers

- Configure and encrypt all passwords.
- Configure a login warning banner.
- Configure enhanced username password security.
- Configure an SSH server on a router.
- Configure an SSH client and verify connectivity.
- Configure an SCP server on a router.

Part 3: Configure Administrative Roles

- Create multiple role views and grant varying privileges.
- Verify and contrast views.

Part 4: Configure Cisco IOS Resilience and Management Reporting

- Secure the Cisco IOS image and configuration files.
- Configure SNMPv3 Security using an ACL.
- Configure a router as a synchronized time source for other devices using NTP.
- Configure Syslog support on a router.
- Install a Syslog server on a PC and enable it.
- Make changes to the router and monitor syslog results on the PC.

Part 5: Secure the Control Plane

- Configure OSPF Authentication using SHA256.
- Verify OSPF Authentication.

Part 6: Configure Automated Security Features

- Lock down a router using AutoSecure and verify the configuration.
- Contrast using AutoSecure with manually securing a router using the command line.

Background / Scenario

The router is a critical component in any network. It controls the movement of data into and out of the network and between devices within the network. It is particularly important to protect network routers because the failure of a routing device could make sections of the network, or the entire network, inaccessible. Controlling access to routers and enabling reporting on routers is critical to network security and should be part of a comprehensive security policy.

In this lab, you will build a multi-router network and configure the routers and hosts. Use various CLI tools to secure local and remote access to the routers, analyze potential vulnerabilities, and take steps to mitigate them. Enable management reporting to monitor router configuration changes.

The router commands and output in this lab are from a Cisco 1941 router using Cisco IOS software, release 15.4(3)M2 (with a Security Technology Package license). Other routers and Cisco IOS versions can be used. See the Router Interface Summary Table at the end of the lab to determine which interface identifiers to use based on the equipment in the lab. Depending on the model of the router, the commands available and output produced may vary from what is shown in this lab.

Note: Before you begin, ensure that the routers and the switches have been erased and have no startup configurations.

Required Resources

- 3 Routers (Cisco 1941 with Cisco IOS Release 15.4(3)M2 image with a Security Technology Package license)
- 2 Switches (Cisco 2960 or comparable) (Not Required)
- 2 PCs (Windows 7 or 8.1, SSH Client, Kiwi or Tftpd32 Syslog server)
- Serial and Ethernet cables as shown in the topology
- Console cables to configure Cisco networking devices

Part 1: Configure Basic Device Settings

In Part 1, set up the network topology and configure basic settings, such as interface IP addresses.

Step 1: Cable the network.

Attach the devices, as shown in the topology diagram, and cable as necessary.

Step 2: Configure basic settings for each router.

a. Configure host names as shown in the topology.

b. Configure interface IP addresses as shown in the IP Addressing Table.

c. Configure a clock rate for routers with a DCE serial cable attached to their serial interface. R1 is shown here as an example.

```
R1(config)# interface S0/0/0
R1(config-if)# clock rate 64000
```

d. To prevent the router from attempting to translate incorrectly entered commands as though they were host names, disable DNS lookup. R1 is shown here as an example.

```
R1(config)# no ip domain-lookup
```

Step 3: Configure OSPF routing on the routers.

a. Use the **router ospf** command in global configuration mode to enable OSPF on R1.

```
R1(config)# router ospf 1
```

b. Configure the **network** statements for the networks on R1. Use an area ID of 0.

```
R1(config-router)# network 192.168.1.0 0.0.0.255 area 0
R1(config-router)# network 10.1.1.0 0.0.0.3 area 0
```

c. Configure OSPF on R2 and R3.

d. Issue the **passive-interface** command to change the G0/1 interface on R1 and R3 to passive.

```
R1(config)# router ospf 1
R1(config-router)# passive-interface g0/1
R3(config)# router ospf 1
R3(config-router)# passive-interface g0/1
```

Step 4: Verify OSPF neighbors and routing information.

a. Issue the **show ip ospf neighbor** command to verify that each router lists the other routers in the network as neighbors.

```
R1# show ip ospf neighbor

Neighbor ID    Pri   State        Dead Time   Address     Interface
10.2.2.2        0   FULL/  -      00:00:31    10.1.1.2    Serial0/0/0
```

b. Issue the **show ip route** command to verify that all networks display in the routing table on all routers.

```
R1# show ip route
Codes: L - local, C - connected, S - static, R - RIP, M - mobile, B - BGP
       D - EIGRP, EX - EIGRP external, O - OSPF, IA - OSPF inter area
       N1 - OSPF NSSA external type 1, N2 - OSPF NSSA external type 2
       E1 - OSPF external type 1, E2 - OSPF external type 2
       i - IS-IS, su - IS-IS summary, L1 - IS-IS level-1, L2 - IS-IS level-2
       ia - IS-IS inter area, * - candidate default, U - per-user static route
       o - ODR, P - periodic downloaded static route, H - NHRP, l - LISP
       a - application route
       + - replicated route, % - next hop override

Gateway of last resort is not set

      10.0.0.0/8 is variably subnetted, 3 subnets, 2 masks
C        10.1.1.0/30 is directly connected, Serial0/0/0
L        10.1.1.1/32 is directly connected, Serial0/0/0
O        10.2.2.0/30 [110/128] via 10.1.1.2, 00:03:03, Serial0/0/0
```

```
           192.168.1.0/24 is variably subnetted, 2 subnets, 2 masks
C             192.168.1.0/24 is directly connected, GigabitEthernet0/1
L             192.168.1.1/32 is directly connected, GigabitEthernet0/1
O          192.168.3.0/24 [110/129] via 10.1.1.2, 00:02:36, Serial0/0/0
```

Step 5: Configure PC host IP settings.

Configure a static IP address, subnet mask, and default gateway for PC-A and PC-C as shown in the IP Addressing Table.

Step 6: Verify connectivity between PC-A and PC-C.

a. Ping from R1 to R3.

   If the pings are not successful, troubleshoot the basic device configurations before continuing.

b. Ping from PC-A, on the R1 LAN, to PC-C, on the R3 LAN.

   If the pings are not successful, troubleshoot the basic device configurations before continuing.

Note: If you can ping from PC-A to PC-C you have demonstrated that OSPF routing is configured and functioning correctly. If you cannot ping but the device interfaces are up and IP addresses are correct, use the **show run, show ip ospf neighbor,** and **show ip route** commands to help identify routing protocol-related problems.

Step 7: Save the basic running configuration for each router.

Save the basic running configuration for the routers as text files on your PC. These text files can be used to restore configurations later in the lab.

Part 2: Control Administrative Access for Routers

In Part 2, you will:

- Configure and encrypt passwords.
- Configure a login warning banner.
- Configure enhanced username password security.
- Configure enhanced virtual login security.
- Configure an SSH server on R1.
- Research terminal emulation client software and configure the SSH client.
- Configure an SCP server on R1.

Note: Perform all tasks on both R1 and R3. The procedures and output for R1 are shown here.

Task 1: Configure and Encrypt Passwords on Routers R1 and R3.

Step 1: Configure a minimum password length for all router passwords.

Use the **security passwords** command to set a minimum password length of 10 characters.

```
R1(config)# security passwords min-length 10
```

Step 2: Configure the enable secret password.

Configure the enable secret encrypted password on both routers. Use the type 9 (SCRYPT) hashing algorithm.

```
R1(config)# enable algorithm-type scrypt secret cisco12345
```

How does configuring an enable secret password help protect a router from being compromised by an attack?

_____

_____

_____

_____

_____

_____

Step 3: Configure basic console, auxiliary port, and virtual access lines.

Note: Passwords in this task are set to a minimum of 10 characters but are relatively simple for the benefit of performing the lab. More complex passwords are recommended in a production network.

a. Configure a console password and enable login for routers. For additional security, the **exec-timeout** command causes the line to log out after 5 minutes of inactivity. The **logging synchronous** command prevents console messages from interrupting command entry.

> **Note**: To avoid repetitive logins during this lab, the **exec-timeout** command can be set to 0 0, which prevents it from expiring. However, this is not considered a good security practice.

```
R1(config)# line console 0
R1(config-line)# password ciscocon
R1(config-line)# exec-timeout 5 0
R1(config-line)# login
R1(config-line)# logging synchronous
```

When you configured the password for the console line, what message was displayed?

_____

_____

b. Configure a new password of **ciscoconpass** for the console.

c. Configure a password for the AUX port for router R1.

```
R1(config)# line aux 0
R1(config-line)# password ciscoauxpass
R1(config-line)# exec-timeout 5 0
R1(config-line)# login
```

d. Telnet from R2 to R1.

```
R2> telnet 10.1.1.1
```

Were you able to login? Explain.

_____

_____

What messages were displayed?

_____

_____

e. Configure the password on the vty lines for router R1.

```
R1(config)# line vty 0 4
R1(config-line)# password ciscovtypass
R1(config-line)# exec-timeout 5 0
R1(config-line)# transport input telnet
R1(config-line)# login
```

Note: The default for vty lines is now **transport input none**.

Telnet from R2 to R1 again. Were you able to login this time?

_____

f. Enter privileged EXEC mode and issue the **show run** command. Can you read the enable secret password? Explain.

_____

_____

Can you read the console, aux, and vty passwords? Explain.

_____

_____

g. Repeat the configuration portion of steps 3a through 3g on router R3.

Step 4: Encrypt clear text passwords.

a. Use the **service password-encryption** command to encrypt the console, aux, and vty passwords.

```
R1(config)# service password-encryption
```

b. Issue the **show run** command. Can you read the console, aux, and vty passwords? Explain.

_____

_____

At what level (number) is the default enable secret password encrypted? _____

At what level (number) are the other passwords encrypted? _____

Which level of encryption is harder to crack and why?

_____

_____

Task 2: Configure a Login Warning Banner on Routers R1 and R3.

Step 1: Configure a warning message to display prior to login.

a. Configure a warning to unauthorized users with a message-of-the-day (MOTD) banner using the **banner motd** command. When a user connects to one of the routers, the MOTD banner appears before the login prompt. In this example, the dollar sign ($) is used to start and end the message.

```
R1(config)# banner motd $Unauthorized access strictly prohibited!$
R1(config)# exit
```

b. Issue the **show run** command. What does the $ convert to in the output?

_____

_____

Task 3: Configure Enhanced Username Password Security on Routers R1 and R3.

Step 1: Investigate the options for the username command.

In global configuration mode, enter the following command:

```
R1(config)# username user01 algorithm-type ?
```

What options are available?

_____

_____

_____

Step 2: Create a new user account with a secret password.

a. Create a new user account with SCRYPT hashing to encrypt the password.

```
R1(config)# username user01 algorithm-type scrypt secret user01pass
```

b. Exit global configuration mode and save your configuration.

c. Display the running configuration. Which hashing method is used for the password?

_____

_____

Step 3: Test the new account by logging in to the console.

a. Set the console line to use the locally defined login accounts.

```
R1(config)# line console 0
R1(config-line)# login local
R1(config-line)# end
R1# exit
```

b. Exit to the initial router screen which displays: R1 con0 is now available, Press RETURN to get started.

c. Log in using the previously defined username **user01** and the password **user01pass**.

What is the difference between logging in at the console now and previously?

_____

_____

d. After logging in, issue the **show run** command. Were you able to issue the command? Explain.

_____

_____

e. Enter privileged EXEC mode using the **enable** command. Were you prompted for a password? Explain.

_____

_____

Step 4: Test the new account by logging in from a Telnet session.

a. From PC-A, establish a Telnet session with R1. Telnet is disabled by default in Windows 7. If necessary, search online for the steps to enable Telnet in Windows 7.

```
PC-A> telnet 192.168.1.1
```

Were you prompted for a user account? Explain.

_____

_____

b. Set the vty lines to use the locally defined login accounts.

```
R1(config)# line vty 0 4
R1(config-line)# login local
```

c. From PC-A, telnet to R1 again.

```
PC-A> telnet 192.168.1.1
```

Were you prompted for a user account? Explain.

_____

_____

.

d. Log in as **user01** with a password of **user01pass**.

e. During the Telnet session to R1, access privileged EXEC mode with the **enable** command.

What password did you use?

_____

f. For added security, set the AUX port to use the locally defined login accounts.

```
R1(config)# line aux 0
R1(config-line)# login local
```

g. End the Telnet session with the **exit** command.

Task 4: Configure the SSH Server on Router R1 and R3.

In this task, use the CLI to configure the router to be managed securely using SSH instead of Telnet. Secure Shell (SSH) is a network protocol that establishes a secure terminal emulation connection to a router or other networking device. SSH encrypts all information that passes over the network link and provides authentication of the remote computer. SSH is rapidly replacing Telnet as the remote login tool of choice for network professionals.

Note: For a router to support SSH, it must be configured with local authentication, (AAA services, or username) or password authentication. In this task, you configure an SSH username and local authentication.

Step 1: Configure a domain name.

Enter global configuration mode and set the domain name.

```
R1# conf t
R1(config)# ip domain-name ccnasecurity.com
```

Step 2: Configure a privileged user for login from the SSH client.

a. Use the **username** command to create the user ID with the highest possible privilege level and a secret password.

```
R1(config)# username admin privilege 15 algorithm-type scrypt secret
cisco12345
```

Note: Usernames are not case sensitive by default. You will learn how to make usernames case sensitive in Chapter 3.

b. Exit to the initial router login screen. Log in with the username admin and the associated password. What was the router prompt after you entered the password?

_____

_____

Step 3: Configure the incoming vty lines.

Specify a privilege level of **15** so that a user with the highest privilege level (15) will default to privileged EXEC mode when accessing the vty lines. Other users will default to user EXEC mode. Use the local user accounts for mandatory login and validation and accept only SSH connections.

```
R1(config)# line vty 0 4
R1(config-line)# privilege level 15
R1(config-line)# login local
R1(config-line)# transport input ssh
R1(config-line)# exit
```

Note: The **login local** command should have been configured in a previous step. It is included here to provide all commands, if you are doing this for the first time.

Note: If you add the keyword **telnet** to the **transport input** command, users can log in using Telnet as well as SSH, however, the router will be less secure. If only SSH is specified, the connecting host must have an SSH client installed.

Step 4: Erase existing key pairs on the router.

```
R1(config)# crypto key zeroize rsa
```

Note: If no keys exist, you might receive this message: `% No Signature RSA Keys found in configuration.`

Step 5: Generate the RSA encryption key pair for the router.

The router uses the RSA key pair for authentication and encryption of transmitted SSH data.

a. Configure the RSA keys with **1024** for the number of modulus bits. The default is 512, and the range is from 360 to 2048.

```
R1(config)# crypto key generate rsa general-keys modulus 1024
The name for the keys will be: R1.ccnasecurity.com

% The key modulus size is 1024 bits
% Generating 1024 bit RSA keys, keys will be non-exportable...[OK]

R1(config)#
*Dec 16 21:24:16.175: %SSH-5-ENABLED: SSH 1.99 has been enabled
```

b. Issue the **ip ssh version 2** command to force the use of SSH version 2.

```
R1(config)# ip ssh version 2
R1(config)# exit
```

Note: The details of encryption methods are covered in Chapter 7.

Step 6: Verify the SSH configuration.

a. Use the **show ip ssh** command to see the current settings.

```
R1# show ip ssh
```

b. Fill in the following information based on the output of the **show ip ssh** command.

SSH version enabled: _____

Authentication timeout: _____

Authentication retries: _____

Step 7: Configure SSH timeouts and authentication parameters.

The default SSH timeouts and authentication parameters can be altered to be more restrictive using the following commands.

```
R1(config)# ip ssh time-out 90
R1(config)# ip ssh authentication-retries 2
```

Step 8: Save the running-config to the startup-config.

```
R1# copy running-config startup-config
```

Task 5: Research Terminal Emulation Client Software and Configure the SSH Client.

Step 1: Research terminal emulation client software.

Conduct a web search for freeware terminal emulation client software, such as TeraTerm or PuTTy. What are some capabilities of each?

_____

_____

_____

_____

_____

_____

_____

_____

_____

Step 2: Install an SSH client on PC-A and PC-C.

a. If the SSH client is not already installed, download either TeraTerm or PuTTY.

b. Save the application to the desktop.

Note: The procedure described here is for PuTTY and pertains to PC-A.

Step 3: Verify SSH connectivity to R1 from PC-A.

a. Launch PuTTY by double-clicking the putty.exe icon.

b. Input the R1 F0/1 IP address **192.168.1.1** in the **Host Name (or IP address)** field.

c. Verify that the **SSH** radio button is selected.

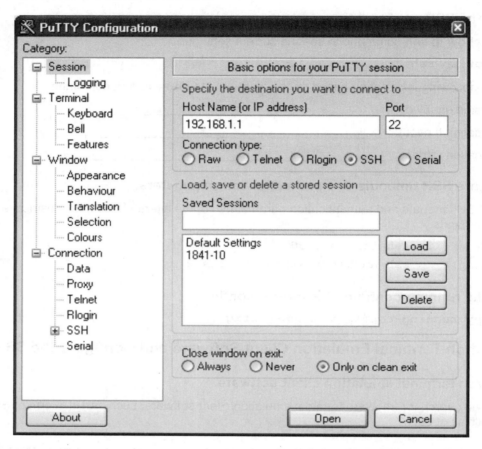

d. Click **Open**.

e. In the PuTTY Security Alert window, click **Yes**.

f. Enter the **admin** username and password **cisco12345** in the PuTTY window.

g. At the R1 privileged EXEC prompt, enter the **show users** command.

```
R1# show users
```

What users are connected to router R1 at this time?

_____

_____

_____

h. Close the PuTTY SSH session window.

i. Try to open a Telnet session to your router from PC-A. Were you able to open the Telnet session? Explain.

_____

_____

j. Open a PuTTY SSH session to the router from PC-A. Enter the **user01** username and password **user01pass** in the PuTTY window to try connecting for a user who does not have privilege level of 15.

If you were able to login, what was the prompt?

_____

_____

k. Use the **enable** command to enter privilege EXEC mode and enter the enable secret password **cisco12345**.

Task 6: Configure an SCP server on R1.

Now that SSH is configured on the router, configure the R1 router as a secure copy (SCP) server.

Step 1: Use the AAA authentication and authorization defaults on R1.

Set the AAA authentication and authorization defaults on R1 to use the local database for logins.

Note: SCP requires the user to have privilege level 15 access.

a. Enable AAA on the router.

```
R1(config)# aaa new-model
```

b. Use the **aaa authentication** command to use the local database as the default login authentication method.

```
R1(config)# aaa authentication login default local
```

c. Use the **aaa authorization** command to use the local database as the default command authorization.

```
R1(config)# aaa authorization exec default local
```

d. Enable SCP server on R1.

```
R1(config)# ip scp server enable
```

Note: AAA is covered in Chapter 3.

Step 2: Copy the running config on R1 to flash.

SCP server allows files to be copied to and from a router's flash. In this step, you will create a copy of the running-config on R1 to flash. You will then use SCP to copy that file to R3.

a. Save the running configuration on R1 to a file on flash called R1-Config.

```
R1# copy running-config R1-Config
```

b. Verify that the new R1-Config file is on flash.

```
R1# show flash
-#- --length-- -----date/time------ path
1      75551300 Feb 16 2015 15:19:22 +00:00 c1900-universalk9-mz.SPA.154-3.M2.bin
2          1643 Feb 17 2015 23:30:58 +00:00 R1-Config

181047296 bytes available (75563008 bytes used)
```

Step 3: Use SCP command on R3 to pull the configuration file from R1.

a. Use SCP to copy the configuration file that you created in Step 2a to R3.

```
R3# copy scp: flash:
Address or name of remote host []? 10.1.1.1
Source username [R3]? admin
Source filename []? R1-Config
Destination filename [R1-Config]? [Enter]
Password: cisco12345
!
2007 bytes copied in 9.056 secs (222 bytes/sec)
```

b. Verify that the file has been copied to R3's flash.

```
R3# show flash
-#- --length-- -----date/time------ path
1      75551300 Feb 16 2015 15:21:38 +00:00 c1900-universalk9-mz.SPA.154-3.M2.bin
2          1338 Feb 16 2015 23:46:10 +00:00 pre_autosec.cfg
3          2007 Feb 17 2015 23:42:00 +00:00 R1-Config

181043200 bytes available (75567104 bytes used)
```

c. Issue the **more** command to view the contents of the R1-Config file.

```
R3# more R1-Config
!
version 15.4
service timestamps debug datetime msec
service timestamps log datetime msec
no service password-encryption
!
hostname R1
!
<Output omitted>
!
end
R3#
```

Step 4: Save the configuration.

Save the running configuration to the startup configuration from the privileged EXEC prompt.

```
R1# copy running-config startup-config
```

Part 3: Configure Administrative Roles

In Part 3 of this lab, you will:

- Create multiple administrative roles, or views, on routers R1 and R3.
- Grant each view varying privileges.
- Verify and contrast the views.

The role-based CLI access feature allows the network administrator to define views, which are a set of operational commands and configuration capabilities that provide selective or partial access to Cisco IOS EXEC and configuration (config) mode commands. Views restrict user access to the Cisco IOS CLI and configuration information. A view can define which commands are accepted and what configuration information is visible.

Note: Perform all tasks on both R1 and R3. The procedures and output for R1 are shown here.

Task 1: Enable Root View on R1 and R3.

If an administrator wants to configure another view to the system, the system must be in root view. When a system is in root view, the user has the same access privileges as a user who has level-15 privileges, but the root view user can also configure a new view and add or remove commands from the view. When you are in a CLI view, you have access only to the commands that have been added to that view by the root view user.

Step 1: Enable AAA on router R1.

To define views, be sure that AAA was enabled with the **aaa new-model** command in Part 2.

Step 2: Enable the root view.

Use the command **enable view** to enable the root view. Use the **enable secret** password **cisco12345**. If the router does not have an enable secret password, create one now.

```
R1# enable view
Password: cisco12345
R1#
```

Task 2: Create New Views for the Admin1, Admin2, and Tech Roles on R1 and R3.

Step 1: Create the admin1 view, establish a password, and assign privileges.

a. The admin1 user is the top-level user below root that is allowed to access this router. It has the most authority. The admin1 user can use all **show**, **config**, and **debug** commands. Use the following command to create the admin1 view while in the root view.

```
R1(config)# parser view admin1
R1(config-view)#
```

Note: To delete a view, use the command **no parser view** *viewname*.

b. Associate the admin1 view with an encrypted password.

```
R1(config-view)# secret admin1pass
R1(config-view)#
```

c. Review the commands that can be configured in the admin1 view. Use the **commands ?** command to see available commands. The following is a partial listing of the available commands.

```
R1(config-view)# commands ?
```

```
    RITE-profile          Router IP traffic export profile command mode
    RMI Node Config       Resource Policy Node Config mode
    RMI Resource Group    Resource Group Config mode
    RMI Resource Manager  Resource Manager Config mode
    RMI Resource Policy   Resource Policy Config mode
    SASL-profile          SASL profile configuration mode
    aaa-attr-list         AAA attribute list config mode
    aaa-user              AAA user definition
    accept-dialin         VPDN group accept dialin configuration mode
    accept-dialout        VPDN group accept dialout configuration mode
    address-family        Address Family configuration mode
<output omitted>
```

d. Add all **config**, **show**, and **debug** commands to the admin1 view and then exit from view configuration mode.

```
R1(config-view)# commands exec include all show
R1(config-view)# commands exec include all config terminal
R1(config-view)# commands exec include all debug
R1(config-view)# end
```

e. Verify the admin1 view.

```
R1# enable view admin1
Password: admin1pass

R1# show parser view
Current view is 'admin1'
```

f. Examine the commands available in the admin1 view.

```
R1# ?
Exec commands:
   <0-0>/<0-4>  Enter card slot/sublot number
   configure    Enter configuration mode
   debug        Debugging functions (see also 'undebug')
   do-exec      Mode-independent "do-exec" prefix support
   enable       Turn on privileged commands
   exit         Exit from the EXEC
   show         Show running system
```

Note: There may be more EXEC commands available than are displayed. This depends on your device and the IOS image used.

g. Examine the **show** commands available in the admin1 view.

```
R1# show ?
   aaa                Show AAA values
   access-expression  List access expression
   access-lists       List access lists
   acircuit           Access circuit info
   adjacency          Adjacent nodes
   aliases            Display alias commands
   alignment          Show alignment information
```

```
    appfw                      Application Firewall information
    archive                    Archive functions
    arp                        ARP table
<output omitted>
```

Step 2: Create the admin2 view, establish a password, and assign privileges.

a. The admin2 user is a junior administrator in training who is allowed to view all configurations but is not allowed to configure the routers or use debug commands.

b. Use the **enable view** command to enable the root view, and enter the enable secret password **cisco12345**.

```
R1# enable view
Password: cisco12345
```

c. Use the following command to create the admin2 view.

```
R1(config)# parser view admin2
R1(config-view)#
```

d. Associate the admin2 view with a password.

```
R1(config-view)# secret admin2pass
R1(config-view)#
```

e. Add all **show** commands to the view, and then exit from view configuration mode.

```
R1(config-view)# commands exec include all show
R1(config-view)# end
```

f. Verify the admin2 view.

```
R1# enable view admin2
Password: admin2pass

R1# show parser view
Current view is 'admin2'
```

g. Examine the commands available in the admin2 view.

```
R1# ?
Exec commands:
   <0-0>/<0-4>  Enter card slot/sublot number
   do-exec       Mode-independent "do-exec" prefix support
   enable        Turn on privileged commands
   exit          Exit from the EXEC
   show          Show running system information
```

Note: There may be more EXEC commands available than are displayed. This depends on your device and the IOS image used.

What is missing from the list of admin2 commands that is present in the admin1 commands?

Step 3: Create the tech view, establish a password, and assign privileges.

a. The tech user typically installs end-user devices and cabling. Tech users are only allowed to use selected **show** commands.

b. Use the enable **view** command to enable the root view, and enter the enable secret password **cisco12345**.

```
R1# enable view
Password: cisco12345
```

c. Use the following command to create the tech view.

```
R1(config)# parser view tech
R1(config-view)#
```

d. Associate the tech view with a password.

```
R1(config-view)# secret techpasswd
R1(config-view)#
```

e. Add the following **show** commands to the view and then exit from view configuration mode.

```
R1(config-view)# commands exec include show version
R1(config-view)# commands exec include show interfaces
R1(config-view)# commands exec include show ip interface brief
R1(config-view)# commands exec include show parser view
R1(config-view)# end
```

f. Verify the tech view.

```
R1# enable view tech
Password: techpasswd

R1# show parser view
Current view is 'tech'
```

g. Examine the commands available in the tech view.

```
R1# ?
Exec commands:
  <0-0>/<0-4>  Enter card slot/sublot number
  do-exec      Mode-independent "do-exec" prefix support
  enable       Turn on privileged commands
  exit         Exit from the EXEC
  show         Show running system information
```

Note: There may be more EXEC commands available than are displayed. This depends on your device and the IOS image used.

h. Examine the **show** commands available in the tech view.

```
R1# show ?
  banner      Display banner information
  flash0:     display information about flash0: file system
  flash1:     display information about flash1: file system
  flash:      display information about flash: file system
  interfaces  Interface status and configuration
```

```
ip          IP information
parser      Display parser information
usbflash0:  display information about usbflash0: file system
version     System hardware and software status
```

Note: There may be more EXEC commands available than are displayed. This depends on your device and the IOS image used.

i. Issue the **show ip interface brief** command. Were you able to do it as the tech user? Explain.

_____

_____

j. Issue the **show ip route** command. Were you able to do it as the tech user?

_____

_____

k. Return to root view with the **enable view** command.

```
R1# enable view
Password: cisco12345
```

l. Issue the **show run** command to see the views you created. For tech view, why are the **show** and **show ip** commands listed as well as **show ip interface** and **show ip interface brief**?

_____

_____

Step 4: Save the configuration on routers R1 and R3.

Save the running configuration to the startup configuration from the privileged EXEC prompt.

Part 4: Configure IOS Resilience and Management Reporting

In Part 4 of this lab, you will:

- Secure the Cisco IOS image and configuration files.
- Configure SNMPv3 security using an ACL.
- Using NTP, configure a router as a synchronized time source for other devices.
- Configure syslog support on a router.
- Install a syslog server on a PC and enable it.
- Configure the logging trap level on a router.
- Make changes to the router and monitor syslog results on the PC.

Note: Perform all tasks on both R1 and R3. The procedure and output for R1 is shown here.

Task 1: Secure Cisco IOS Image and Configuration Files on R1 and R3.

The Cisco IOS resilient configuration feature enables a router to secure the running image and maintain a working copy of the configuration. This ensures that those files can withstand malicious attempts to erase the contents of persistent storage (NVRAM and flash). This feature secures the smallest working set of files to preserve persistent storage space. No extra space is required to secure the primary Cisco IOS image file. In this task, you configure the Cisco IOS Resilient Configuration feature.

Note: Cisco IOS resilient configuration feature is not available on the Cisco 1921 router.

Note: The output of the commands in this Task are for example purposes only. Your output will be different.

Step 1: Display the files in flash memory for R1.

The **show flash:** command displays the contents of sub-directories. The **dir** command only displays contents of the current directory.

```
R1# show flash:
-#- --length-- -----date/time------ path
1      75551300 Feb 5 2015 16:53:34 +00:00 c1900-universalk9-mz.SPA.154-3.M2.bin
2             0 Jan 6 2009 01:28:44 +00:00 ipsdir
3        334531 Jan 6 2009 01:35:40 +00:00 ipsdir/R1-sigdef-default.xml
4           461 Jan 6 2009 01:37:42 +00:00 ipsdir/R1-sigdef-delta.xml
5          8509 Jan 6 2009 01:33:42 +00:00 ipsdir/R1-sigdef-typedef.xml
6         38523 Jan 6 2009 01:33:46 +00:00 ipsdir/R1-sigdef-category.xml
7           304 Jan 6 2009 01:31:48 +00:00 ipsdir/R1-seap-delta.xml
8           491 Jan 6 2009 01:31:48 +00:00 ipsdir/R1-seap-typedef.xml
9          1410 Oct 26 2014 04:44:08 +00:00 pre_autosec.cfg

76265535 bytes available (180221889 bytes used)


R1# dir
Directory of flash:/

    1  -rw-      75551300 Feb 5 2015 16:53:34 +00:00 c1900-universalk9-mz.SPA.154-
3.M2.bin
    2  drw-             0  Jan 6 2009 01:28:44 +00:00  ipsdir
    9  -rw-          1410  Oct 26 2014 04:44:08 +00:00  pre_autosec.cfg

256487424 bytes total (180221889 bytes free)
```

Step 2: Secure the Cisco IOS image and archive a copy of the running configuration.

a. The **secure boot-image** command enables Cisco IOS image resilience, which hides the file from the **dir** command and **show** commands. The file cannot be viewed, copied, modified, or removed using EXEC mode commands. (It can be viewed in ROMMON mode.) When turned on for the first time, the running image is secured.

```
R1(config)# secure boot-image
.Feb 11 25:40:13.170: %IOS_RESILIENCE-5-IMAGE_RESIL_ACTIVE: Successfully secured
running image
```

b. The **secure boot-config** command takes a snapshot of the router running configuration and securely archives it in persistent storage (flash).

```
R1(config)# secure boot-config
.Feb 11 25:42:18.691: %IOS_RESILIENCE-5-CONFIG_RESIL_ACTIVE: Successfully secured
config archive [flash:.runcfg-20150211-224218.ar]
```

Step 3: Verify that your image and configuration are secured.

You can use only the **show secure bootset** command to display the archived filename. Display the status of configuration resilience and the primary bootset filename.

```
R1# show secure bootset
```

```
IOS resilience router id FTX1111W0QF

IOS image resilience version 15.4 activated at 25:40:13 UTC Wed Feb 11 2015
Secure archive flash: c1900-universalk9-mz.SPA.154-3.M2.bin type is image (elf)
[]
   file size is 75551300 bytes, run size is 75730352 bytes
   Runnable image, entry point 0x8000F000, run from ram

IOS configuration resilience version 15.4 activated at 25:42:18 UTC Wed Feb 11 2015
Secure archive flash:.runcfg-20150211-224218.ar type is config
configuration archive size 3293 bytes
```

What is the name of the archived running config file and on what is the name based?

_____

_____

Step 4: Display the files in flash memory for R1.

a. Display the contents of flash using the **show flash** command.

```
R1# show flash:
-#- --length-- -----date/time------ path
2              0 Jan 6 2009 01:28:44 +00:00 ipsdir
3         334531 Jan 6 2009 01:35:40 +00:00 ipsdir/R1-sigdef-default.xml
4            461 Jan 6 2009 01:37:42 +00:00 ipsdir/R1-sigdef-delta.xml
5           8509 Jan 6 2009 01:33:42 +00:00 ipsdir/R1-sigdef-typedef.xml
6          38523 Jan 6 2009 01:33:46 +00:00 ipsdir/R1-sigdef-category.xml
7            304 Jan 6 2009 01:31:48 +00:00 ipsdir/R1-seap-delta.xml
8            491 Jan 6 2009 01:31:48 +00:00 ipsdir/R1-seap-typedef.xml
9           1410 Oct 26 2014 04:44:08 +00:00 pre_autosec.cfg

76265535 bytes available (180221889 bytes used)
```

Is the Cisco IOS image or the archived running config file listed?

_____

_____

b. How can you tell that the Cisco IOS image is still there?

_____

_____

Step 5: Disable the IOS Resilient Configuration feature.

a. Disable the Resilient Configuration feature for the Cisco IOS image.

```
R1# config t
R1(config)# no secure boot-image
.Feb 11 25:48:23.009: %IOS_RESILIENCE-5-IMAGE_RESIL_INACTIVE: Disabled secure
image archival
```

b. Disable the Resilient Configuration feature for the running config file.

```
R1(config)# no secure boot-config
.Feb 11 25:48:47.972: %IOS_RESILIENCE-5-CONFIG_RESIL_INACTIVE: Disabled
secure config archival [removed flash:.runcfg-20150211-224218.ar]
```

Step 6: Verify that the Cisco IOS image is now visible in flash.

Use the **show flash:** command to display the files in flash.

```
R1# show flash:
-#- --length-- -----date/time------ path
1     75551300 Feb 5 2015 16:53:34 +00:00 c1900-universalk9-mz.SPA.154-3.M2.bin
2            0 Jan 6 2009 01:28:44 +00:00 ipsdir
3       334531 Jan 6 2009 01:35:40 +00:00 ipsdir/R1-sigdef-default.xml
4          461 Jan 6 2009 01:37:42 +00:00 ipsdir/R1-sigdef-delta.xml
5         8509 Jan 6 2009 01:33:42 +00:00 ipsdir/R1-sigdef-typedef.xml
6        38523 Jan 6 2009 01:33:46 +00:00 ipsdir/R1-sigdef-category.xml
7          304 Jan 6 2009 01:31:48 +00:00 ipsdir/R1-seap-delta.xml
8          491 Jan 6 2009 01:31:48 +00:00 ipsdir/R1-seap-typedef.xml
9         1410 Oct 26 2014 04:44:08 +00:00 pre_autosec.cfg

76265535 bytes available (180221889 bytes used)
```

Step 7: Save the configuration on both routers.

Save the running configuration to the startup configuration from the privileged EXEC prompt.

Task 2: Configure SNMPv3 Security using an ACL.

Simple Network Management Protocol (SNMP) enables network administrators to monitor network performance, mange network devices, and troubleshoot network problems. SNMPv3 provides secure access by authenticating and encrypting SNMP management packets over the network. You will configure SNMPv3 using an ACL on R1.

Step 1: Configure an ACL on R1 that will restrict access to SNMP on the 192.168.1.0 LAN.

a. Create a standard access-list named **PERMIT-SNMP**.

```
R1(config)# ip access-list standard PERMIT-SNMP
```

b. Add a permit statement to allow only packets on R1's LAN.

```
R1(config-std-nacl)# permit 192.168.1.0 0.0.0.255
R1(config-std-nacl)# exit
```

Step 2: Configure the SNMP view.

Configure a SNMP view called **SNMP-RO** to include the ISO MIB family.

```
R1(config)# snmp-server view SNMP-RO iso included
```

Step 3: Configure the SNMP group.

Call the group name **SNMP-G1**, and configure the group to use SNMPv3 and require both authentication and encryption by using the **priv** keyword. Associate the view you created in Step 2 to the group, giving it read only access with the **read** parameter. Finally specify the ACL **PERMIT-SNMP**, configured in Step 1, to restrict SNMP access to the local LAN.

```
R1(config)# snmp-server group SNMP-G1 v3 priv read SNMP-RO access PERMIT-SNMP
```

Step 4: Configure the SNMP user.

Configure an **SNMP-Admin** user and associate the user to the **SNMP-G1** group you configured in Step 3. Set the authentication method to **SHA** and the authentication password to **Authpass**. Use AES-128 for encryption with a password of **Encrypass**.

```
R1(config)# snmp-server user SNMP-Admin SNMP-G1 v3 auth sha Authpass priv aes
128 Encrypass
R1(config)# end
```

Step 5: Verify your SNMP configuration.

a. Use the show **snmp group** command in privilege EXEC mode to view the SNMP group configuration. Verify that your group is configured correctly.

Note: If you need to make changes to the group, use the command **no snmp group** to remove the group from the configuration and then re-add it with the correct parameters.

```
R1# show snmp group
groupname: ILMI                                security model:v1
contextname: <no context specified>            storage-type: permanent
readview : *ilmi                               writeview: *ilmi
notifyview: <no notifyview specified>
row status: active


groupname: ILMI                                security model:v2c
contextname: <no context specified>            storage-type: permanent
readview : *ilmi                               writeview: *ilmi
notifyview: <no notifyview specified>
row status: active


groupname: SNMP-G1                             security model:v3 priv
contextname: <no context specified>            storage-type: nonvolatile
readview : SNMP-RO                             writeview: <no writeview specified>
notifyview: <no notifyview specified>
row status: active  access-list: PERMIT-SNMP
```

b. Use the command **show snmp user** to view the SNMP user information.

Note: The **snmp-server user** command is hidden from view in the configuration for security reasons. However, if you need to make changes to a SNMP user, you can issue the command **no snmp-server user** to remove the user from the configuration, and then re-add the user with the new parameters.

```
R1# show snmp user

User name: SNMP-Admin
Engine ID: 80000009030030F70DA30DA0
storage-type: nonvolatile  active
Authentication Protocol: SHA
Privacy Protocol: AES128
Group-name: SNMP-G1
```

Task 3: Configure a Synchronized Time Source Using NTP.

R2 will be the master NTP clock source for routers R1 and R3.

Note: R2 could also be the master clock source for switches S1 and S3, but it is not necessary to configure them for this lab.

Step 1: Set Up the NTP Master using Cisco IOS commands.

R2 is the master NTP server in this lab. All other routers and switches learn the time from it, either directly or indirectly. For this reason, you must ensure that R2 has the correct Coordinated Universal Time set.

a. Use the **show clock** command to display the current time set on the router.

```
R2# show clock
*19:48:38.858 UTC Wed Feb 18 2015
```

b. To set the time on the router, use the **clock set** *time* command.

```
R2# clock set 20:12:00 Dec 17 2014
R2#
*Dec 17 20:12:18.000: %SYS-6-CLOCKUPDATE: System clock has been updated from
01:20:26 UTC Mon Dec 15 2014 to 20:12:00 UTC Wed Dec 17 2014, configured from
console by admin on console.
```

c. Configure NTP authentication by defining the authentication key number, hashing type, and password that will be used for authentication. The password is case sensitive.

```
R2# config t
R2(config)# ntp authentication-key 1 md5 NTPpassword
```

d. Configure the trusted key that will be used for authentication on R2.

```
R2(config)# ntp trusted-key 1
```

e. Enable the NTP authentication feature on R2.

```
R2(config)# ntp authenticate
```

f. Configure R2 as the NTP master using the **ntp master** *stratum-number* command in global configuration mode. The stratum number indicates the distance from the original source. For this lab, use a stratum number of **3** on R2. When a device learns the time from an NTP source, its stratum number becomes one greater than the stratum number of its source.

```
R2(config)# ntp master 3
```

Step 2: Configure R1 and R3 as NTP clients using the CLI.

a. Configure NTP authentication by defining the authentication key number, hashing type, and password that will be used for authentication.

```
R1# config t
R1(config)# ntp authentication-key 1 md5 NTPpassword
```

b. Configure the trusted key that will be used for authentication. This command provides protection against accidentally synchronizing the device to a time source that is not trusted.

```
R1(config)# ntp trusted-key 1
```

c. Enable the NTP authentication feature.

```
R1(config)# ntp authenticate
```

d. R1 and R3 will become NTP clients of R2. Use the command **ntp server** *hostname*. The host name can also be an IP address. The command **ntp update-calendar** periodically updates the calendar with the NTP time.

```
R1(config)# ntp server 10.1.1.2
R1(config)# ntp update-calendar
```

e. Verify that R1 has made an association with R2 with the **show ntp associations** command. You can also use the more verbose version of the command by adding the **detail** argument. It might take some time for the NTP association to form.

```
R1# show ntp associations

address      ref clock     st   when   poll reach  delay  offset    disp
~10.1.1.2  127.127.1.1    3    14     64     3  0.000  -280073   3939.7
*sys.peer, # selected, +candidate, -outlyer, x falseticker, ~ configured
```

f. Issue the **debug ntp all** command to see NTP activity on R1 as it synchronizes with R2.

```
R1# debug ntp all
NTP events debugging is on
NTP core messages debugging is on
NTP clock adjustments debugging is on
NTP reference clocks debugging is on
NTP packets debugging is on


Dec 17 20.12:18.554: NTP message sent to 10.1.1.2, from interface 'Serial0/0/0'
(10.1.1.1).
Dec 17 20.12:18.574: NTP message received from 10.1.1.2 on interface 'Serial0/0/0'
(10.1.1.1).
Dec 17 20:12:18.574: NTP Core(DEBUG): ntp_receive: message received
Dec 17 20:12:18.574: NTP Core(DEBUG): ntp_receive: peer is 0x645A3120, next action is
1.
Dec 17 20:12:18.574: NTP Core(DEBUG): receive: packet given to process_packet
Dec 17 20:12:18.578: NTP Core(INFO): system event 'event_peer/strat_chg' (0x04)
status 'sync_alarm, sync_ntp, 5 events, event_clock_reset' (0xC655)
Dec 17 20:12:18.578: NTP Core(INFO): synchronized to 10.1.1.2, stratum 3
Dec 17 20:12:18.578: NTP Core(INFO): system event 'event_sync_chg' (0x03) status
 'leap_none, sync_ntp, 6 events, event_peer/strat_chg' (0x664)
Dec 17 20:12:18.578: NTP Core(NOTICE): Clock is synchronized.
Dec 17 20:12:18.578: NTP Core(INFO): system event 'event_peer/strat_chg' (0x04)
status 'leap_none, sync_ntp, 7 events, event_sync_chg' (0x673)
Dec 17 20:12:23.554: NTP: Calendar updated.
```

g. Issue the **undebug all** or the **no debug ntp all** command to turn off debugging.

```
R1# undebug all
```

h. Verify the time on R1 after it has made an association with R2.

```
R1# show clock
*20:12:24.859 UTC Wed Dec 17 2014
```

Task 4: Configure syslog Support on R1 and PC-A.

Step 1: Install the syslog server.

Tftpd32 includes a TFTP server, TFTP client, and a syslog server and viewer. The Kiwi Syslog Daemon is only a dedicated syslog server. You can use either with this lab. Both are available as free versions and run on Microsoft Windows.

If a syslog server is not currently installed on the host, download the latest version of Tftpd32 from http://tftpd32.jounin.net or Kiwi from http://www.kiwisyslog.com and install it on your desktop. If it is already installed, go to Step 2.

Note: This lab uses the Ttftpd32 application for the syslog server functionality.

Step 2: Configure R1 to log messages to the syslog server using the CLI.

a. Verify that you have connectivity between R1 and PC-A by pinging the R1 G0/1 interface IP address 192.168.1.1. If it is not successful, troubleshoot as necessary before continuing.

b. NTP was configured in Task 2 to synchronize the time on the network. Displaying the correct time and date in syslog messages is vital when using syslog to monitor a network. If the correct time and date of a message is not known, it can be difficult to determine what network event caused the message.

Verify that the timestamp service for logging is enabled on the router using the **show run** command. Use the following command if the timestamp service is not enabled.

```
R1(config)# service timestamps log datetime msec
```

c. Configure the syslog service on the router to send syslog messages to the syslog server.

```
R1(config)# logging host 192.168.1.3
```

Step 3: Configure the logging severity level on R1.

Logging traps can be set to support the logging function. A trap is a threshold that when reached, triggers a log message. The level of logging messages can be adjusted to allow the administrator to determine what kinds of messages are sent to the syslog server. Routers support different levels of logging. The eight levels range from 0 (emergencies), indicating that the system is unstable, to 7 (debugging), which sends messages that include router information.

Note: The default level for syslog is 6, informational logging. The default for console and monitor logging is 7, debugging.

a. Use the **logging trap** command to determine the options for the command and the various trap levels available.

```
R1(config)# logging trap ?
<0-7>          Logging severity level
alerts         Immediate action needed              (severity=1)
critical       Critical conditions                  (severity=2)
debugging      Debugging messages                   (severity=7)
emergencies    System is unusable                   (severity=0)
errors         Error conditions                     (severity=3)
informational  Informational messages               (severity=6)
notifications  Normal but significant conditions (severity=5)
warnings       Warning conditions                   (severity=4)
<cr>
```

b. Define the level of severity for messages sent to the syslog server. To configure the severity levels, use either the keyword or the severity level number (0–7).

Severity Level	Keyword	Meaning
0	emergencies	System is unusable
1	alerts	Immediate action required
2	critical	Critical conditions
3	errors	Error conditions
4	warnings	Warning conditions
5	notifications	Normal but significant condition
6	informational	Informational messages
7	debugging	Debugging messages

Note: The severity level includes the level specified and anything with a lower severity number. For example, if you set the level to 4, or use the keyword **warnings**, you capture messages with severity level 4, 3, 2, 1, and 0.

c. Use the **logging trap** command to set the severity level for R1.

```
R1(config)# logging trap warnings
```

d. What is the problem with setting the level of severity too high or too low?

_____

_____

e. If the command **logging trap critical** were issued, which severity levels of messages would be logged?

_____

_____

Step 4: Display the current status of logging for R1.

Use the **show logging** command to see the type and level of logging enabled.

```
R1# show logging
Syslog logging: enabled (0 messages dropped, 3 messages rate-limited, 0 flushes, 0
overruns, xml disabled, filtering disabled)

No Active Message Discriminator.



No Inactive Message Discriminator.


    Console logging: level debugging, 72 messages logged, xml disabled,
                     filtering disabled
    Monitor logging: level debugging, 0 messages logged, xml disabled,
                     filtering disabled
    Buffer logging:  level debugging, 72 messages logged, xml disabled,
                     filtering disabled
    Exception Logging: size (4096 bytes)
    Count and timestamp logging messages: disabled
    Persistent logging: disabled

No active filter modules.
```

```
     Trap logging: level warnings, 54 message lines logged
         Logging to 192.168.1.13  (udp port 514, audit disabled,
             link up),
             3 message lines logged,
             0 message lines rate-limited,
             0 message lines dropped-by-MD,
             xml disabled, sequence number disabled
             filtering disabled
         Logging to 192.168.1.3  (udp port 514, audit disabled,
             link up),
             3 message lines logged,
             0 message lines rate-limited,
             0 message lines dropped-by-MD,
             xml disabled, sequence number disabled
             filtering disabled
         Logging Source-Interface:       VRF Name:
<output omitted>
```

At what level is console logging enabled?

_____

At what level is trap logging enabled?

_____

What is the IP address of the syslog server?

_____

What port is syslog using?

_____

Part 5: Securing the Control Plane

In Part 5 of this lab, you will do as follows:

- Configure OSPF routing protocol authentication using SHA256.
- Verify that OSPF routing protocol authentication is working.

Task 1: Configure OSPF Routing Protocol Authentication using SHA256 Hashing.

Step 1: Configure a key chain on all three routers.

a. Assign a key chain name and number.

```
R1(config)# key chain NetAcad
R1(config-keychain)# key 1
```

b. Assign the authentication key string.

```
R1(config-keychain-key)# key-string CCNASkeystring
```

c. Configure the encryption algorithm to be used for authentication, use SHA256 encryption.

```
R1(config-keychain-key)#cryptographic-algorithm hmac-sha-256
```

Step 2: Configure the serial interfaces to use OSPF authentication.

a. Use the **ip ospf authentication** command to assign the key-chain to the serial interface on R1 and R3.

```
R1(config)# interface s0/0/0
R1(config-if)# ip ospf authentication key-chain NetAcad
R1(config)#
Feb 17 21:24:45.309: %OSPF-5-ADJCHG: Process 1, Nbr 10.2.2.2 on Serial0/0/0 from FULL
to DOWN, Neighbor Down: Dead timer expired

R3(config)# interface s0/0/1
R3(config-if)# ip ospf authentication key-chain NetAcad
R3(config)#
*Feb 17 21:23:14.078: %OSPF-5-ADJCHG: Process 1, Nbr 10.2.2.2 on Serial0/0/1 from FULL
to DOWN, Neighbor Down: Dead timer expired
```

b. Use the **ip ospf authentication** command to assign the key-chain to both serial interfaces on R2.

```
R2(config)# interface s0/0/0
R2(config-if)# ip ospf authentication key-chain NetAcad
R2(config)# interface serial 0/0/1
R2(config-if)# ip ospf authentication key-chain NetAcad
R2(config-if)#
Feb 17 21:36:25.114: %OSPF-5-ADJCHG: Process 1, Nbr 192.168.1.1 on Serial0/0/0 from
LOADING to FULL, Loading Done
Feb 17 21:36:30.686: %OSPF-5-ADJCHG: Process 1, Nbr 192.168.3.1 on Serial0/0/1 from
LOADING to FULL, Loading Done
```

Step 3: Verify OSPF Routing and Authentication is Correct.

a. Issue the show **ip ospf interface** command to verify that Authentication Key has been assigned to the serial interfaces on all routers.

```
R1# show ip ospf interface s0/0/0
Serial0/0/0 is up, line protocol is up
  Internet Address 10.1.1.1/30, Area 0, Attached via Network Statement
  Process ID 1, Router ID 192.168.1.1, Network Type POINT_TO_POINT, Cost: 64
  Topology-MTID    Cost    Disabled    Shutdown      Topology Name
       0            64        no          no             Base
  Transmit Delay is 1 sec, State POINT_TO_POINT
  Timer intervals configured, Hello 10, Dead 40, Wait 40, Retransmit 5
    oob-resync timeout 40
    Hello due in 00:00:02
  Supports Link-local Signaling (LLS)
  Cisco NSF helper support enabled
  IETF NSF helper support enabled
  Index 2/2, flood queue length 0
  Next 0x0(0)/0x0(0)
  Last flood scan length is 1, maximum is 1
  Last flood scan time is 0 msec, maximum is 0 msec
  Neighbor Count is 1, Adjacent neighbor count is 1
```

```
     Adjacent with neighbor 10.2.2.2
  Suppress hello for 0 neighbor(s)
  Cryptographic authentication enabled
     Sending SA: Key 1, Algorithm HMAC-SHA-256 - key chain NetAcad
R1#
```

b. Issue the **show ip ospf** neighbor command to verify that each router lists the other routers in the network as neighbors.

R2# **show ip ospf neighbor**

```
Neighbor ID     Pri   State        Dead Time   Address      Interface
192.168.3.1       0   FULL/ -      00:00:39    10.2.2.1     Serial0/0/1
192.168.1.1       0   FULL/ -      00:00:37    10.1.1.1     Serial0/0/0
R2#
```

c. Issue the **show ip route** command to verify that all networks display in the routing table on all routers.

R3# **show ip route**

```
Codes: L - local, C - connected, S - static, R - RIP, M - mobile, B - BGP
       D - EIGRP, EX - EIGRP external, O - OSPF, IA - OSPF inter area
       N1 - OSPF NSSA external type 1, N2 - OSPF NSSA external type 2
       E1 - OSPF external type 1, E2 - OSPF external type 2
       i - IS-IS, su - IS-IS summary, L1 - IS-IS level-1, L2 - IS-IS level-2
       ia - IS-IS inter area, * - candidate default, U - per-user static route
       o - ODR, P - periodic downloaded static route, H - NHRP, l - LISP
       a - application route
       + - replicated route, % - next hop override

Gateway of last resort is not set

      10.0.0.0/8 is variably subnetted, 3 subnets, 2 masks
O        10.1.1.0/30 [110/1562] via 10.2.2.2, 00:01:56, Serial0/0/1
C        10.2.2.0/30 is directly connected, Serial0/0/1
L        10.2.2.1/32 is directly connected, Serial0/0/1
O     192.168.1.0/24 [110/1563] via 10.2.2.2, 00:01:46, Serial0/0/1
      192.168.3.0/24 is variably subnetted, 2 subnets, 2 masks
C        192.168.3.0/24 is directly connected, GigabitEthernet0/1
L        192.168.3.1/32 is directly connected, GigabitEthernet0/1
```

d. Use the **ping** command to verify connectivity between PC-A and PC-C.

    If the pings are not successful, troubleshoot before continuing.

Part 6: Configure Automated Security Features

In Part 6 of this lab, you will do as follows:

•   Use AutoSecure to secure R3.

•   Review router security configurations with CLI.

Task 1: Use AutoSecure to Secure R3.

By using a single command in CLI mode, the AutoSecure feature allows you to disable common IP services that can be exploited for network attacks. It can also enable IP services and features that can aid in the defense of a network when under attack. AutoSecure simplifies the security configuration of a router and hardens the router configuration.

Step 1: Use the AutoSecure Cisco IOS feature.

a. Enter privileged EXEC mode using the **enable** command.

b. Issue the **auto secure** command on R3 to lock down the router. R2 represents an ISP router, so assume that R3 S0/0/1 is connected to the Internet when prompted by the AutoSecure questions. Respond to the AutoSecure questions as shown in the following output. The responses are bolded.

```
R3# auto secure
                --- AutoSecure Configuration ---

*** AutoSecure configuration enhances the security of
the router, but it will not make it absolutely resistant
to all security attacks ***

AutoSecure will modify the configuration of your device.
All configuration changes will be shown. For a detailed
explanation of how the configuration changes enhance security
and any possible side effects, please refer to Cisco.com for
Autosecure documentation.
At any prompt you may enter '?' for help.
Use ctrl-c to abort this session at any prompt.

Gathering information about the router for AutoSecure

Is this router connected to internet? [no]: yes
Enter the number of interfaces facing the internet [1]: [Enter]

Interface                   IP-Address     OK? Method Status                      Protocol
Embedded-Service-Engine0/0  unassigned     YES NVRAM  administratively down down
GigabitEthernet0/0          unassigned     YES manual administratively down down
GigabitEthernet0/1          192.168.3.1    YES manual up                          up
Serial0/0/0                 unassigned     YES NVRAM  administratively down down
Serial0/0/1                 10.2.2.1       YES manual up                          up
Enter the interface name that is facing the internet: Serial0/0/1

Securing Management plane services...

Disabling service finger
Disabling service pad
Disabling udp & tcp small servers
Enabling service password encryption
Enabling service tcp-keepalives-in
Enabling service tcp-keepalives-out
```

Disabling the cdp protocol

Disabling the bootp server
Disabling the http server
Disabling the finger service
Disabling source routing
Disabling gratuitous arp

Here is a sample Security Banner to be shown
at every access to device. Modify it to suit your
enterprise requirements.

Authorized Access only
  This system is the property of So-&-So-Enterprise.
  UNAUTHORIZED ACCESS TO THIS DEVICE IS PROHIBITED.
  You must have explicit permission to access this
  device. All activities performed on this device
  are logged. Any violations of access policy will result
  in disciplinary action.

Enter the security banner {Put the banner between
k and k, where k is any character}:
 # Unauthorized Access Prohibited #
Enter the new enable password: **cisco67890**
Confirm the enable password: **cisco67890**
Configuring AAA local authentication
Configuring console, Aux and vty lines for
local authentication, exec-timeout, transport
Securing device against Login Attacks
Configure the following parameters

Blocking Period when Login Attack detected: **60**

Maximum Login failures with the device: **2**

Maximum time period for crossing the failed login attempts: **30**

Configure SSH server? [yes]: **[Enter]**

Configuring interface specific AutoSecure services
Disabling the following ip services on all interfaces:

 no ip redirects
 no ip proxy-arp
 no ip unreachables
 no ip directed-broadcast
 no ip mask-reply
Disabling mop on Ethernet interfaces

Securing Forwarding plane services...

Enabling unicast rpf on all interfaces connected
to internet

Configure CBAC Firewall feature? [yes/no]: **no**

This is the configuration generated:

```
no service finger
no service pad
no service udp-small-servers
no service tcp-small-servers
service password-encryption
service tcp-keepalives-in
service tcp-keepalives-out
no cdp run
no ip bootp server
no ip http server
no ip finger
no ip source-route
no ip gratuitous-arps
no ip identd
banner motd ^C  Unaauthorized Access Prohibited ^C
security authentication failure rate 10 log
enable password 7 121A0C0411045A53727274
aaa new-model
aaa authentication login local_auth local
line console 0
 login authentication local_auth
 exec-timeout 5 0
 transport output telnet
line aux 0
 login authentication local_auth
 exec-timeout 10 0
 transport output telnet
line vty 0 4
 login authentication local_auth
 transport input telnet
line tty 1 2
 login authentication local_auth
 exec-timeout 15 0
login block-for 60 attempts 2 within 30
crypto key generate rsa general-keys modulus 1024
ip ssh time-out 60
ip ssh authentication-retries 2
line vty 0 4
```

```
 transport input ssh telnet
service timestamps debug datetime msec localtime show-timezone
service timestamps log datetime msec localtime show-timezone
logging facility local2
logging trap debugging
service sequence-numbers
logging console critical
logging buffered
interface Embedded-Service-Engine0/0
 no ip redirects
 no ip proxy-arp
 no ip unreachables
 no ip directed-broadcast
 no ip mask-reply
 no mop enabled
interface GigabitEthernet0/0
 no ip redirects
 no ip proxy-arp
 no ip unreachables
 no ip directed-broadcast
 no ip mask-reply
 no mop enabled
interface GigabitEthernet0/1
 no ip redirects
 no ip proxy-arp
 no ip unreachables
 no ip directed-broadcast
 no ip mask-reply
 no mop enabled
interface Serial0/0/0
 no ip redirects
 no ip proxy-arp
 no ip unreachables
 no ip directed-broadcast
 no ip mask-reply
interface Serial0/0/1
 no ip redirects
 no ip proxy-arp
 no ip unreachables
 no ip directed-broadcast
 no ip mask-reply
access-list 100 permit udp any any eq bootpc
interface Serial0/0/1
 ip verify unicast source reachable-via rx allow-default 100
!
end
```

```
Apply this configuration to running-config? [yes]: [Enter]

Applying the config generated to running-config
% You already have RSA keys defined named R3.ccnasecurity.com.
% They will be replaced.

% The key modulus size is 1024 bits
% Generating 1024 bit RSA keys, keys will be non-exportable...
[OK] (elapsed time was 1 seconds)

*Feb 18 20:29:18.159: %SSH-5-DISABLED: SSH 2.0 has been disabled
R3#
000066: *Feb 18 20:29:21.023 UTC: %AUTOSEC-1-MODIFIED: AutoSecure configuration has
been Modified on this device
R3#
```

Note: The questions asked and the output may vary depend on the features on the IOS image and device.

Step 2: Establish an SSH connection from PC-C to R3.

a. Start PuTTy or another SSH client, and log in with the **admin** account and password **cisco12345** created when AutoSecure was run. Enter the IP address of the R3 G0/1 interface **192.168.3.1**.

b. Because SSH was configured using AutoSecure on R3, you will receive a PuTTY security warning. Click **Yes** to connect anyway.

c. Enter privileged EXEC mode, and verify the R3 configuration using the **show run** command.

d. Issue the **show flash** command. Is there a file that might be related to AutoSecure, and if so what is its name and when was it created?

_____

_____

e. Issue the command **more flash:pre_autosec.cfg**. What are the contents of this file, and what is its purpose?

_____

_____

f. How would you restore this file if AutoSecure did not produce the desired results?

_____

_____

Step 3: Contrast the AutoSecure-generated configuration of R3 with the manual configuration of R1.

    a.   What security-related configuration changes were performed on R3 by AutoSecure that were not performed in previous sections of the lab on R1?

        _____

        _____

        _____

        _____

        _____

        _____

        _____

    b.   What security-related configuration changes were performed in previous sections of the lab that were not performed by AutoSecure?

        _____

        _____

        _____

        _____

        _____

        _____

    c.   Identify at least five unneeded services that were locked down by AutoSecure and at least three security measures applied to each interface.

        Note: Some of the services listed as being disabled in the AutoSecure output above might not appear in the **show running-config** output because they are already disabled by default for this router and Cisco IOS version.

        Services disabled include:

        _____

        _____

        _____

        _____

        _____

        For each interface, the following were disabled:

        _____

        _____

        _____

_____

_____

_____

Step 4: Test connectivity.

Ping from PC-A on the R1 LAN to PC-C on the router R3 LAN. If pings from PC-A to PC-C are not successful, troubleshoot before continuing.

Reflection

1. Explain the importance of securing router access and monitoring network devices.

_____

_____

_____

_____

_____

_____

2. What advantages does SSH have over Telnet?

_____

_____

3. How scalable is setting up usernames and using the local database for authentication?

_____

_____

_____

_____

_____

_____

4. Why it is better to have centralized logging servers rather than to have the routers only log locally?

_____

_____

_____

_____

_____

_____

5. What are some advantages to using AutoSecure?

_____

_____

_____

_____

_____

_____

Router Interface Summary Table

Router Interface Summary				
Router Model	**Ethernet Interface #1**	**Ethernet Interface #2**	**Serial Interface #1**	**Serial Interface #2**
1800	Fast Ethernet 0/0 (F0/0)	Fast Ethernet 0/1 (F0/1)	Serial 0/0/0 (S0/0/0)	Serial 0/0/1 (S0/0/1)
1900	Gigabit Ethernet 0/0 (G0/0)	Gigabit Ethernet 0/1 (G0/1)	Serial 0/0/0 (S0/0/0)	Serial 0/0/1 (S0/0/1)
2801	Fast Ethernet 0/0 (F0/0)	Fast Ethernet 0/1 (F0/1)	Serial 0/1/0 (S0/1/0)	Serial 0/1/1 (S0/1/1)
2811	Fast Ethernet 0/0 (F0/0)	Fast Ethernet 0/1 (F0/1)	Serial 0/0/0 (S0/0/0)	Serial 0/0/1 (S0/0/1)
2900	Gigabit Ethernet 0/0 (G0/0)	Gigabit Ethernet 0/1 (G0/1)	Serial 0/0/0 (S0/0/0)	Serial 0/0/1 (S0/0/1)

Note: To find out how the router is configured, look at the interfaces to identify the type of router and how many interfaces the router has. There is no way to effectively list all the combinations of configurations for each router class. This table includes identifiers for the possible combinations of Ethernet and Serial interfaces in the device. The table does not include any other type of interface, even though a specific router may contain one. An example of this might be an ISDN BRI interface. The string in parenthesis is the legal abbreviation that can be used in Cisco IOS commands to represent the interface.

Chapter 3: Authentication, Authorization, and Accounting

Lab 3.6.1.1 – Securing Administrative Access Using AAA and RADIUS

Topology

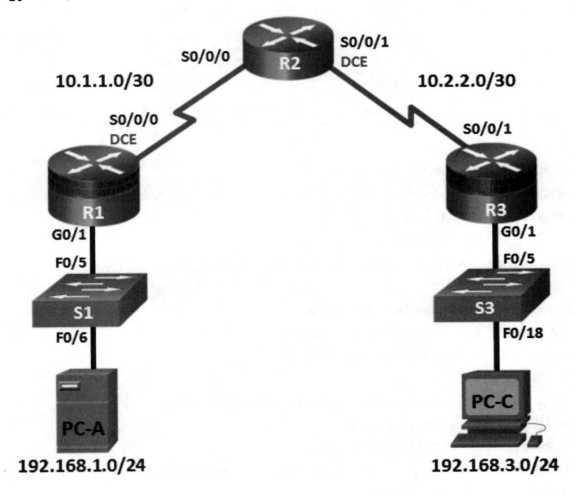

Note: ISR G1 devices use FastEthernet interfaces instead of GigabitEthernet Interfaces.

Addressing Table

Device	Interface	IP Address	Subnet Mask	Default Gateway	Switch Port
R1	G0/1	192.168.1.1	255.255.255.0	N/A	S1 F0/5
	S0/0/0 (DCE)	10.1.1.1	255.255.255.252	N/A	N/A
R2	S0/0/0	10.1.1.2	255.255.255.252	N/A	N/A
	S0/0/1 (DCE)	10.2.2.2	255.255.255.252	N/A	N/A
R3	G0/1	192.168.3.1	255.255.255.0	N/A	S3 F0/5
	S0/0/1	10.2.2.1	255.255.255.252	N/A	N/A
PC-A	NIC	192.168.1.3	255.255.255.0	192.168.1.1	S1 F0/6
PC-C	NIC	192.168.3.3	255.255.255.0	192.168.3.1	S3 F0/18

Objectives

Part 1: Configure Basic Device Settings

- Configure basic settings such as host name, interface IP addresses, and access passwords.
- Configure static routing.

Part 2: Configure Local Authentication

- Configure a local database user and local access for the console, vty, and aux lines.
- Test the configuration.

Part 3: Configure Local Authentication Using AAA

- Configure the local user database using Cisco IOS.
- Configure AAA local authentication using Cisco IOS.
- Test the configuration.

Part 4: Configure Centralized Authentication Using AAA and RADIUS

- Install a RADIUS server on a computer.
- Configure users on the RADIUS server.
- Use Cisco IOS to configure AAA services on a router to access the RADIUS server for authentication.
- Test the AAA RADIUS configuration.

Background / Scenario

The most basic form of router access security is to create passwords for the console, vty, and aux lines. A user is prompted for only a password when accessing the router. Configuring a privileged EXEC mode enable secret password further improves security, but still only a basic password is required for each mode of access.

In addition to basic passwords, specific usernames or accounts with varying privilege levels can be defined in the local router database that can apply to the router as a whole. When the console, vty, or aux lines are configured to refer to this local database, the user is prompted for a username and a password when using any of these lines to access the router.

Additional control over the login process can be achieved using authentication, authorization, and accounting (AAA). For basic authentication, AAA can be configured to access the local database for user logins, and fallback procedures can also be defined. However, this approach is not very scalable because it must be configured on every router. To take full advantage of AAA and achieve maximum scalability, AAA is used in conjunction with an external TACACS+ or RADIUS server database. When a user attempts to log in, the router references the external server database to verify that the user is logging in with a valid username and password.

In this lab, you build a multi-router network and configure the routers and hosts. You will then use CLI commands to configure routers with basic local authentication by means of AAA. You will install RADIUS software on an external computer and use AAA to authenticate users with the RADIUS server.

Note: The router commands and output in this lab are from a Cisco 1941 router with Cisco IOS Release 15.4(3)M2 (with a Security Technology Package license). Other routers and Cisco IOS versions can be used. See the Router Interface Summary Table at the end of the lab to determine which interface identifiers to use based on the equipment in the lab. Depending on the router model and Cisco IOS version, the commands available and output produced might vary from what is shown in this lab.

Note: Before beginning, ensure that the routers and switches have been erased and have no startup configurations.

Required Resources

- 3 Routers (Cisco 1941 with Cisco IOS Release 15.4(3)M2 image with a Security Technology Package license)
- 2 Switches (Cisco 2960 or comparable) (Not Required)
- 2 PCs (Windows 7 or Windows 8.1, SSH Client, and WinRadius)
- Serial and Ethernet cables, as shown in the topology
- Console cables to configure Cisco networking devices

Part 1: Configure Basic Device Settings

In Part 1 of this lab, you set up the network topology and configure basic settings, such as the interface IP addresses, static routing, device access, and passwords.

All steps should be performed on routers R1 and R3. Only steps 1, 2, 3 and 6 need to be performed on R2. The procedure for R1 is shown here as an example.

Step 1: Cable the network as shown in the topology.

Attach the devices as shown in the topology diagram, and then cable as necessary.

Step 2: Configure basic settings for each router.

a. Configure host names as shown in the topology.

b. Configure the interface IP addresses as shown in the IP addressing table.

c. Configure a clock rate for the routers with a DCE serial cable attached to their serial interfaces.

```
R1(config)# interface S0/0/0
R1(config-if)# clock rate 64000
```

d. To prevent the router from attempting to translate incorrectly entered commands as though they were host names, disable DNS lookup.

```
R1(config)# no ip domain-lookup
```

Step 3: Configure static routing on the routers.

    a.   Configure a static default route from R1 to R2 and from R3 to R2.

    b.   Configure a static route from R2 to the R1 LAN and from R2 to the R3 LAN.

Step 4: Configure PC host IP settings.

Configure a static IP address, subnet mask, and default gateway for PC-A and PC-C, as shown in the IP addressing table.

Step 5: Verify connectivity between PC-A and R3.

    a.   Ping from R1 to R3.

    If the pings are not successful, troubleshoot the basic device configurations before continuing.

    b.   Ping from PC-A on the R1 LAN to PC-C on the R3 LAN.

    If the pings are not successful, troubleshoot the basic device configurations before continuing.

    Note: If you can ping from PC-A to PC-C, you have demonstrated that static routing is configured and functioning correctly. If you cannot ping but the device interfaces are up and IP addresses are correct, use the **show run** and **show ip route** commands to help identify routing protocol-related problems.

Step 6: Save the basic running configuration for each router.

Step 7: Configure and encrypt passwords on R1 and R3.

Note: Passwords in this task are set to a minimum of 10 characters but are relatively simple for the benefit of performing the lab. More complex passwords are recommended in a production network.

For this step, configure the same settings for R1 and R3. Router R1 is shown here as an example.

    a.   Configure a minimum password length.

    Use the **security passwords** command to set a minimum password length of 10 characters.

```
R1(config)# security passwords min-length 10
```

    b.   Configure the **enable secret** password on both routers. Use the type 9 (SCRYPT) hashing algorithm.

```
R1(config)# enable algorithm-type scrypt secret cisco12345
```

Step 8: Configure the basic console, auxiliary port, and vty lines.

    a.   Configure a console password and enable login for router R1. For additional security, the **exec-timeout** command causes the line to log out after **5** minutes of inactivity. The **logging synchronous** command prevents console messages from interrupting command entry.

    Note: To avoid repetitive logins during this lab, the exec timeout can be set to 0 0, which prevents it from expiring. However, this is not considered a good security practice.

```
R1(config)# line console 0
R1(config-line)# password ciscoconpass
R1(config-line)# exec-timeout 5 0
R1(config-line)# login
R1(config-line)# logging synchronous
```

b. Configure a password for the aux port for router R1.

```
R1(config)# line aux 0
R1(config-line)# password ciscoauxpass
R1(config-line)# exec-timeout 5 0
R1(config-line)# login
```

c. Configure the password on the vty lines for router R1.

```
R1(config)# line vty 0 4
R1(config-line)# password ciscovtypass
R1(config-line)# exec-timeout 5 0
R1(config-line)# login
```

d. Encrypt the console, aux, and vty passwords.

```
R1(config)# service password-encryption
```

e. Issue the **show run** command. Can you read the console, aux, and vty passwords? Explain.

_____

_____

Step 9: Configure a login warning banner on routers R1 and R3.

a. Configure a warning to unauthorized users using a message-of-the-day (MOTD) banner with the **banner motd** command. When a user connects to the router, the MOTD banner appears before the login prompt. In this example, the dollar sign ($) is used to start and end the message.

```
R1(config)# banner motd $Unauthorized access strictly prohibited!$
R1(config)# exit
```

b. Exit privileged EXEC mode by using the **disable** or **exit** command and press **Enter** to get started.

If the banner does not appear correctly, re-create it using the **banner motd** command.

Step 10: Save the basic configurations on all routers.

Save the running configuration to the startup configuration from the privileged EXEC prompt.

```
R1# copy running-config startup-config
```

Part 2: Configure Local Authentication

In Part 2 of this lab, you configure a local username and password and change the access for the console, aux, and vty lines to reference the router's local database for valid usernames and passwords. Perform all steps on R1 and R3. The procedure for R1 is shown here.

Step 1: Configure the local user database.

a. Create a local user account with MD5 hashing to encrypt the password. Use the type 9 (SCRYPT) hashing algorithm.

```
R1(config)# username user01 algorithm-type scrypt secret user01pass
```

b. Exit global configuration mode and display the running configuration. Can you read the user's password?

_____

_____

Step 2: Configure local authentication for the console line and login.

a. Set the console line to use the locally defined login usernames and passwords.

```
R1(config)# line console 0
R1(config-line)# login local
```

b. Exit to the initial router screen that displays:

```
R1 con0 is now available. Press RETURN to get started.
```

c. Log in using the **user01** account and password previously defined.

What is the difference between logging in at the console now and previously?

_____

_____

d. After logging in, issue the **show run** command. Were you able to issue the command? Explain.

_____

_____

Enter privileged EXEC mode using the **enable** command. Were you prompted for a password? Explain.

_____

_____

Step 3: Test the new account by logging in from a Telnet session.

a. From PC-A, establish a Telnet session with R1.

```
PC-A> telnet 192.168.1.1
```

b. Were you prompted for a user account? Explain.

_____

_____

c. Set the vty lines to use the locally defined login accounts and configure the **transport input** command to allow Telnet.

```
R1(config)# line vty 0 4
R1(config-line)# login local
R1(config-line)# transport input telnet
R1(config-line)# exit
```

d. From PC-A, telnet R1 to R1 again.

```
PC-A> telnet 192.168.1.1
```

Were you prompted for a user account? Explain.

_____

e. Log in as **user01** with a password of **user01pass**.

f. While connected to R1 via Telnet, access privileged EXEC mode with the **enable** command.

What password did you use?

_____

g. For added security, set the aux port to use the locally defined login accounts.

```
R1(config)# line aux 0
R1(config-line)# login local
```

h. End the Telnet session with the **exit** command.

Step 4: Save the configuration on R1.

Save the running configuration to the startup configuration from the privileged EXEC prompt.

```
R1# copy running-config startup-config
```

Step 5: Perform steps 1 through 4 on R3 and save the configuration.

Save the running configuration to the startup configuration from the privileged EXEC prompt.

Part 3: Configure Local Authentication Using AAA on R3

Task 1: Configure the Local User Database Using Cisco IOS.

Step 1: Configure the local user database.

a. Create a local user account with SCRYPT hashing to encrypt the password.

```
R3(config)# username Admin01 privilege 15 algorithm-type scrypt secret
Admin01pass
```

b. Exit global configuration mode and display the running configuration. Can you read the user's password?

_____

_____

Task 2: Configure AAA Local Authentication Using Cisco IOS.

On R3, enable services with the global configuration **aaa new-model** command. Because you are implementing local authentication, use local authentication as the first method, and no authentication as the secondary method.

If you were using an authentication method with a remote server, such as TACACS+ or RADIUS, you would configure a secondary authentication method for fallback if the server is unreachable. Normally, the secondary method is the local database. In this case, if no usernames are configured in the local database, the router allows all users login access to the device.

Step 1: Enable AAA services.

```
R3(config)# aaa new-model
```

Step 2: Implement AAA services for console access using the local database.

a. Create the default login authentication list by issuing the **aaa authentication login default** *method1[method2][method3]* command with a method list using the **local** and **none** keywords.

```
R3(config)# aaa authentication login default local-case none
```

Note: If you do not set up a default login authentication list, you could get locked out of the router and be forced to use the password recovery procedure for your specific router.

Note: The **local-case** parameter is used to make usernames case-sensitive.

b. Exit to the initial router screen that displays:

```
R3 con0 is now available

Press RETURN to get started.
```

Log in to the console as **Admin01** with a password of **Admin01pass**. Remember that usernames and passwords are both case-sensitive now. Were you able to log in? Explain.

_____

_____

Note: If your session with the console port of the router times out, you might have to log in using the default authentication list.

c. Exit to the initial router screen that displays:

```
R3 con0 is now available

Press RETURN to get started.
```

d. Attempt to log in to the console as **baduser** with any password. Were you able to log in? Explain.

_____

_____

e. If no user accounts are configured in the local database, which users are permitted to access the device?

_____

_____

Step 3: Create an AAA authentication profile for Telnet using the local database.

a. Create a unique authentication list for Telnet access to the router. This does not have the fallback of no authentication, so if there are no usernames in the local database, Telnet access is disabled. To create an authentication profile that is not the default, specify a list name of TELNET_LINES and apply it to the vty lines.

```
R3(config)# aaa authentication login TELNET_LINES local
R3(config)# line vty 0 4
R3(config-line)# login authentication TELNET_LINES
```

b. Verify that this authentication profile is used by opening a Telnet session from PC-C to R3.

```
PC-C> telnet 192.168.3.1
Trying 192.168.3.1 ... Open
```

c. Log in as **Admin01** with a password of **Admin01pass**. Were you able to login? Explain.

_____

_____

d. Exit the Telnet session with the **exit** command, and Telnet to R3 again.

e. Attempt to log in as **baduser** with any password. Were you able to login? Explain.

_____

_____

Task 3: Observe AAA Authentication Using Cisco IOS Debug.

In this task, you use the **debug** command to observe successful and unsuccessful authentication attempts.

Step 1: Verify that the system clock and debug time stamps are configured correctly.

a. From the R3 user or privileged EXEC mode prompt, use the **show clock** command to determine what the current time is for the router. If the time and date are incorrect, set the time from privileged EXEC mode with the command **clock set HH:MM:SS DD month YYYY**. An example is provided here for R3.

```
R3# clock set 14:15:00 26 December 2014
```

b. Verify that detailed time-stamp information is available for your debug output using the **show run** command. This command displays all lines in the running config that include the text "timestamps".

```
R3# show run | include timestamps
service timestamps debug datetime msec
service timestamps log datetime msec
```

c. If the **service timestamps debug** command is not present, enter it in global config mode.

```
R3(config)# service timestamps debug datetime msec
R3(config)# exit
```

d. Save the running configuration to the startup configuration from the privileged EXEC prompt.

```
R3# copy running-config startup-config
```

Step 2: Use debug to verify user access.

a. Activate debugging for AAA authentication.

```
R3# debug aaa authentication
AAA Authentication debugging is on
```

b. Start a Telnet session from R2 to R3.

c. Log in with username **Admin01** and password **Admin01pass**. Observe the AAA authentication events in the console session window. Debug messages similar to the following should be displayed.

```
R3#
Feb 20 08:45:49.383: AAA/BIND(0000000F): Bind i/f
Feb 20 08:45:49.383: AAA/AUTHEN/LOGIN (0000000F): Pick method list 'TELNET_LINES'
```

d. From the Telnet window, enter privileged EXEC mode. Use the enable secret password of **cisco12345**. Debug messages similar to the following should be displayed. In the third entry, note the username (Admin01), virtual port number (tty132), and remote Telnet client address (10.2.2.2). Also note that the last status entry is "PASS."

```
R3#
Feb 20 08:46:43.223: AAA: parse name=tty132 idb type=-1 tty=-1
Feb 20 08:46:43.223: AAA: name=tty132 flags=0x11 type=5 shelf=0 slot=0 adapter=0
port=132 channel=0
Feb 20 08:46:43.223: AAA/MEMORY: create_user (0x32716AC8) user='Admin01' ruser='NULL'
ds0=0 port='tty132' rem_addr='10.2.2.2' authen_type=ASCII service=ENABLE priv=15
initial_task_id='0', vrf= (id=0)
Feb 20 08:46:43.223: AAA/AUTHEN/START (2655524682): port='tty132' list='' action=LOGIN
service=ENABLE
Feb 20 08:46:43.223: AAA/AUTHEN/START (2
R3#655524682): non-console enable - default to enable password
Feb 20 08:46:43.223: AAA/AUTHEN/START (2655524682): Method=ENABLE
```

```
Feb 20 08:46:43.223: AAA/AUTHEN (2655524682): status = GETPASS
R3#
Feb 20 08:46:46.315: AAA/AUTHEN/CONT (2655524682): continue_login (user='(undef)')
Feb 20 08:46:46.315: AAA/AUTHEN (2655524682): status = GETPASS
Feb 20 08:46:46.315: AAA/AUTHEN/CONT (2655524682): Method=ENABLE
Feb 20 08:46:46.543: AAA/AUTHEN (2655524682): status = PASS
```

e. From the Telnet window, exit privileged EXEC mode using the **disable** command. Try to enter privileged EXEC mode again, but use a bad password this time. Observe the debug output on R3, noting that the status is "FAIL" this time.

```
Feb 20 08:47:36.127: AAA/AUTHEN (4254493175): status = GETPASS
Feb 20 08:47:36.127: AAA/AUTHEN/CONT (4254493175): Method=ENABLE
Feb 20 08:47:36.355: AAA/AUTHEN(4254493175): password incorrect
Feb 20 08:47:36.355: AAA/AUTHEN (4254493175): status = FAIL
Feb 20 08:47:36.355: AAA/MEMORY: free_user (0x32148CE4) user='NULL' ruser='NULL'
port='tty132' rem_addr='10.2.2.2' authen_type=ASCII service=ENABLE priv=15 vrf= (id=0)
R3#
```

f. From the Telnet window, exit the Telnet session to the router. Then try to open a Telnet session to the router again, but this time try to log in with the username **Admin01** and a bad password. From the console window, the debug output should look similar to the following.

```
Feb 20 08:48:17.887: AAA/AUTHEN/LOGIN (00000010): Pick method list 'TELNET_LINES'
```

What message was displayed on the Telnet client screen?

_____

_____

g. Turn off all debugging using the **undebug all** command at the privileged EXEC prompt.

Part 4: Configure Centralized Authentication Using AAA and RADIUS

In Part 4 of the lab, you install RADIUS server software on PC-A. You then configure R1 to access the external RADIUS server for user authentication. The freeware server WinRadius is used for this section of the lab.

Task 1: Restore R1 to the Basic Configuration.

To avoid confusion as to what was already entered in the AAA RADIUS configuration, start by restoring router R1 to its basic configuration as performed in Parts 1 and 2 of this lab.

Step 1: Reload and restore saved configuration on R1.

In this step, restore the router back to the basic configuration saved in Parts 1 and 2.

a. Connect to the R1 console, and log in with the username **user01** and password **user01pass**.

b. Enter privileged EXEC mode with the password **cisco12345**.

c. Reload the router and enter **no** when prompted to save the configuration.

```
R1# reload
```

```
System configuration has been modified. Save? [yes/no]: no
Proceed with reload? [confirm]
```

Step 2: Verify connectivity.

a.   Test connectivity by pinging from host PC-A to PC-C. If the pings are not successful, troubleshoot the router and PC configurations until they are.

b.   If you are logged out of the console, log in again as **user01** with password **user01pass**, and access privileged EXEC mode with the password **cisco12345**.

Task 2: Download and Install a RADIUS Server on PC-A.

There are a number of RADIUS servers available, both freeware and for cost. This lab uses WinRadius, a freeware standards-based RADIUS server that runs on Windows operating systems. The free version of the software can support only five usernames.

Note: A zipped file containing the WinRadius software can be obtained from your instructor.

Step 1: Download the WinRadius software.

a.   Create a folder named **WinRadius** on your desktop or other location in which to store the files.

b.   Extract the WinRadius zipped files to the folder you created in Step 1a. There is no installation setup. The extracted **WinRadius.exe** file is executable.

c.   You may create a shortcut on your desktop for WinRadius.exe.

Note: If WinRadius is used on a PC that uses the Microsoft Windows Vista operating system or the Microsoft Windows 7 operating system, ODBC (Open Database Connectivity) may fail to create successfully because it cannot write to the registry.

Possible solutions:

a.   Compatibility settings:

1)   Right click on the **WinRadius.exe** icon and select **Properties**.

2)   While in the **Properties** dialog box, select the **Compatibility** tab. In this tab, select the checkbox for **Run this program in compatibility mode for**. Then, in the drop down menu below, choose the operating system that is appropriate for your computer (e.g. Windows 7).

3)   Click **OK**.

b.   Run as Administrator settings:

1)   Right click on the WinRadius.exe icon and select **Properties**.

2)   While in the **Properties** dialog box, select the **Compatibility** tab. In this tab, select the checkbox for **Run this program as administrator** in the Privilege Level section.

3)   Click **OK**.

c.   Run as Administration for each launch:

1)   Right click on the WinRadius.exe icon and select **Run as Administrator**.

2)   When WinRadius launches, click **Yes** in the User Account Control dialog box.

Step 2: Configure the WinRadius server database.

a.   Start the WinRadius.exe application. WinRadius uses a local database in which it stores user information. When the application is started for the first time, the following messages are displayed:

```
Please go to "Settings/Database and create the ODBC for your RADIUS database.
Launch ODBC failed.
```

b. Choose **Settings > Database** from the main menu. The following screen is displayed. Click the **Configure ODBC Automatically** button and then click **OK**. You should see a message that the ODBC was created successfully. Exit WinRadius and restart the application for the changes to take effect.

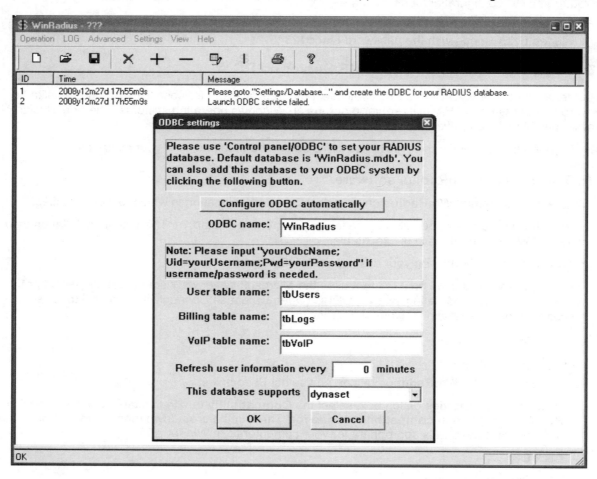

c. When WinRadius starts again, you should see messages similar to the following.

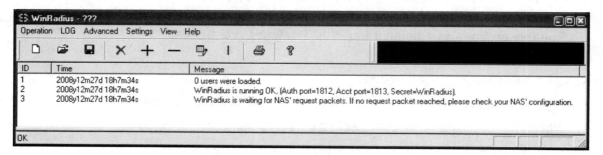

Note about WinRadius Server:

The free version of WinRadius only supports five usernames. If the first message in the above screen shows something other than 0 users were loaded, then you will need to remove the previously added users from the WinRadius database.

To determine what usernames are in the database, click on **Operation** > **Query** then click **OK**. A list of usernames contained in the database is displayed in the bottom section of the WinRadius window.

To delete a user, click **Operation** > **Delete User**, and then enter the username exactly as listed. Usernames are case sensitive.

d. On which ports is WinRadius listening for authentication and accounting?

_____

_____

Step 3: Configure users and passwords on the WinRadius server.

a. From the main menu, select **Operation** > **Add User**.

b. Enter the username **RadUser** with a password of **RadUserpass**. Remember that passwords are case-sensitive.

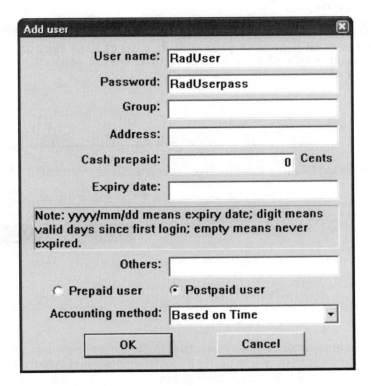

c. Click **OK**. You should see a message on the log screen that the user was added successfully.

Step 4: Clear the log display.

From the main menu, choose **Log** > **Clear**.

Step 5: Test the new user added using the WinRadius test utility.

a. A WinRadius testing utility is included in the downloaded zip file. Navigate to the folder where you unzipped the WinRadius.zip file and locate the file named RadiusTest.exe.

b. Start the RadiusTest application, and enter the IP address of this RADIUS server (**192.168.1.3**), username **RadUser**, and password **RadUserpass** as shown. Do not change the default RADIUS port number of 1813 and the RADIUS password of **WinRadius**.

c. Click **Send** and you should see a Send Access_Request message indicating the server at 192.168.1.3, port number 1813, received 44 hexadecimal characters.

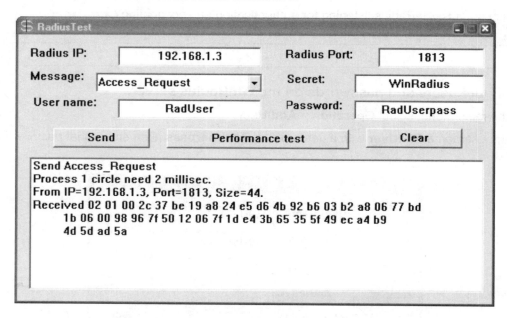

d. Review the WinRadius log to verify that RadUser successfully authenticated.

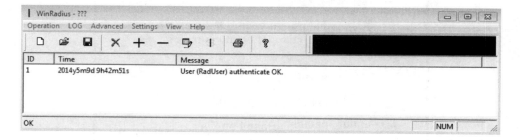

Note: The WinRadius application may be minimized to the system tray. It is still running during the RadiusTest application and will display an error indicating the service failed if it is launched a second time. Make certain to bring the WinRadius back to the top by clicking the icon in the system tray.

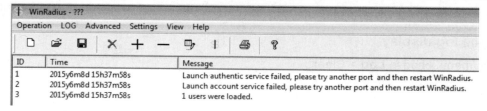

e. Close the RadiusTest application.

Task 3: Configure R1 AAA Services and Access the RADIUS Server Using Cisco IOS.

Step 1: Enable AAA on R1.

Use the **aaa new-model** command in global configuration mode to enable AAA.

```
R1(config)# aaa new-model
```

Step 2: Configure the default login authentication list.

a. Configure the list to first use RADIUS for the authentication service, and then none. If no RADIUS server can be reached and authentication cannot be performed, the router globally allows access without authentication. This is a safeguard measure in case the router starts up without connectivity to an active RADIUS server.

```
R1(config)# aaa authentication login default group radius none
```

b. You could alternatively configure local authentication as the backup authentication method instead.

Note: If you do not set up a default login authentication list, you could get locked out of the router and need to use the password recovery procedure for your specific router.

Step 3: Specify a RADIUS server.

a. Use the **radius server** command to enter RADIUS server configuration mode.

```
R1(config)# radius server CCNAS
```

b. Use the ? to view the sub-mode commands available for configuring a Radius server.

```
R1(config-radius-server)# ?
RADIUS server sub-mode commands:
   address          Specify the radius server address
   automate-tester  Configure server automated testing.
   backoff          Retry backoff pattern(Default is retransmits with constant
                    delay)
   exit             Exit from RADIUS server configuration mode
   key              Per-server encryption key
   no               Negate a command or set its defaults
   non-standard     Attributes to be parsed that violate RADIUS standard
   pac              Protected Access Credential key
   retransmit       Number of retries to active server (overrides default)
   timeout          Time to wait (in seconds) for this radius server to reply
                    (overrides default)
```

c. Use the **address** command to configure this IP address for PC-A

```
R1(config-radius-server)# address ipv4 192.168.1.3
```

d. The **key** command is used for the secret password that is shared between the RADIUS server and the router (R1 in this case) and is used to authenticate the connection between the router and the server before the user authentication process takes place. Use the default NAS secret password of **WinRadius** specified on the Radius server (see Task 2, Step 5). Remember that passwords are case-sensitive.

```
R1(config-radius-server)# key WinRadius
R1(config-redius-server)# end
```

Task 4: Test the AAA RADIUS Configuration.

Step 1: Verify connectivity between R1 and the computer running the RADIUS server.

Ping from R1 to PC-A.

```
R1# ping 192.168.1.3
```

If the pings were not successful, troubleshoot the PC and router configuration before continuing.

Step 2: Test your configuration.

a. If you restarted the WinRadius server, you must re-create the user **RadUser** with a password of **RadUserpass** by choosing **Operation** > **Add User**.

b. Clear the log on the WinRadius server by choosing **Log** > **Clear** from the main menu.

c. On R1, exit to the initial router screen that displays:

```
R1 con0 is now available

Press RETURN to get started.
```

d. Test your configuration by logging in to the console on R1 using the username **RadUser** and the password of **RadUserpass**. Were you able to gain access to the user EXEC prompt and, if so, was there any delay?

_____

e. Exit to the initial router screen that displays:

```
R1 con0 is now available

Press RETURN to get started.
```

f. Test your configuration again by logging in to the console on R1 using the nonexistent username of **Userxxx** and the password of **Userxxxpass**. Were you able to gain access to the user EXEC prompt? Explain.

_____

_____

g. Were any messages displayed on the RADIUS server log for either login? _____

h. Why was a nonexistent username able to access the router and no messages are displayed on the RADIUS server log screen?

_____

_____

i. When the RADIUS server is unavailable, messages similar to the following may display after attempted logins.

```
*Dec 26 16:46:54.039: %RADIUS-4-RADIUS_DEAD: RADIUS server 192.168.1.3:1645,1646 is
not responding.
*Dec 26 15:46:54.039: %RADIUS-4-RADIUS_ALIVE: RADIUS server 192.168.1.3:1645,1646 is
being marked alive.
```

Step 3: Troubleshoot router-to-RADIUS server communication.

a. Check the default Cisco IOS RADIUS UDP port numbers used on R1 by entering into radius server configuration mode again using the **radius server** command and then use the Cisco IOS Help function on the **address** sub-mode command.

```
R1(config)# radius server CCNAS
R1(config-radius-server)# address ipv4 192.168.1.3 ?
  acct-port   UDP port for RADIUS acco/unting server (default is 1646)
  alias       1-8 aliases for this server (max. 8)
  auth-port   UDP port for RADIUS authentication server (default is 1645)
  <cr>
```

What are the default R1 Cisco IOS UDP port numbers for the RADIUS server?

_____

Step 4: Check the default port numbers on the WinRadius server on PC-A.

From the WinRadius main menu, choose **Settings** > **System**.

What are the default WinRadius UDP port numbers? _____

Note: RFC 2865 officially assigned port numbers 1812 and 1813 for RADIUS.

Step 5: Change the RADIUS port numbers on R1 to match the WinRadius server.

Unless specified otherwise, the Cisco IOS RADIUS configuration defaults to UDP port numbers 1645 and 1646. Either the router Cisco IOS port numbers must be changed to match the port number of the RADIUS server or the RADIUS server port numbers must be changed to match the port numbers of the Cisco IOS router.

Re-issue the address sub-mode command again. This time specify port numbers **1812** and **1813**, along with the IPv4 address.

```
R1(config-radius-server)# address ipv4 192.168.1.3 auth-port 1812 acct-port
1813
```

Step 6: Test your configuration by logging into the console on R1.

    a.   Exit to the initial router screen that displays: R1 con0 is now available, Press **RETURN** to get started.

    b.   Log in again with the username of **RadUser** and password of **RadUserpass**. Were you able to login? Was there any delay this time?

_____

_____

    c.   The following message should display on the RADIUS server log.

```
User (RadUser) authenticate OK.
```

    d.   Exit to the initial router screen that displays:

```
R1 con0 is now available, Press RETURN to get started.
```

    e.   Log in again using an invalid username of **Userxxx** and the password of **Userxxxpass**. Were you able to login?

_____

_____

        What message was displayed on the router?

_____

        The following messages should display on the RADIUS server log.

```
Reason: Unknown username
User (Userxxx) authenticate failed
```

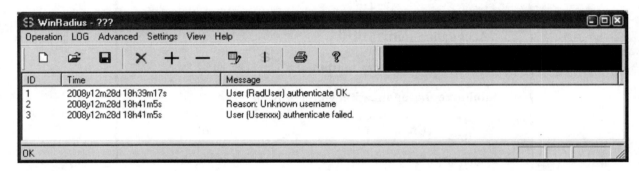

Step 7: Create an authentication method list for Telnet and test it.

    a.   Create a unique authentication method list for Telnet access to the router. This does not have the fallback of no authentication, so if there is no access to the RADIUS server, Telnet access is disabled. Name the authentication method list **TELNET_LINES**.

```
R1(config)# aaa authentication login TELNET_LINES group radius
```

    b.   Apply the list to the vty lines on the router using the login authentication command.

```
R1(config)# line vty 0 4
R1(config-line)# login authentication TELNET_LINES
```

    c.   Telnet from PC-A to R1, and log in with the username **RadUser** and the password of **RadUserpass**. Were you able to gain access to log in? Explain.

_____

_____

   d. Exit the Telnet session, and use Telnet from PC-A to R1 again. Log in with the username **Userxxx** and the password of **Userxxxpass**. Were you able to log in? Explain.

_____

_____

Reflection

1. Why would an organization want to use a centralized authentication server rather than configuring users and passwords on each individual router?

_____

_____

_____

_____

_____

_____

_____

_____

2. Contrast local authentication and local authentication with AAA.

_____

_____

_____

_____

_____

_____

_____

_____

3. Based on the Academy online course content, web research, and the use of RADIUS in this lab, compare and contrast RADIUS with TACACS+.

_____

_____

_____

_____

_____

_____

Router Interface Summary Table

Router Interface Summary				
Router Model	**Ethernet Interface #1**	**Ethernet Interface #2**	**Serial Interface #1**	**Serial Interface #2**
1800	Fast Ethernet 0/0 (F0/0)	Fast Ethernet 0/1 (F0/1)	Serial 0/0/0 (S0/0/0)	Serial 0/0/1 (S0/0/1)
1900	Gigabit Ethernet 0/0 (G0/0)	Gigabit Ethernet 0/1 (G0/1)	Serial 0/0/0 (S0/0/0)	Serial 0/0/1 (S0/0/1)
2801	Fast Ethernet 0/0 (F0/0)	Fast Ethernet 0/1 (F0/1)	Serial 0/1/0 (S0/1/0)	Serial 0/1/1 (S0/1/1)
2811	Fast Ethernet 0/0 (F0/0)	Fast Ethernet 0/1 (F0/1)	Serial 0/0/0 (S0/0/0)	Serial 0/0/1 (S0/0/1)
2900	Gigabit Ethernet 0/0 (G0/0)	Gigabit Ethernet 0/1 (G0/1)	Serial 0/0/0 (S0/0/0)	Serial 0/0/1 (S0/0/1)

Note: To find out how the router is configured, look at the interfaces to identify the type of router and how many interfaces the router has. There is no way to effectively list all the combinations of configurations for each router class. This table includes identifiers for the possible combinations of Ethernet and Serial interfaces in the device. The table does not include any other type of interface, even though a specific router may contain one. An example of this might be an ISDN BRI interface. The string in parenthesis is the legal abbreviation that can be used in Cisco IOS commands to represent the interface.

Chapter 4: Implementing Firewall Technologies

Lab 4.4.1.2 – Configuring Zone-Based Policy Firewalls

Topology

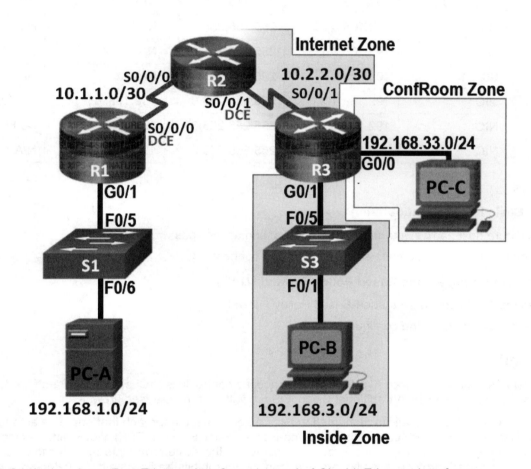

Note: ISR G1 devices have Fast Ethernet interfaces instead of Gigabit Ethernet Interfaces.

IP Addressing Table

Device	Interface	IP Address	Subnet Mask	Default Gateway	Switch Port
R1	G0/1	192.168.1.1	255.255.255.0	N/A	S1 F0/5
	S0/0/0 (DCE)	10.1.1.1	255.255.255.252	N/A	N/A
R2	S0/0/0	10.1.1.2	255.255.255.252	N/A	N/A
	S0/0/1 (DCE)	10.2.2.2	255.255.255.252	N/A	N/A
R3	G0/0	192.168.33.1	255.255.255.0	N/A	N/A
	G0/1	192.168.3.1	255.255.255.0	N/A	S3 F0/5
	S0/0/1	10.2.2.1	255.255.255.252	N/A	N/A
PC-A	NIC	192.168.1.3	255.255.255.0	192.168.1.1	S1 F0/6
PC-B	NIC	192.168.3.3	255.255.255.0	192.168.3.1	S3 F0/1
PC-C	NIC	192.168.33.3	255.255.255.0	192.168.33.1	N/A

Objectives

Part 1: Basic Router Configuration

- Configure host names, interface IP addresses, and access passwords.
- Configure the static routes to enable end-to-end connectivity.

Part 2: Configuring a Zone-Based Policy Firewall (ZPF)

- Use the CLI to configure a Zone-Based Policy Firewall.
- Use the CLI to verify the configuration.

Background

The most basic form of a Cisco IOS firewall uses access control lists (ACLs) to filter IP traffic and monitor established traffic patterns. A traditional Cisco IOS firewall is an ACL-based firewall.

The newer Cisco IOS Firewall implementation uses a zone-based approach that operates as a function of interfaces instead of access control lists. A Zone-Based Policy Firewall (ZPF) allows different inspection policies to be applied to multiple host groups connected to the same router interface. It can be configured for extremely advanced, protocol specific, granular control. It prohibits traffic via a default deny-all policy between different firewall zones. ZPF is suited for multiple interfaces that have similar or varying security requirements.

In this lab, you build a multi-router network, configure the routers and PC hosts, and configure a Zone-Based Policy Firewall using the Cisco IOS command line interface (CLI).

Note: The router commands and output in this lab are from a Cisco 1941 with Cisco IOS Release 15.4(3)M2 (UniversalK9-M). Other routers and Cisco IOS versions can be used. See the Router Interface Summary Table at the end of the lab to determine which interface identifiers to use based on the equipment in the lab. Depending on the router model and Cisco IOS version, the commands available and output produced might vary from what is shown in this lab.

Note: Make sure that the routers and switches have been erased and have no startup configurations.

Required Resources

- 3 Routers (Cisco 1941 with Cisco IOS Release 15.4(3)M2 image or comparable)
- 2 Switches (Cisco 2960 or comparable)
- 3 PCs (Windows Vista or Windows 7)
- Serial and Ethernet cables, as shown in the topology
- Console cables to configure Cisco networking devices

Part 1: Basic Router Configuration

In Part 1 of this lab, you set up the network topology and configure basic settings, such as the interface IP addresses, static routing, device access, and passwords.

Note: All tasks should be performed on routers R1, R2, and R3. The procedures are shown for only one of the routers.

Step 1: Cable the network as shown in the topology.

Attach the devices as shown in the topology diagram, and cable as necessary.

Step 2: Configure basic settings for each router.

a. Configure host names as shown in the topology.

b. Configure the interface IP addresses as shown in the IP addressing table.

c. Configure a clock rate for the serial router interfaces with a DCE serial cable attached.

```
R2(config)# interface S0/0/0
R2(config-if)# clock rate 64000
```

Step 3: Disable DNS lookup.

To prevent the router from attempting to translate incorrectly entered commands, disable DNS lookup.

```
R2(config)# no ip domain-lookup
```

Step 4: Configure static routes on R1, R2, and R3.

a. In order to achieve end-to-end IP reachability, proper static routes must be configured on R1, R2 and R3. R1 and R3 are stub routers, and as such, only need a default route pointing to R2. R2, behaving as the ISP, must know how to reach R1's and R3's internal networks before end-to-end IP reachability is achieved. Below is the static route configuration for R1, R2 and R3. On R1, use the following command:

```
R1(config)# ip route 0.0.0.0 0.0.0.0 10.1.1.2
```

b. On R2, use the following commands.

```
R2(config)# ip route 192.168.1.0 255.255.255.0 10.1.1.1
R2(config)# ip route 192.168.3.0 255.255.255.0 10.2.2.1
R2(config)# ip route 192.168.33.0 255.255.255.0 10.2.2.1
```

c. On R3, use the following command.

```
R3(config)# ip route 0.0.0.0 0.0.0.0 10.2.2.2
```

Step 5: Configure PC host IP settings.

Configure a static IP address, subnet mask, and default gateway for PC-A, PC-B, and PC-C as shown in the IP addressing table.

Step 6: Verify basic network connectivity.

a. Ping from R1 to R3.

If the pings are not successful, troubleshoot the basic device configurations before continuing.

b. Ping from PC-A on the R1 LAN to PC-C on the R3 LAN.

If the pings are not successful, troubleshoot the basic device configurations before continuing.

Note: If you can ping from PC-A to PC-C, you have demonstrated that the end-to-end IP reachability has been achieved. If you cannot ping but the device interfaces are UP and IP addresses are correct, use the **show interface**, **show ip interface,** and **show ip route** commands to help identify problems.

Step 7: Configure a user account, encrypted passwords and crypto keys for SSH.

Note: Passwords in this task are set to a minimum of 10 characters, but are relatively simple for the benefit of performing the lab. More complex passwords are recommended in a production network.

a. Configure a minimum password length using the **security passwords** command to set a minimum password length of 10 characters.

```
R1(config)# security passwords min-length 10
```

b. Configure a domain name.

```
R1(config)# ip domain-name ccnasecurity.com
```

c. Configure crypto keys for SSH

```
R1(config)# crypto key generate rsa general-keys modulus 1024
```

d. Configure an admin01 user account using **algorithm-type scrypt** for encryption and a password of cisco12345.

```
R1(config)# username admin01 algorithm-type scrypt secret cisco12345
```

e. Configure line console 0 to use the local user database for logins. For additional security, the **exec-timeout** command causes the line to log out after **5** minutes of inactivity. The **logging synchronous** command prevents console messages from interrupting command entry.

Note: To avoid repetitive logins during this lab, the **exec-timeout** command can be set to **0 0**, which prevents it from expiring; however, this is not considered to be a good security practice.

```
R1(config)# line console 0
R1(config-line)# login local
R1(config-line)# exec-timeout 5 0
R1(config-line)# logging synchronous
```

f. Configure line aux 0 to use the local user database for logins.

```
R1(config)# line aux 0
R1(config-line)# login local
R1(config-line)# exec-timeout 5 0
```

g. Configure line vty 0 4 to use the local user database for logins and restrict access to SSH connections only.

```
R1(config)# line vty 0 4
R1(config-line)# login local
R1(config-line)# transport input ssh
R1(config-line)# exec-timeout 5 0
```

h. Configure the enable password with strong encryption.

```
R1(config)# enable algorithm-type scrypt secret class12345
```

Step 8: Save the basic running configuration for all three routers.

Save the running configuration to the startup configuration from the privileged EXEC prompt.

```
R1# copy running-config startup-config
```

Part 2: Configuring a Zone-Based Policy Firewall (ZPF)

In Part 2 of this lab, you configure a zone-based policy firewall (ZPF) on R3 using the command line interface (CLI).

Task 1: Verify Current Router Configurations.

In this task, you will verify end-to-end network connectivity before implementing ZPF.

Step 1: Verify end-to-end network connectivity.

a. Ping from R1 to R3 Using both of R3's Gigabit Ethernet interface IP addresses.

    If the pings are not successful, troubleshoot the basic device configurations before continuing.

b. Ping from PC-A on the R1 LAN to PC-C on the R3 conference room LAN.

    If the pings are not successful, troubleshoot the basic device configurations before continuing.

c. Ping from PC-A on the R1 LAN to PC-B on the R3 internal LAN.

    If the pings are not successful, troubleshoot the basic device configurations before continuing.

Step 2: Display the R3 running configurations.

a. Issue the **show ip interface brief** command on R3 to verify the correct IP addresses were assigned. Use the IP Address Table to verify the addresses.

b. Issue the **show ip route** command on R3 to verify it has a static default route pointing to R2's serial 0/0/1 interface.

c. Issue the **show run** command to review the current basic configuration on R3.

d. Verify the R3 basic configuration as performed in Part 1 of the lab. Are there any security commands related to access control?

Task 2: Create a Zone-Based Policy Firewall

In this task, you will create a zone-based policy firewall on R3, making it act not only as a router but also as a firewall. R3 is currently responsible for routing packets for the three networks connected to it. R3's interface roles are configured as follows:

Serial 0/0/1 is connected to the Internet. Because this is a public network, it is considered an *untrusted* network and should have the lowest security level.

G0/1 is connected to the internal network. Only authorized users have access to this network. In addition, vital institution resources also reside in this network. The internal network is to be considered a *trusted* network and should have the highest security level.

G0/0 is connected to a conference room. The conference room is used to host meetings with people who are not part of the organization.

The security policy to be enforced by R3 when it is acting as a firewall dictates that:

- No traffic initiated from the Internet should be allowed into the internal or conference room networks.

- Returning Internet traffic (return packets coming from the Internet into the R3 site, in response to requests originating from any of the R3 networks) should be allowed.

- Computers in the R3 internal network are considered *trusted* and are allowed to initiate any type traffic (TCP, UDP or ICMP based traffic).

- Computers in the R3 conference room network are considered *untrusted* and are allowed to initiate only web traffic (HTTP or HTTPS) to the Internet.

- No traffic is allowed between the internal network and the conference room network. There is no guarantee regarding the condition of guest computers in the conference room network. Such machines could be infected with malware and might attempt to send out spam or other malicious traffic.

Step 1: Creating the security zones.

A security zone is a group of interfaces with similar security properties and requirements. For example, if a router has three interfaces connected to internal networks, all three interfaces can be placed under the same zone named "internal". Because all security properties are configured to the zone instead of to the individual router interfaces, the firewall design is much more scalable.

In this lab, the R3 site has three interfaces; one connected to an internal trusted network, one connected to the conference room network and another connected to the Internet. Because all three networks have different security requirements and properties, we will create three different security zones.

a. Security zones are created in global configuration mode, and the command allows for zone name definition. In R3, create three zones named **INSIDE**, **CONFROOM** and **INTERNET**:

```
R3(config)# zone security INSIDE
R3(config)# zone security CONFROOM
R3(config)# zone security INTERNET
```

Step 2: Creating Security Policies

Before ZPF can decide if some specific traffic should be allowed or denied, it must be told *what* traffic is to be considered. Cisco IOS uses class-maps to select traffic. *Interesting traffic* is a common denomination for traffic that has been selected by a class-map.

While class-maps select traffic, it is not their job to decide what happens to the selected traffic; Policy-maps decide the *fate* of the selected traffic.

ZPF traffic policies are defined as policy-maps and use class-maps to select traffic. In other words, class-maps define *what* traffic is to be policed while policy-maps define the *action* to be taken upon the selected traffic.

Policy-maps can drop, pass or inspect traffic. Because we want the firewall to *watch* traffic moving in the direction of zone-pairs, we will create inspect policy-maps. Inspect policy-maps allow for dynamic handling of the return traffic.

First, you will create class-maps. After the class-maps are created, you will create policy-maps and attach the class-maps to the policy-maps.

a. Create an inspect class-map to match traffic to be allowed from the INSIDE zone to the **INTERNET** zone. Because we trust the INSIDE zone, we allow all the main protocols.

In the commands below, the first line creates an inspect class-map. The **match-any** keyword instructs the router that any of the **match** protocol statements will qualify as a successful match resulting in a policy being applied. The result is a match for TCP or UDP or ICMP packets.

The **match** commands refer to specific Cisco NBAR supported protocols. For more information on Cisco NBAR visit Cisco Network-Based Application Recognition.

```
R3(config)# class-map type inspect match-any INSIDE_PROTOCOLS
R3(config-cmap)# match protocol tcp
R3(config-cmap)# match protocol udp
R3(config-cmap)# match protocol icmp
```

b. Similarly, create a class-map to match the traffic to be allowed from the **CONFROOM** zone to the **INTERNET** zone. Because we do not fully trust the **CONFROOM** zone, we must limit what the server can send out to the Internet:

```
R3(config)# class-map type inspect match-any CONFROOM_PROTOCOLS
R3(config-cmap)# match protocol http
R3(config-cmap)# match protocol https
R3(config-cmap)# match protocol dns
```

c. Now that the class-maps are created, you can create the policy-maps.

In the commands below, the first line creates an inspect policy-map named **INSIDE_TO_INTERNET**. The second line binds the previously created **INSIDE_PROTOCOLS** class-map to the policy-map. All packets matched by the **INSIDE_PROTOCOLS** class-map will be subjected to the action taken by the **INSIDE_TO_INTERNET** policy-map. Finally, the third line defines the actual action this policy-map will apply to the matched packets. In this case, the matched packets will be inspected.

The next three lines creates a similar policy-map named **CONFROOM_TO_INTERNET** and attaches the **CONFROOM_PROTOCOLS** class-map.

The commands are as follows:

```
R3(config)# policy-map type inspect INSIDE_TO_INTERNET
R3(config-pmap)# class type inspect INSIDE_PROTOCOLS
R3(config-pmap-c)# inspect
R3(config)# policy-map type inspect CONFROOM_TO_INTERNET
R3(config-pmap)# class type inspect CONFROOM_PROTOCOLS
R3(config-pmap-c)# inspect
```

Step 3: Create the Zone Pairs

A zone pair allows you to specify a unidirectional firewall policy between two security zones.

For example, a commonly used security policy dictates that the internal network can initiate any traffic towards the Internet but no traffic originating from the Internet should be allowed to reach the internal network.

This traffic policy requires only one zone pair, **INTERNAL to INTERNET**. Because zone-pairs define unidirectional traffic flow, another zone-pair must be created if Internet-initiated traffic must flow in the **INTERNET to INTERNAL** direction.

Notice that Cisco ZPF can be configured to inspect traffic that moves in the direction defined by the zone pair. In that situation, the firewall *watches* the traffic and dynamically creates rules allowing the return or related traffic to flow back through the router.

To define a zone pair, use the **zone-pair security** command. The direction of the traffic is specified by the source and destination zones.

For this lab, you will create two zone-pairs:

INSIDE_TO_INTERNET: Allows traffic leaving the internal network towards the Internet.

CONFROOM_TO_INTERNET: Allows Internet access from the ConfRoom network.

a. Creating the zone-pairs:

```
R3(config)# zone-pair security INSIDE_TO_INTERNET source INSIDE destination
INTERNET
R3(config)# zone-pair security CONFROOM_TO_INTERNET source CONFROOM
destination INTERNET
```

b. Verify the zone-pairs were correctly created by issuing the **show zone-pair security** command. Notice that no policies are associated with the zone-pairs yet. The security policies will be applied to zone-pairs in the next step.

```
R3# show zone-pair security
Zone-pair name INSIDE_TO_INTERNET
    Source-Zone INSIDE  Destination-Zone INTERNET
    service-policy not configured
Zone-pair name CONFROOM_TO_INTERNET
    Source-Zone CONFROOM  Destination-Zone INTERNET
    service-policy not configured
```

Step 4: Applying Security Policies

a. As the last configuration step, apply the policy-maps to the zone-pairs:

```
R3(config)# zone-pair security INSIDE_TO_INTERNET
R3(config-sec-zone-pair)# service-policy type inspect INSIDE_TO_INTERNET
R3(config)# zone-pair security CONFROOM_TO_INTERNET
R3(config-sec-zone-pair)# service-policy type inspect CONFROOM_TO_INTERNET
```

b. Issue the **show zone-pair security** command once again to verify the zone-pair configuration. Notice that the service-polices are now displayed:

```
R3#show zone-pair security
Zone-pair name INSIDE_TO_INTERNET
    Source-Zone INSIDE  Destination-Zone INTERNET
    service-policy INSIDE_TO_INTERNET
Zone-pair name CONFROOM_TO_INTERNET
    Source-Zone CONFROOM  Destination-Zone INTERNET
    service-policy CONFROOM_TO_INTERNET
```

To obtain more information about the zone-pairs, their policy-maps, the class-maps and match counters, use the **show policy-map type inspect zone-pair** command:

```
R3#show policy-map type inspect zone-pair
policy exists on zp INSIDE_TO_INTERNET
  Zone-pair: INSIDE_TO_INTERNET

  Service-policy inspect : INSIDE_TO_INTERNET

    Class-map: INSIDE_PROTOCOLS (match-any)
      Match: protocol tcp
        0 packets, 0 bytes
        30 second rate 0 bps
      Match: protocol udp
        0 packets, 0 bytes
        30 second rate 0 bps
      Match: protocol icmp
        0 packets, 0 bytes
        30 second rate 0 bps

    Inspect
        Session creations since subsystem startup or last reset 0
        Current session counts (estab/half-open/terminating) [0:0:0]
        Maxever session counts (estab/half-open/terminating) [0:0:0]
        Last session created never
        Last statistic reset never
        Last session creation rate 0
        Maxever session creation rate 0
        Last half-open session total 0
        TCP reassembly statistics
        received 0 packets out-of-order; dropped 0
        peak memory usage 0 KB; current usage: 0 KB
        peak queue length 0

    Class-map: class-default (match-any)
      Match: any
      Drop
```

```
                      0 packets, 0 bytes
[output omitted]
```

Step 5: Assign Interfaces to the Proper Security Zones

Interfaces (physical and logical) are assigned to security zones with the **zone-member security** interface command.

a. Assign R3's G0/0 to the **CONFROOM** security zone:

```
R3(config)# interface g0/0
R3(config-if)# zone-member security CONFROOM
```

b. Assign R3's G0/1 to the INSIDE security zone:

```
R3(config)# interface g0/1
R3(config-if)# zone-member security INSIDE
```

c. Assign R3's S0/0/1 to the **INTERNET** security zone:

```
R3(config)# interface s0/0/1
R3(config-if)# zone-member security INTERNET
```

Step 6: Verify Zone Assignment

a. Issue the show zone security command to ensure the zones were properly created, and the interfaces were correctly assigned:

```
R3# show zone security
zone self
  Description: System defined zone

zone CONFROOM
  Member Interfaces:
    GigEthernet0/0

zone INSIDE
  Member Interfaces:
    GigEthernet0/1

zone INTERNET
  Member Interfaces:
    Serial0/0/1
```

b. Even though no commands were issued to create a "self" zone, the output above still displays it. Why is R3 displaying a zone named "self"? What is the significance of this zone?

_____

_____

_____

_____

Part 3: ZPF Verification

Task 1: Verify ZPF Firewall Functionality

Step 1: Traffic originating on the Internet

    a. To test the firewall's effectiveness, ping PC-B from PC-A. In PC-A, open a command prompt and issue:

```
C:\Users\NetAcad> ping 192.168.3.3
```

        Was the ping successful? Explain.

_____

_____

_____

_____

    b. Ping PC-C from PC-A. In PC-A, open a command window and issue

```
C:\Users\NetAcad> ping 192.168.33.3
```

        Was the ping successful? Explain.

_____

_____

_____

_____

    c. Ping PC-A from PC-B. In PC-B, open a command window and issue

```
C:\Users\NetAcad> ping 192.168.1.3
```

    d. Was the ping successful? Explain.

_____

_____

_____

_____

        Ping PC-A from PC-C. In PC-C, open a command window and issue

```
C:\Users\NetAcad> ping 192.168.1.3
```

    e. Was the ping successful? Explain.

_____

_____

_____

_____

Step 2: The Self Zone Verification

a. From PC-A ping R3's G0/1 interface:

    `C:\Users\NetAcad> ping 192.168.3.1`

    Was the ping successful? Is this the correct behavior? Explain.

    _____

    _____

    _____

    _____

b. From PC-C ping R3's G0/1 interface:

    `C:\Users\NetAcad> ping 192.168.3.1`

    Was the ping successful? Is this the correct behavior? Explain.

    _____

    _____

    _____

    _____

Challenge (optional)

Create the proper zone-pair, class-maps, and policy-maps and configure R3 to prevent Internet originating traffic from reaching the Self Zone.

Appendix – Multiple Interfaces under the Same Zone (optional)

One benefit of ZPF firewalls is that they scale well compared to the classic firewall. If a new interface with the same security requirements is added to the firewall, the administrator can simply add the new interface as a member of an existing security zone. However, some IOS versions will not allow devices connected to different interfaces of the same zone to communicate by default. In those cases, a zone-pair must be created using the same zone as source and destination.

Traffic between similarly zoned interfaces will always be bidirectional due the fact that the zone-pair's source and destination zones are the same. Because of that, there is no need to inspect traffic to allow for automatic return traffic handling; return traffic will always be allowed because it will always conform to the zone-pair definition. In this case, the policy-map should have a **pass** action instead of **inspect**. Because of the **pass** action, the router will not inspect packets matched by the policy-map, it will simply forward it to its destination.

In the context of this lab, if R3 had a G0/2 interface also assigned to the INSIDE zone, and the router IOS version did not support allowing traffic between interfaces configured to the same zone, the extra configuration would look like this:

New zone-pair: **Inside to Inside**; allows routing of traffic among the internal trusted interfaces.

Creating the policy-map (notice that no explicit class-map is needed because we use the default "catch-all" class):

```
R3(config)# policy-map type inspect inside
R3(config-pmap)# class class-default
R3(config-pmap-c)# pass
```

Creating the zone-pair and assigning the new policy-map to it. Notice that the INSIDE zone is both the source and the destination of the zone-pair:

```
R3(config)# zone-pair security INSIDE source INSIDE destination INSIDE
R3(config-sec-zone-pair)# service-policy type inspect inside
```

To verify the existence of the new pair, use **show zone-pair security**:

```
R3# show zone-pair security
    Zone-pair name INSIDE_TO_INTERNET
        Source-Zone INSIDE Destination-Zone INTERNET
        service-policy INSIDE_TO_INTERNET
    Zone-pair name CONFROOM_TO_INTERNET
        Source-Zone CONFROOM  Destination-Zone INTERNET
        service-policy CONFROOM_TO_INTERNET
    Zone-pair name INSIDE
        Source-Zone INSIDE Destination-Zone INSIDE
        service-policy inside
```

Router Interface Summary Table

Router Interface Summary				
Router Model	**Ethernet Interface #1**	**Ethernet Interface #2**	**Serial Interface #1**	**Serial Interface #2**
1800	Fast Ethernet 0/0 (F0/0)	Fast Ethernet 0/1 (F0/1)	Serial 0/0/0 (S0/0/0)	Serial 0/0/1 (S0/0/1)
1900	Gigabit Ethernet 0/0 (G0/0)	Gigabit Ethernet 0/1 (G0/1)	Serial 0/0/0 (S0/0/0)	Serial 0/0/1 (S0/0/1)
2801	Fast Ethernet 0/0 (F0/0)	Fast Ethernet 0/1 (F0/1)	Serial 0/1/0 (S0/1/0)	Serial 0/1/1 (S0/1/1)
2811	Fast Ethernet 0/0 (F0/0)	Fast Ethernet 0/1 (F0/1)	Serial 0/0/0 (S0/0/0)	Serial 0/0/1 (S0/0/1)
2900	Gigabit Ethernet 0/0 (G0/0)	Gigabit Ethernet 0/1 (G0/1)	Serial 0/0/0 (S0/0/0)	Serial 0/0/1 (S0/0/1)
Note: To find out how the router is configured, look at the interfaces to identify the type of router and how many interfaces the router has. There is no way to effectively list all the combinations of configurations for each router class. This table includes identifiers for the possible combinations of Ethernet and Serial interfaces in the device. The table does not include any other type of interface, even though a specific router may contain one. An example of this might be an ISDN BRI interface. The string in parenthesis is the legal abbreviation that can be used in Cisco IOS commands to represent the interface.				

Chapter 5: Implementing Intrusion Prevention

Lab 5.4.1.1 – Configure an Intrusion Prevention System (IPS)

Topology

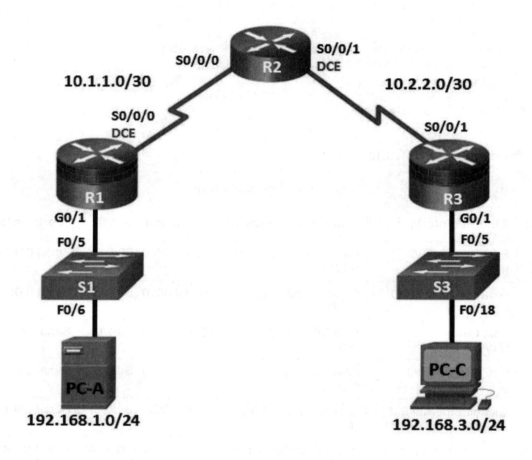

IP Addressing Table

Device	Interface	IP Address	Subnet Mask	Default Gateway	Switch Port
R1	G0/1	192.168.1.1	255.255.255.0	N/A	S1 F0/5
	S0/0/0 (DCE)	10.1.1.1	255.255.255.252	N/A	N/A
R2	S0/0/0	10.1.1.2	255.255.255.252	N/A	N/A
	S0/0/1 (DCE)	10.2.2.2	255.255.255.252	N/A	N/A
R3	G0/1	192.168.3.1	255.255.255.0	N/A	S3 F0/5
	S0/0/1	10.2.2.1	255.255.255.252	N/A	N/A
PC-A	NIC	192.168.1.3	255.255.255.0	192.168.1.1	S1 F0/6
PC-C	NIC	192.168.3.3	255.255.255.0	192.168.3.1	S3 F0/18

Objectives

Part 1: Configure Basic Router Settings

- Configure hostname, interface IP addresses, and access passwords.
- Configure the static routing.

Part 2: Use CLI to Configure an IOS IPS

- Configure IOS IPS using CLI.
- Modify IPS signatures.
- Examine the resulting IPS configuration.
- Verify IPS functionality.
- Log IPS messages to a syslog server.

Part 3: Simulate an Attack

- Use a scanning tool to simulate an attack.

Background/Scenario

In this lab, you will configure the Cisco IOS IPS, which is part of the Cisco IOS Firewall feature set. IPS examines certain attack patterns and alerts or mitigates when those patterns occur. IPS alone is not enough to make a router into a secure Internet firewall, but when added to other security features, it can be a powerful defense.

You will configure IPS using the Cisco IOS CLI and then test IPS functionality. You will load the IPS Signature package from a TFTP server and configure the public crypto key using the Cisco IOS.

Note: The router commands and output in this lab are from a Cisco 1941 router with Cisco IOS Release 15.4(3)M2. Other routers and Cisco IOS versions can be used. See the Router Interface Summary Table at the end of the lab to determine which interface identifiers to use based on the equipment in the lab. The commands available and output produced are determined by the router model and Cisco IOS version used. Therefore, they might vary from what is shown in this lab.

Note: Ensure that the routers and switches have been erased and have no startup configurations.

Required Resources

- 3 routers (Cisco 1941 with Cisco IOS Release 15.4(3)M2)
- 2 switches (Cisco 2960 or comparable)
- 2 PCs (Windows Vista or Windows 7, Tftpd32 server, Nmap/Zenmap, the latest version of Java, Internet Explorer, and Flash Player)
- Serial and Ethernet cables as shown in the topology
- Console cables to configure Cisco networking devices
- IPS Signature package and public crypto key files on PC-A and PC-C (provided by the instructor)

Part 1: Configure Basic Router Settings

In Part 1, you will set up the network topology and configure basic settings, such as hostnames, interface IP addresses, static routing, device access, and passwords.

Note: Perform the steps listed in Part 1 on all three routers. Only R1 is shown below.

Step 1: Cable the network as shown in the topology.

Attach the devices, as shown in the topology diagram, and cable as necessary.

Step 2: Configure the basic settings for each router.

a. Configure the hostnames, as shown in the topology.

b. Configure the interface IP addresses, as shown in the IP Addressing table.

c. Configure a clock rate for serial router interfaces with a DCE serial cable attached.

```
R1(config)# interface S0/0/0
R1(config-if)# clock rate 64000
```

d. Disable DNS lookup to prevent the router from attempting to translate incorrectly entered commands.

```
R1(config)# no ip domain-lookup
```

Step 3: Configure static routing on the routers.

a. Configure a static default route using a next-hop IPv4 address from R1 to R2 and from R3 to R2.

b. Configure a static route from R2 to the R1 LAN (192.168.1.0) and from R2 to the R3 LAN (192.168.3.0) using the appropriate next-hop IPv4 address.

Step 4: Configure PC host IP settings.

Configure a static IP address, subnet mask, and default gateway for PC-A and PC-C, as shown in the IP Addressing table.

Step 5: Verify basic network connectivity.

a. Ping from R1 to R3.

If the pings are unsuccessful, troubleshoot the basic device configurations before continuing.

b. Ping from PC-A on the R1 LAN to PC-C on the R3 LAN.

If the pings are unsuccessful, troubleshoot the basic device configurations before continuing.

Note: If you can ping from PC-A to PC-C, you have demonstrated that the static routing protocol is configured and functioning correctly. If you cannot ping, but the device interfaces are up and IP addresses are correct, use the **show run** and **show ip route** commands to identify routing protocol-related problems.

Step 6: Configure a user account, encrypted passwords, and crypto keys for SSH.

Note: Passwords in this task are set to a minimum of 10 characters but are relatively simple for the benefit of performing the lab. More complex passwords are recommended in a production network.

a. Configure a minimum password length using the **security passwords** command to set a minimum password length of 10 characters.

```
R1(config)# security passwords min-length 10
```

b. Configure a domain name.

```
R1(config)# ip domain-name ccnasecurity.com
```

c. Configure crypto keys for SSH

```
R1(config)# crypto key generate rsa general-keys modulus 1024
```

d. Configure an admin01 user account using **algorithm-type scrypt** for encryption and a password of cisco12345.

```
R1(config)# username admin01 algorithm-type scrypt secret cisco12345
```

e. Configure line console 0 to use the local user database for logins. For additional security, the **exec-timeout** command causes the line to log out after five minutes of inactivity. The **logging synchronous** command prevents console messages from interrupting command entry.

Note: To avoid repetitive logins during this lab, the **exec-timeout** command can be set to **0 0**, which prevents it from expiring. However, this is not considered a good security practice.

```
R1(config)# line console 0
R1(config-line)# login local
R1(config-line)# exec-timeout 5 0
R1(config-line)# logging synchronous
```

f. Configure line aux 0 to use the local user database for logins.

```
R1(config)# line aux 0
R1(config-line)# login local
R1(config-line)# exec-timeout 5 0
```

g. Configure line vty 0 4 to use the local user database for logins and restrict access to only SSH connections.

```
R1(config)# line vty 0 4
R1(config-line)# login local
R1(config-line)# transport input ssh
R1(config-line)# exec-timeout 5 0
```

h. Configure the enable password with strong encryption.

```
R1(config)# enable algorithm-type scrypt secret class12345
```

Step 7: Save the basic configurations for all three routers.

Save the running configuration to the startup configuration from the privileged EXEC mode prompt.

```
R1# copy running-config startup-config
```

Part 2: Configuring IPS Using the Cisco IOS CLI

In Part 2 of this lab, you will configure IPS on R1 using the Cisco IOS CLI. You then review and test the resulting configuration.

Task 1: Verify Access to the R1 LAN from R2

In this task, you will verify that without IPS configured, the external R2 can ping the R1 S0/0/0 interface and PC-A on the R1 internal LAN.

Step 1: Ping from R2 to R1.

From R2, ping R1 interface S0/0/0 at IP address 10.1.1.1.

```
R2# ping 10.1.1.1
```

If the pings are unsuccessful, troubleshoot the basic device configurations before continuing.

Step 2: Ping from R2 to PC-A on the R1 LAN.

From R2, ping PC-A on the R1 LAN at IP address 192.168.1.3.

```
R2# ping 192.168.1.3
```

If the pings are unsuccessful, troubleshoot the basic device configurations before continuing.

Step 3: Display the R1 running configuration prior to configuring IPS.

Issue the **show run** command to review the current basic configuration on R1.

Are there any security commands related to IPS?

_____

_____

_____

Task 2: Prepare the Router and TFTP Server

Step 1: Verify the availability of Cisco IOS IPS files.

To configure Cisco IOS IPS 5.x, the IOS IPS Signature package file and public crypto key file must be available on PC-A. Check with your instructor if these files are not on the PC. These files can be downloaded from www.cisco.com with a valid user account that has proper authorization.

a.   Verify that the IOS-S*xxx*-CLI.pkg file is in a TFTP folder. This is the signature package. The *xxx* is the version number and varies depending on which file was downloaded.

b.   Verify that the realm-cisco.pub.key.txt file is available and note its location on PC-A. This is the public crypto key used by IOS IPS.

Step 2: Verify or create the IPS directory in router flash on R1.

a.   In this step, you will verify the existence of, or create a directory in, the router flash memory where the required signature files and configurations will be stored.

Note: Alternatively, you can use a USB flash drive connected to the router USB port to store the signature files and configurations. The USB flash drive must remain connected to the router USB port if it is used as the IOS IPS configuration directory location. IOS IPS also supports any Cisco IOS file system as its configuration location with proper write access.

b. From the R1 CLI, display the contents of flash memory using the **show flash** command and check for the **ipsdir** directory.

```
R1# show flash
```

c. If the **ipsdir** directory is not listed, create it in privileged EXEC mode.

```
R1# mkdir ipsdir
Create directory filename [ipsdir]? <Enter>
Created dir flash:ipsdir
```

d. If the directory already exists, the following message displays:

```
%Error Creating dir flash:ipsdir (Can't create a file that exists)
```

Use the **delete** command to erase the content of **ipsdir** directory.

```
R1# delete flash:ipsdir/*
Delete filename [/ipsdir/*]?
Delete flash:/ipsdir/R1-sigdef-default.xml? [confirm]
Delete flash:/ipsdir/R1-sigdef-delta.xml? [confirm]
Delete flash:/ipsdir/R1-sigdef-typedef.xml? [confirm]
Delete flash:/ipsdir/R1-sigdef-category.xml? [confirm]
Delete flash:/ipsdir/R1-seap-delta.xml? [confirm]
Delete flash:/ipsdir/R1-seap-typedef.xml? [confirm]
```

Note: Use this command with caution. If there are no files in the **ipsdir** directory, the following message displays:

```
R1# delete flash:ipsdir/*
Delete filename [/ipsdir/*]?
No such file
```

e. From the R1 CLI, verify that the directory is present using the **dir flash:** or **dir flash:ipsdir** command.

```
R1# dir flash:
Directory of flash:/

    1  -rw-    75551300  Feb 16 2015 01:53:10 +00:00  c1900-univeralk9-mz.SPA.154-
3.M2.bin
    2  drw-           0  Mar 8  2015 12:38:14 +00:00  ipsdir
```

or

```
R1# dir flash:ipsdir

Directory of flash:/ipsdir/

No files in directory
```

Note: The directory exists, but there are currently no files in it.

Task 3: Configure the IPS Crypto Key

The crypto key verifies the digital signature for the master signature file (sigdef-default.xml). The contents are signed by a Cisco private key to guarantee the authenticity and integrity at every release.

Step 1: Copy and paste the crypto key file into R1.

In global configuration mode, select and copy the crypto key file named **realm-cisco.pub.key.txt**.

```
crypto key pubkey-chain rsa
  named-key realm-cisco.pub signature
   key-string
    30820122 300D0609 2A864886 F70D0101 01050003 82010F00 3082010A 02820101
    00C19E93 A8AF124A D6CC7A24 5097A975 206BE3A2 06FBA13F 6F12CB5B 4E441F16
    17E630D5 C02AC252 912BE27F 37FDD9C8 11FC7AF7 DCDD81D9 43CDABC3 6007D128
    B199ABCB D34ED0F9 085FADC1 359C189E F30AF10A C0EFB624 7E0764BF 3E53053E
    5B2146A9 D7A5EDE3 0298AF03 DED7A5B8 9479039D 20F30663 9AC64B93 C0112A35
    FE3F0C87 89BCB7BB 994AE74C FA9E481D F65875D6 85EAF974 6D9CC8E3 F0B08B85
    50437722 FFBE85B9 5E4189FF CC189CB9 69C46F9C A84DFBA5 7A0AF99E AD768C36
    006CF498 079F88F8 A3B3FB1F 9FB7B3CB 5539E1D1 9693CCBB 551F78D2 892356AE
    2F56D826 8918EF3C 80CA4F4D 87BFCA3B BFF668E9 689782A5 CF31CB6E B4B094D3
    F3020301 0001
   quit
```

Step 2: Apply the contents of the text file to the router.

a. At the R1 privileged EXEC mode prompt, enter global configuration mode using the **config t** command.

b. Paste the copied crypto key content at the global configuration mode prompt.

```
R1(config)#
R1(config)# crypto key pubkey-chain rsa
R1(config-pubkey-chain)# named-key realm-cisco.pub signature
R1(config-pubkey-key)# key-string
Enter a public key as a hexidecimal number ....

R1(config-pubkey)#$2A864886 F70D0101 01050003 82010F00 3082010A 02820101
R1(config-pubkey)#$D6CC7A24 5097A975 206BE3A2 06FBA13F 6F12CB5B 4E441F16
R1(config-pubkey)#$912BE27F 37FDD9C8 11FC7AF7 DCDD81D9 43CDABC3 6007D128
R1(config-pubkey)#$085FADC1 359C189E F30AF10A C0EFB624 7E0764BF 3E53053E
R1(config-pubkey)#$0298AF03 DED7A5B8 9479039D 20F30663 9AC64B93 C0112A35
R1(config-pubkey)#$994AE74C FA9E481D F65875D6 85EAF974 6D9CC8E3 F0B08B85
R1(config-pubkey)#$5E4189FF CC189CB9 69C46F9C A84DFBA5 7A0AF99E AD768C36
R1(config-pubkey)#$A3B3FB1F 9FB7B3CB 5539E1D1 9693CCBB 551F78D2 892356AE
R1(config-pubkey)#$80CA4F4D 87BFCA3B BFF668E9 689782A5 CF31CB6E B4B094D3
R1(config-pubkey)#   F3020301 0001
R1(config-pubkey)#  quit
R1(config-pubkey-key)#
```

c. Exit global configuration mode and issue the **show run** command to confirm that the crypto key is configured.

Task 4: Configure IPS

Step 1: Create an IPS rule.

a.   On R1, create an IPS rule name using the **ip ips name name** command in global configuration mode. Name the IPS rule **iosips**. This will be used later on an interface to enable IPS.

```
R1(config)# ip ips name iosips
```

b.   You can specify an optional extended or standard access control list (ACL) to filter the traffic that will be scanned by this rule name. All traffic permitted by the ACL is subject to inspection by the IPS. Traffic that is denied by the ACL is not inspected by the IPS.

c.   To see the options available for specifying an ACL with the rule name, use the **ip ips name** command and the CLI help function (**?**).

```
R1(config)# ip ips name ips list ?
  <1-199>  Numbered access list
  WORD     Named access list
```

Step 2: Configure the IPS Signature storage location in router flash memory.

The IPS files will be stored in the **ipsdir** directory that was created in Task 2, Step 2. Configure the location using the **ip ips config location** command.

```
R1(config)# ip ips config location flash:ipsdir
```

Step 3: Enable IPS SDEE event notification.

The Cisco Security Device Event Exchange (SDEE) server is a Simple Object Access Protocol (SOAP) based, IDS alert format and transport protocol specification. SDEE replaces Cisco RDEP.

To use SDEE, the HTTP server must be enabled with the **ip http server** command. If the HTTP server is not enabled, the router cannot respond to the SDEE clients because it cannot see the requests. SDEE notification is disabled by default, and must be explicitly enabled.

```
R1(config)# ip http server
```

To enable SDEE, use the following command:

```
R1(config)# ip ips notify sdee
```

Step 4: Enable IPS syslog support.

IOS IPS also supports the use of syslog to send event notifications. SDEE and syslog can be used independently or enabled at the same time to send IOS IPS event notification. Syslog notification is enabled by default.

a.   If console logging is enabled, IPS syslog messages display. Enable syslog if it is not enabled.

```
R1(config)# ip ips notify log
```

b.   Use the **show clock** command to verify the current time and date for the router. Use the **clock set** command in privileged EXEC mode to reset the clock if necessary. The following example shows how to set the clock.

```
R1# clock set 01:20:00 8 march 2015
```

c.   Verify that the timestamp service for logging is enabled on the router using the **show run** command. Enable the timestamp service if it is not enabled.

```
R1(config)# service timestamps log datetime msec
```

d. To send log messages to the syslog server on PC-A, use the following command:

    `R1(config)# logging 192.168.1.3`

e. To see the type and level of logging enabled on R1, use the **show logging** command.

    `R1# show logging`

Note: Verify that you have connectivity between R1 and PC-A by pinging from PC-A to the R1 Fa0/1 interface IP address **192.168.1.1**. If it is not successful, troubleshoot as necessary before continuing.

The next step describes how to download one of the freeware syslog servers if one is unavailable on PC-A.

Step 5: (Optional) Download and start the syslog server.

If a syslog server is not currently available on PC-A, you can download the Tftpd32 from http://tftpd32.jounin.net/. If the syslog server is available on the PC, go to Step 6.

Start the syslog server software on PC-A to send log messages to it.

Step 6: Configure IOS IPS to use one of the pre-defined signature categories.

IOS IPS with Cisco 5.x format signatures operates with signature categories, just like Cisco IPS appliances do. All signatures are pre-grouped into categories, and the categories are hierarchical. This helps classify signatures for easy grouping and tuning.

Warning: The "all" signature category contains *all* signatures in a signature release. Do not unretired the "all" category because IOS IPS cannot compile and use all the signatures contained in a signature release at one time. The router will run out of memory.

Note: When configuring IOS IPS, it is required to first retire all the signatures in the "all" category and then unretire selected signature categories.

In the following example, all signatures in the **all** category are retired, and then the **ios_ips basic** category is unretired.

```
R1(config)# ip ips signature-category
R1(config-ips-category)# category all
R1(config-ips-category-action)# retired true
R1(config-ips-category-action)# exit
R1(config-ips-category)# category ios_ips basic
R1(config-ips-category-action)# retired false
R1(config-ips-category-action)# exit
R1(config-ips-category)# exit
Do you want to accept these changes? [confirm] <Enter>

Jan  6 01:32:37.983: Applying Category configuration to signatures ...
```

Step 7: Apply the IPS rule to an interface.

a. Apply the IPS rule to an interface with the **ip ips** *name direction* command in interface configuration mode. Apply the rule you just created for inbound traffic on the S0/0/0 interface. After you enable IPS, some log messages will be sent to the console line, which indicates that the IPS engines are being initialized.

    Note: The direction **in** means that IPS inspects only traffic going into the interface. Similarly, **out** means only traffic going out the interface. To enable IPS to inspect both in and out traffic, enter the IPS rule name for in and out separately on the same interface.

```
R1(config)# interface serial0/0/0
R1(config-if)# ip ips iosips in

Jan  6 03:03:30.495: %IPS-6-ENGINE_BUILDS_STARTED:  03:03:30 UTC Jan 6 2008
Jan  6 03:03:30.495: %IPS-6-ENGINE_BUILDING: atomic-ip - 3 signatures - 1 of 13
engines
Jan  6 03:03:30.511: %IPS-6-ENGINE_READY: atomic-ip - build time 16 ms - packets for
this engine will be scanned
Jan  6 03:03:30.511: %IPS-6-ALL_ENGINE_BUILDS_COMPLETE: elapsed time 16 ms
```

The message also displays on the syslog server if it is enabled. The Tftpd32 syslog server is shown here.

Note: The following message may display if the router does not have a built-in IOS signature file.

```
***********************************************************************
The signature package is missing or was saved by a previous version
IPS Please load a new signature package
***********************************************************************

Jan  6 01:22:17.383: %IPS-3-SIG_UPDATE_REQUIRED: IOS IPS requires a signature update
package to be loaded
```

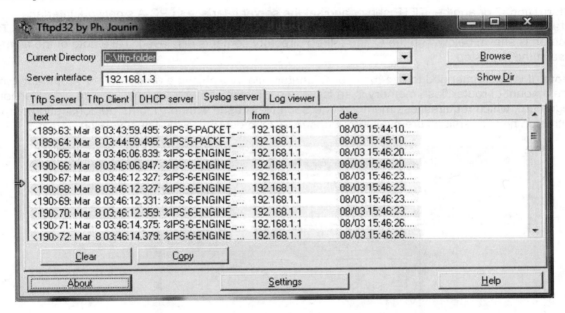

b. Although the R1 Fa0/1 interface is an internal interface, configure it with IPS to respond to internal attacks. Apply the IPS rule to the R1 Fa0/1 interface in the inbound direction.

```
R1(config)# interface g0/1
R1(config-if)# ip ips iosips in
```

Step 8: Save the running configuration.

Enter privileged EXEC mode and save the running configuration to the startup-config file.

```
R1# copy run start
```

Task 5: Load the IOS IPS Signature Package to the Router

The most common way to load the signature package to the router is to use TFTP. Refer to Step 4 for alternative methods of loading the IOS IPS signature package. The alternative methods include the use of FTP and a USB flash drive.

Step 1: (Optional) Download the TFTP server.

The Tftpd32 freeware TFTP server is used in this task. Many other free TFTP servers are also available. If a TFTP server is currently unavailable on PC-A, you can download the latest version of Tftpd32 from http://tftpd32.jounin.net/. If it is already installed, go to Step 2.

Note: This lab uses the Tftpd32 TFTP server. This software also includes a syslog server, which runs simultaneously with the TFTP server.

Step 2: Start the TFTP server on PC-A and verify the IPS file directory.

a. Verify connectivity between R1 and PC-A and the TFTP server using the **ping** command.

b. Verify that the PC has the IPS Signature package file in a directory on the TFTP server. This file is typically named IOS-S*xxx*-CLI.pkg, where *xxx* is the signature file version.

   Note: If this file is not present, contact your instructor before continuing.

c. Start Tftpd32 or another TFTP server and set the server interface to PC-A's network interface (192.168.1.3), and set the default directory to the one with the IPS Signature package in it. The Tftpd32 screen is shown below with the C:\tftp-folder\ directory contents displayed. Take note of the filename for use in the next step.

   Note: It is recommended to use the latest signature file available in a production environment. However, if the amount of router flash memory is an issue in a lab environment, you may use an older version 5.x signature, which requires less memory. The S364 file is used with this lab for demonstration purposes, although newer versions are available. Consult CCO to determine the latest version.

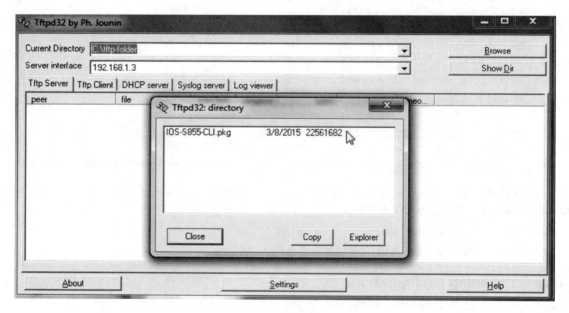

Step 3: Copy the signature package from the TFTP server to the router.

If you do not have a TFTP server available, and you are using a router with a USB port, go to Step 5 and use the procedure described there.

a. Use the **copy tftp** command to retrieve the signature file and load it into the Intrusion Detection Configuration. Use the **idconf** keyword at the end of the **copy** command.

Note: Signature compiling begins immediately after the signature package is loaded to the router. You can see the messages on the router with logging level 6 or above enabled.

```
# copy tftp://192.168.1.3/IOS-S855-CLI.pkg idconf
Loading IOS-S855-CLI.pkg from 192.168.1.3 (via GigabitEthernet0/1): !!!!!OO!!
Mar  8 03:43:59.495: %IPS-5-PACKET_UNSCANNED: atomic-ip - fail open - packets
passed
unscanned!!!!!!!!!!!!!!!!!!!!!!!!!!!!!!!!!!!!!!!!!!!!!!!!!!!!!!!!!!!!!!!!!!!!!!!!!
Mar  8 03:44:59.495: %IPS-5-PACKET_UNSCANNED: atomic-ip - fail open - packets
passed unscanned!!!!!!!!!!!!!!!!!!
[OK - 22561682 bytes]


Mar  8 03:46:06.839: %IPS-6-ENGINE_BUILDS_STARTED:  03:46:06 UTC Mar 8 2015
Mar  8 03:46:06.847: %IPS-6-ENGINE_BUILDING: atomic-ip - 539 signatures - 1
of 13 engines
Mar  8 03:46:12.327: %IPS-6-ENGINE_READY: atomic-ip - build time 5480 ms -
packets for this engine will be scanned
Mar  8 03:46:12.327: %IPS-6-ENGINE_BUILDING: normalizer - 10 signatures - 2
of 13 engines
Mar  8 03:46:12.331: %IPS-6-ENGINE_READY: normalizer - build time 4 ms -
packets for this engine will be scanned
Mar  8 03:46:12.359: %IPS-6-ENGINE_BUILDING: service-http - 1837 signatures -
3 of 13 engines
Mar  8 03:46:14.375: %IPS-6-ENGINE_READY: service-http - build time 2016 ms -
packets for this engine will be scanned
Mar  8 03:46:14.379: %IPS-6-ENGINE_BUILDING: service-smb-advanced - 76
signatures - 4 of 13 engines
Mar  8 03:46:15.003: %IPS-6-ENGINE_READY: service-smb-advanced - build time
624 ms - packets for this engine will be scanned
Mar  8 03:46:15.003: %IPS-6-ENGINE_BUILDING: service-msrpc - 37 signatures -
5 of 13 engines
Mar  8 03:46:15.107: %IPS-6-ENGINE_READY: service-msrpc - build time 104 ms -
packets for this engine will be scanned
Mar  8 03:46:15.111: %IPS-6-ENGINE_BUILDING: state - 39 signatures - 6 of 13
engines
Mar  8 03:46:15.203: %IPS-6-ENGINE_READY: state - build time 92 ms - packets
for this engine will be scanned
Mar  8 03:46:15.203: %IPS-6-ENGINE_BUILDING: service-ftp - 3 signatures - 7
of 13 engines
Mar  8 03:46:15.207: %IPS-6-ENGINE_READY: service-ftp - build time 4 ms -
packets for this engine will be scanned
Mar  8 03:46:15.271: %IPS-6-ENGINE_BUILDING: string-tcp - 3782 signatures - 8
of 13 engines
```

```
Mar  8 03:46:19.887: %IPS-6-ENGINE_READY: string-tcp - build time 4616 ms -
packets for this engine will be scanned
Mar  8 03:46:19.895: %IPS-6-ENGINE_BUILDING: service-rpc - 79 signatures - 9
of 13 engines
Mar  8 03:46:19.991: %IPS-6-ENGINE_READY: service-rpc - build time 96 ms -
packets for this engine will be scanned
Mar  8 03:46:19.991: %IPS-6-ENGINE_BUILDING: service-dns - 39 signatures - 10
of 13 engines
Mar  8 03:46:20.027: %IPS-6-ENGINE_READY: service-dns - build time 36 ms -
packets for this
R1#
R1# engine will be scanned
Mar  8 03:46:20.027: %IPS-6-ENGINE_BUILDING: string-udp - 80 signatures - 11
of 13 engines
Mar  8 03:46:20.087: %IPS-6-ENGINE_READY: string-udp - build time 60 ms -
packets for this engine will be scanned
Mar  8 03:46:20.099: %IPS-6-ENGINE_BUILDING: multi-string - 614 signatures -
12 of 13 engines
Mar  8 03:46:20.803: %IPS-6-ENGINE_READY: multi-string - build time 700 ms -
packets for this engine will be scanned
Mar  8 03:46:20.803: %IPS-6-ENGINE_BUILDING: string-icmp - 3 signa
R1#tures - 13 of 13 engines
Mar  8 03:46:20.803: %IPS-6-ENGINE_READY: string-icmp - build time 0 ms -
packets for this engine will be scanned
Mar  8 03:46:20.803: %IPS-6-ALL_ENGINE_BUILDS_COMPLETE: elapsed time 13964 ms
```

b. Use the **dir flash** command to see the contents of the **ipsdir** directory created earlier. There should be six files, as shown here.

```
R1# dir flash:ipsdir
Directory of flash0:/ipsdir/

    4  -rw-          255    Mar 8 2015 02:45:40 +00:00  iosips-sig-delta.xmz
    5  -rw-        16625    Mar 8 2015 03:43:52 +00:00  iosips-sig-typedef.xmz
    6  -rw-       143832    Mar 8 2015 03:43:58 +00:00  iosips-sig-category.xmz
    7  -rw-          304    Mar 8 2015 02:45:42 +00:00  iosips-seap-delta.xmz
    8  -rw-          835    Mar 8 2015 02:45:42 +00:00  iosips-seap-typedef.xmz
    9  -rw-      1632555    Mar 8 2015 03:45:18 +00:00  iosips-sig-default.xmz
```

Step 4: Verify that the signature package is properly compiled.

a. Use the **show ip ips signature count** command to see the counts for the signature package compiled.

```
R1# show ip ips signature count

Cisco SDF release version S364.0
Trend SDF release version V0.0

Signature Micro-Engine: multi-string: Total Signatures 11
      multi-string enabled signatures: 9
      multi-string retired signatures: 11
```

```
Signature Micro-Engine: service-http: Total Signatures 662
      service-http enabled signatures: 163
      service-http retired signatures: 565
      service-http compiled signatures: 97
      service-http obsoleted signatures: 1

Signature Micro-Engine: string-tcp: Total Signatures 1148
      string-tcp enabled signatures: 622
      string-tcp retired signatures: 1031
      string-tcp compiled signatures: 117
      string-tcp obsoleted signatures: 21

<Output Omitted>

Total Signatures: 2435
   Total Enabled Signatures: 1063
   Total Retired Signatures: 2097
   Total Compiled Signatures: 338
   Total Obsoleted Signatures: 25
```

Note: If you see an error message during signature compilation, such as "%IPS-3-INVALID_DIGITAL_SIGNATURE: Invalid Digital Signature found (key not found)," it means the public crypto key is invalid. Refer to Task 3, Configure the IPS Crypto Key, to reconfigure the public crypto key.

b. Use the **show ip ips all** command to view the IPS configuration status summary. To which interfaces and in which direction is the iosips rule applied?

_____

_____

```
R1# show ip ips all

IPS Signature File Configuration Status
    Configured Config Locations: flash:ipsdir/
    Last signature default load time: 18:47:52 UTC Jan 6 2009
    Last signature delta load time: 20:11:35 UTC Jan 6 2009
    Last event action (SEAP) load time: -none-

    General SEAP Config:
    Global Deny Timeout: 3600 seconds
    Global Overrides Status: Enabled
    Global Filters Status: Enabled

IPS Auto Update is not currently configured

IPS Syslog and SDEE Notification Status
    Event notification through syslog is enabled
    Event notification through SDEE is enabled

IPS Signature Status
```

```
      Total Active Signatures: 339
      Total Inactive Signatures: 2096

  IPS Packet Scanning and Interface Status
      IPS Rule Configuration
        IPS name iosips
      IPS fail closed is disabled
      IPS deny-action ips-interface is false
      Interface Configuration
        Interface Serial0/0/0
          Inbound IPS rule is iosips
          Outgoing IPS rule is not set
  Interface FastEthernet0/1
          Inbound IPS rule is iosips
          Outgoing IPS rule is not set

  IPS Category CLI Configuration:
      Category all:
          Retire: True
      Category ios_ips basic:
          Retire: False
```

Step 5: (Optional) Alternative methods of copying the signature package to the router.

If you used TFTP to copy the file and will not use one of these alternative methods, read through the procedures described here to become familiar with them. If you use one of these methods instead of TFTP, return to Step 4 to verify that the signature package loaded properly.

FTP method: Although the TFTP method is generally adequate, the signature file is rather large and FTP can provide another method of copying the file. You can use an FTP server to copy the signature file to the router with this command:

```
copy ftp://<ftp_user:password@Server_IP_address>/<signature_package> idconf
```

In the following example, the user **admin** must be defined on the FTP server with a password of **cisco**.

```
R1# copy ftp://admin:cisco@192.168.1.3/IOS-S855-CLI.pkg idconf
Loading IOS-S855-CLI.pkg !!!!!!!!!!!!!!!!!!!!!!!!!!!!!!!!
[OK - 7608873/4096 bytes]
```

USB method: If there is no access to an FTP or a TFTP server, you can use a USB flash drive to load the signature package to the router.

a. Copy the signature package onto the USB drive.

b. Connect the USB drive to one of the USB ports on the router.

c. Use the **show file systems** command to see the name of the USB drive. In the following output, a 4 GB USB drive is connected to the USB port on the router as file system usbflash0:

```
R1# show file systems
File Systems:

          Size(b)        Free(b)     Type  Flags  Prefixes
              -              -      opaque    rw   archive:
```

```
           -            -       opaque    rw   system:
           -            -       opaque    rw   tmpsys:
           -            -       opaque    rw   null:
           -            -       network   rw   tftp:
      196600       185972       nvram     rw   nvram:
*   64012288     14811136       disk      rw   flash:#
           -            -       opaque    wo   syslog:
           -            -       opaque    rw   xmodem:
           -            -       opaque    rw   ymodem:
           -            -       network   rw   rcp:
           -            -       network   rw   pram:
           -            -       network   rw   http:
           -            -       network   rw   ftp:
           -            -       network   rw   scp:
           -            -       opaque    ro   tar:
           -            -       network   rw   https:
           -            -       opaque    ro   cns:
  4001378304   3807461376       usbflash  rw   usbflash0:
```

d. Verify the contents of the flash drive using the **dir** command.

```
R1# dir usbflash0:
Directory of usbflash0:/

  1  -rw-         807   Mar 8 2015 13:20:12 +00:00  realm-cisco.pub.key
  2  -rw-    22561682   Mar 8 2015 09:57:38 +00:00  IOS-S855-CLI.pkg
```

e. Use the **copy** command with the **idconf** keyword to copy the signature package to the router.

```
R1# copy usbflash0:IOS-S855-CLI.pkg idconf
```

The USB copy process can take 60 seconds or more, and no progress indicator displays. When the copy process is complete, numerous engine building messages display. These must finish before the command prompt returns.

Task 6: Test the IPS Rule and Modify a Signature

You can work with signatures in many ways. They can be retired and unretired, enabled and disabled, and their characteristics and actions can be changed. In this task, you first test the default behavior of IOS IPS by pinging it from the outside.

Step 1: Ping from R2 to the R1 serial 0/0/0 interface.

From the CLI on R2, ping R1 S0/0/0 at IP address **10.1.1.1**. The pings are successful because the ICMP Echo Request signature 2004:0 is retired.

Step 2: Ping from R2 to PC-A.

From the CLI on R2, ping PC-A at IP address **192.168.1.3**. These pings are also successful because of the retired signature. This is the default behavior of the IPS signatures.

```
R2# ping 192.168.1.3

Type escape sequence to abort.
Sending 5, 100-byte ICMP Echos to 192.168.1.3, timeout is 2 seconds:
!!!!!
Success rate is 100 percent (5/5), round-trip min/avg/max = 1/1/4 ms
```

Step 3: Modify the signature.

You can use the Cisco IOS CLI to change signature status and actions for one signature or a group of signatures based on signature categories.

The following example shows how to unretire the echo request signature, enable it, change the signature action to alert, and drop and reset for signature 2004 with a subsig ID of 0.

```
R1(config)# ip ips signature-definition
R1(config-sigdef)# signature 2004 0
R1(config-sigdef-sig)#status
R1(config-sigdef-sig-status)# retired false
R1(config-sigdef-sig-status)# enabled true
R1(config-sigdef-sig-status)# engine
R1(config-sigdef-sig-engine)# event-action produce-alert
R1(config-sigdef-sig-engine)# event-action deny-packet-inline
R1(config-sigdef-sig-engine)# event-action reset-tcp-connection
R1(config-sigdef-sig-engine)# exit
R1(config-sigdef-sig)# exit
R1(config-sigdef)# exit
Do you want to accept these changes? [confirm] <Enter>

Mar  8 05:37:45.775: %IPS-6-ENGINE_BUILDS_STARTED:  05:37:45 UTC Mar 8 2015
Mar  8 05:37:46.099: %IPS-6-ENGINE_BUILDING: atomic-ip - 539 signatures - 1
of 13 engines
R1(config)#
Mar  8 05:37:51.219: %IPS-6-ENGINE_READY: atomic-ip - build time 5120 ms -
packets for this engine will be scanned
Mar  8 05:37:51.427: %IPS-6-ALL_ENGINE_BUILDS_COMPLETE: elapsed time 5652 ms
```

Step 4: Ping from R2 to R1 serial 0/0/0 interface.

a. Start the syslog server.

b. From the CLI on R2, ping R1 S0/0/0 at IP address 10.1.1.1. Were the pings successful? Explain.

_____

_____

Step 5: Ping from R2 to PC-A.

a. From the CLI on R2, ping PC-A at IP address 192.168.1.3. Were the pings successful? Explain.

_____

_____

b. Notice the IPS messages from R1 on the syslog server screen below. How many messages were generated from the R2 pings to R1 and PC-A?

_____

_____

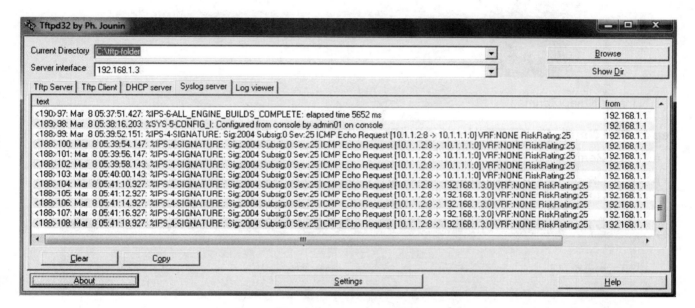

Note: The ICMP echo request IPS risk rating (severity level) is relatively low at 25. Risk rating can range from 0 to 100.

Part 3: Simulate an Attack

Task 1: Verify IPS with Zenmap

Nmap/Zenmap is a network scanning tool that allows you to discover network hosts and resources, including services, ports, operating systems, and other fingerprinting information. Zenmap is the graphical interface for Nmap. Nmap **should not** be used to scan networks without prior permission. The act of network scanning can be considered a form of network attack.

Nmap/Zenmap will test the IPS capabilities on R1. You will run the scanning program from PC-A and attempt to scan open ports on router R2 before and after applying IPS rule iosips on R1.

Step 1: Download and install Nmap/Zenmap.

a. If Nmap/Zenmap is not installed on PC-A, download **Nmap/Zenmap** at http://nmap.org/download.html.

b. Search for the appropriate binaries for your operating system.

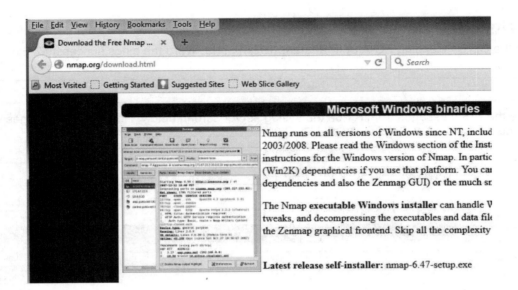

c.   Install Nmap/Zenmap.

Step 2: Run Nmap/Zenmap and set scanning options.

a.   Start **Zenmap** on PC-A.

b.   Enter IP address **10.1.1.2** as the Target and verify that **Intense scan** is selected as the Profile. Click **Scan** to begin the scan.

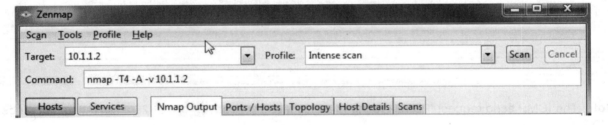

c.   After the scan is complete, review the results displayed in the **Nmap Output** tab.

d.   Click the **Ports/Hosts** tab. How many open ports did Nmap find on R2? What are the associated port numbers and services?

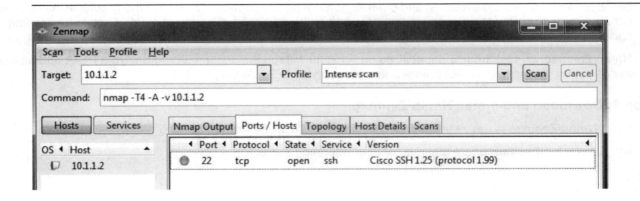

e.   Exit Zenmap.

Task 2: Observe the syslog messages on R1.

You should see syslog entries on the R1 console and on the syslog server if it is enabled. The descriptions should include phrases, such as TCP NULL Packet and TCP SYN/FIN Packet.

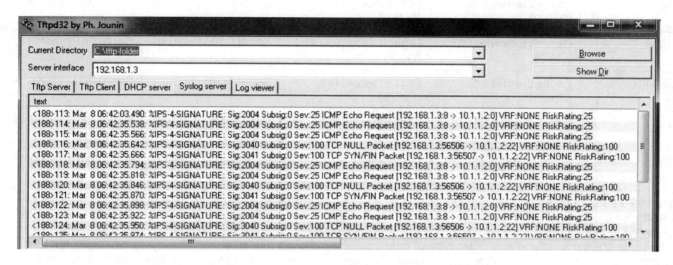

a.   What is the IPS risk rating or severity level (Sev:) of the TCP NULL Packet, signature 3040?

_____

b.   What is the IPS risk rating or severity level (Sev:) of the TCP SYN/FIN packet, signature 3041?

_____

Reflection

1.   If changes are made to a signature while using version 5.x signature files, are they visible in the router running the configuration?

_____

_____

_____

_____

_____

_____

_____

_____

Router Interface Summary Table

Router Interface Summary				
Router Model	**Ethernet Interface #1**	**Ethernet Interface #2**	**Serial Interface #1**	**Serial Interface #2**
1800	Fast Ethernet 0/0 (Fa0/0)	Fast Ethernet 0/1 (Fa0/1)	Serial 0/0/0 (S0/0/0)	Serial 0/0/1 (S0/0/1)
1900	Gigabit Ethernet 0/0 (G0/0)	Gigabit Ethernet 0/1 (G0/1)	Serial 0/0/0 (S0/0/0)	Serial 0/0/1 (S0/0/1)
2801	Fast Ethernet 0/0 (Fa0/0)	Fast Ethernet 0/1 (Fa0/1)	Serial 0/1/0 (S0/1/0)	Serial 0/1/1 (S0/1/1)
2811	Fast Ethernet 0/0 (Fa0/0)	Fast Ethernet 0/1 (Fa0/1)	Serial 0/0/0 (S0/0/0)	Serial 0/0/1 (S0/0/1)
2900	Gigabit Ethernet 0/0 (G0/0)	Gigabit Ethernet 0/1 (G0/1)	Serial 0/0/0 (S0/0/0)	Serial 0/0/1 (S0/0/1)

Note: To find out how the router is configured, look at the interfaces to identify the type of router and how many interfaces the router has. There is no way to effectively list all the combinations of configurations for each router class. This table includes identifiers for the possible combinations of Ethernet and Serial interfaces in the device. The table does not include any other type of interface, even though a specific router may contain one. An example of this might be an ISDN BRI interface. The string in parenthesis is the legal abbreviation that can be used in Cisco IOS commands to represent the interface.

Chapter 6: Securing the Local Area Network

Lab 6.3.1.1 – Securing Layer 2 Switches

Topology

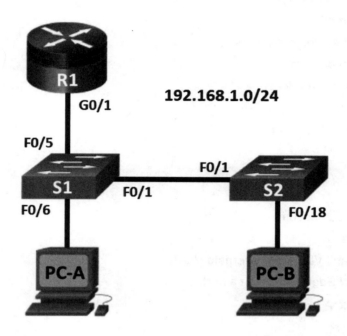

Note: ISR G1 devices use FastEthernet interfaces instead of GigabitEthernet interfaces.

IP Addressing Table

Device	Interface	IP Address	Subnet Mask	Default Gateway	Switch Port
R1	G0/1	192.168.1.1	255.255.255.0	N/A	S1 F0/5
S1	VLAN 1	192.168.1.2	255.255.255.0	N/A	N/A
S2	VLAN 1	192.168.1.3	255.255.255.0	N/A	N/A
PC-A	NIC	192.168.1.10	255.255.255.0	192.168.1.1	S1 F0/6
PC-B	NIC	192.168.1.11	255.255.255.0	192.168.1.1	S2 F0/18

Objectives

Part 1: Configure Basic Switch Settings

- Build the topology.
- Configure the hostname, IP address, and access passwords.

Part 2: Configure SSH Access to the Switches

- Configure SSH version 2 access on the switch.
- Configure an SSH client to access the switch.
- Verify the configuration.

Part 3: Configure Secure Trunks and Access Ports

- Configure trunk port mode.
- Change the native VLAN for trunk ports.
- Verify trunk configuration.
- Enable storm control for broadcasts.
- Configure access ports.
- Enable PortFast and BPDU guard.
- Verify BPDU guard.
- Enable root guard.
- Enable loop guard.
- Configure and verify port security.
- Disable unused ports.
- Move ports from default VLAN 1 to alternate VLAN.
- Configure the PVLAN Edge feature on a port.

Part 4: Configure IP DHCP Snooping

- Configure DHCP on R1.
- Configure Inter-VLAN communication on R1.
- Configure S1 interface F0/5 as a trunk.
- Verify DHCP operation on PC- A and B.
- Enable DHCP Snooping.
- Verify DHCP Snooping.

Background / Scenario

The Layer 2 infrastructure consists mainly of interconnected Ethernet switches. Most end-user devices, such as computers, printers, IP phones, and other hosts, connect to the network via Layer 2 access switches. As a result, switches can present a network security risk. Similar to routers, switches are subject to attack from malicious internal users. The switch Cisco IOS software provides many security features that are specific to switch functions and protocols.

In this lab, you will configure SSH access and Layer 2 security for S1 and S2. You will also configure various switch protection measures, including access port security and Spanning Tree Protocol (STP) features, such as BPDU guard and root guard.

Note: The router commands and output in this lab are from a Cisco 1941 router using Cisco IOS software, release 15.4(3)M2 (with a Security Technology Package license). The switch commands and output are from Cisco WS-C2960-24TT-L switches with Cisco IOS Release 15.0(2)SE4 (C2960-LANBASEK9-M image). Other routers, switches, and Cisco IOS versions can be used. See the Router Interface Summary Table at the end of the lab to determine which interface identifiers to use based on the equipment in the lab. The commands available to the user and the output produced may vary depending on which router, switch, and Cisco IOS version is used.

Note: Make sure that the routers and switches have been erased and have no startup configurations.

Required Resources

- 1 Router (Cisco 1941 with Cisco IOS Release 15.4(3)M2 image with a Security Technology Package license)
- 2 Switches (Cisco 2960 with cryptography IOS image for SSH support – Release 15.0(2)SE7 or comparable)
- 2 PCs (Windows 7 or Windows 8 with SSH client software
- Ethernet cables as shown in the topology
- Console cables to configure Cisco networking devices

Part 1: Configure Basic Switch Settings

In Part 1, you will set up the network topology and configure basic settings, such as the hostnames, IP addresses, and device access passwords.

Step 1: Cable the network as shown in the topology.

Attach the devices, as shown in the topology diagram, and cable as necessary.

Step 2: Configure basic settings for the router and each switch.

Perform all tasks on R1, S1, and S2. The procedure for S1 is shown here as an example.

a. Configure hostnames, as shown in the topology.

b. Configure interface IP addresses, as shown in the IP Addressing Table. The following configuration displays the VLAN 1 management interface on S1:

```
S1(config)# interface vlan 1
S1(config-if)# ip address 192.168.1.2 255.255.255.0
S1(config-if)# no shutdown
```

c. Prevent the router or switch from attempting to translate incorrectly entered commands by disabling DNS lookup. S1 is shown here as an example.

```
S1(config)# no ip domain-lookup
```

d. HTTP access to the switch is enabled by default. Prevent HTTP access by disabling the HTTP server and HTTP secure server.

```
S1(config)# no ip http server
S1(config)# no ip http secure-server
```

Note: The switch must have a cryptography IOS image to support the **ip http secure-server** command. HTTP access to the router is disabled by default.

e. Configure the enable secret password.

```
S1(config)# enable algorithm-type scrypt secret cisco12345
```

f.   Configure console password.

```
S1(config)# line console 0
S1(config-line)# password ciscoconpass
S1(config-line)# exec-timeout 5 0
S1(config-line)# login
S1(config-line)# logging synchronous
```

Step 3: Configure PC host IP settings.

Configure a static IP address, subnet mask, and default gateway for PC-A and PC-B, as shown in the IP Addressing Table.

Step 4: Verify basic network connectivity.

a.   Ping from PC-A and PC-B to the R1 F0/1 interface at IP address **192.168.1.1**.

If the pings are unsuccessful, troubleshoot the basic device configurations before continuing.

b.   Ping from PC-A to PC-B.

If the pings are unsuccessful, troubleshoot the basic device configurations before continuing.

Step 5: Save the basic configurations for the router and both switches.

Save the running configuration to the startup configuration from the privileged EXEC mode prompt.

```
S1# copy running-config startup-config
```

Part 2: Configure SSH Access to the Switches

In Part 2, you will configure S1 and S2 to support SSH connections and install SSH client software on the PCs.

Note: A switch IOS image that supports encryption is required to configure SSH. If this version of image is not used you cannot specify SSH as an input protocol for the vty lines and the **crypto** commands are unavailable.

Task 1: Configure the SSH Server on S1 and S2 Using the CLI.

In this task, use the CLI to configure the switch to be managed securely using SSH instead of Telnet. SSH is a network protocol that establishes a secure terminal emulation connection to a switch or other networking device. SSH encrypts all information that passes over the network link and provides authentication of the remote computer. SSH is rapidly replacing Telnet as the preferred remote login tool for network professionals. It is strongly recommended that SSH be used in place of Telnet on production networks.

Note: A switch must be configured with local authentication or AAA in order to support SSH.

Step 1: Configure a domain name.

Enter global configuration mode and set the domain name.

```
S1# conf t
S1(config)# ip domain-name ccnasecurity.com
```

Step 2: Configure a privileged user for login from the SSH client.

Use the **username** command to create the user ID with the highest possible privilege level and a secret password.

```
S1(config)# username admin privilege 15 algorithm-type scrypt secret
cisco12345
```

Step 3: Generate the RSA encryption key pair for the router.

The switch uses the RSA key pair for authentication and encryption of transmitted SSH data.

Configure the RSA keys with **1024** modulus bits. The default number of modulus bits is 512, and the range is from 360 to 2,048.

```
S1(config)# crypto key generate rsa general-keys modulus 1024
  The name for the keys will be: S1.ccnasecurity.com

% The key modulus size is 1024 bits
% Generating 1024 bit RSA keys, keys will be non-exportable...[OK]

S1(config)#
00:15:36: %SSH-5-ENABLED: SSH 1.99 has been enabled
```

Step 4: Configure SSH version 2

```
S1(config)# ip ssh version 2
```

Step 5: Verify the SSH configuration.

a. Use the **show ip ssh** command to see the current settings.

```
S1# show ip ssh
```

b. Fill in the following information based on the output of the **show ip ssh** command:

SSH version enabled: _____

Authentication timeout: _____

Authentication retries: _____

Step 6: Configure SSH timeouts and authentication parameters.

The default SSH timeouts and authentication parameters can be altered to be more restrictive using the following commands.

```
S1(config)# ip ssh time-out 90
S1(config)# ip ssh authentication-retries 2
```

Step 7: Configure the incoming vty lines.

a. Configure vty access on lines 0 to 4. Specify a privilege level of 15. This will ensure that a user with the highest privilege level (**15**) will default to privileged EXEC mode when accessing the vty lines. Other users will default to user EXEC mode. Specify the use of local user accounts for mandatory login and validation and accept only SSH connections.

```
S1(config)# line vty 0 4
S1(config-line)# privilege level 15
S1(config-line)# exec-timeout 5 0
S1(config-line)# login local
S1(config-line)# transport input ssh
S1(config-line)# exit
```

b. Disable login for switch vty lines 5 to 15 by allowing no transport input.

```
S1(config)# line vty 5 15
S1(config-line)# transport input none
```

Step 8: Save the running configuration to the startup configuration.

```
S1# copy running-config startup-config
```

Task 2: Configure the SSH Client

PuTTy and Tera Term are two terminal emulation programs that can support SSHv2 client connections. This lab uses PuTTY.

Step 1: (Optional) Download and install an SSH client on PC-A and PC-B.

If the SSH client is not already installed, download PuTTY from the following link:

http://www.chiark.greenend.org.uk/~sgtatham/putty/download.html

Note: The procedure described here is for PuTTY and pertains to PC-A.

Step 2: Verify SSH connectivity to S1 from PC-A.

a. Launch PuTTY by double-clicking the **putty.exe** icon (and clicking **Run** if prompted).

b. Input the S1 IP address **192.168.1.2** in the **Host Name (or IP address)** field.

c. Verify that the **SSH** radio button is selected. PuTTY defaults to SSH version 2.

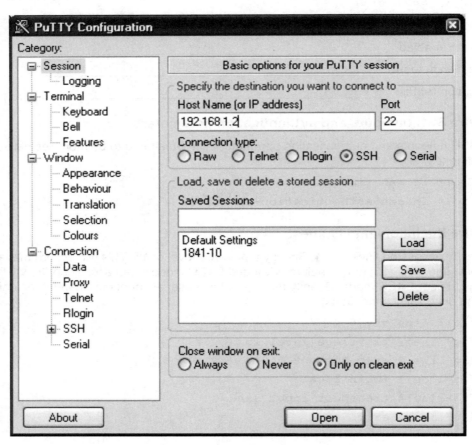

d. Click **Open**.

Note: Upon first connection, the user is prompted with a PuTTY Security Alert stating that the server's host key is not cached in the registry.

e. In the PuTTY Security Alert window, click **Yes** to cache the server's host key.

f. In the PuTTY window, enter **admin** as the username and **cisco12345** as the password.

g. At the S1 privileged EXEC mode prompt, enter the **show users** command.

    S1# **show users**

    Which users are connected to S1 at this time?

    _____

    _____

h. Close the PuTTy SSH session window with the **exit** or **quit** command.

    Try to open a Telnet session to S1 from PC-A. Were you able to open the Telnet session? Explain.

    _____

    _____

Step 3: Save the configuration.

Save the running configuration to the startup configuration from the privileged EXEC mode prompt.

    S1# **copy running-config startup-config**

Part 3: Configure Secure Trunks and Access Ports

In Part 3, you will configure trunk ports, change the native VLAN for trunk ports, and verify trunk configuration.

Securing trunk ports can help stop VLAN hopping attacks. The best way to prevent a basic VLAN hopping attack is to explicitly disable trunking on all ports except the ports that specifically require trunking. On the required trunking ports, disable DTP (auto trunking) negotiations and manually enable trunking. If no trunking is required on an interface, configure the port as an access port. This disables trunking on the interface.

Note: Tasks should be performed on S1 or S2, as indicated.

Task 1: Secure Trunk Ports

Step 1: Configure S1 as the root switch.

For the purposes of this lab, S2 is currently the root bridge. You will configure S1 as the root bridge by changing the bridge ID priority level.

a. From the console on S1, enter global configuration mode.

b. The default priority for S1 and S2 is 32769 (32768 + 1 with System ID Extension). Set S1 priority to **0** so that it becomes the root switch.

```
S1(config)# spanning-tree vlan 1 priority 0
S1(config)# exit
```

Note: You can also use the **spanning-tree vlan 1 root primary** command to make S1 the root switch for VLAN 1.

c. Issue the **show spanning-tree** command to verify that S1 is the root bridge, to see the ports in use, and to see their status.

```
S1# show spanning-tree


VLAN0001
  Spanning tree enabled protocol ieee
  Root ID    Priority    1
             Address      001d.4635.0c80
             This bridge is the root
             Hello Time    2 sec  Max Age 20 sec  Forward Delay 15 sec

  Bridge ID  Priority    1        (priority 0 sys-id-ext 1)
             Address      001d.4635.0c80
             Hello Time    2 sec  Max Age 20 sec  Forward Delay 15 sec
             Aging Time 300

Interface         Role Sts Cost      Prio.Nbr Type
---------------- ---- --- --------- -------- --------------------------------
Fa0/1             Desg FWD 19        128.1    P2p
Fa0/5             Desg FWD 19        128.5    P2p
Fa0/6             Desg FWD 19        128.6    P2p
```

d. What is the S1 priority?

_____

Which ports are in use and what is their status?

_____

_____

Step 2: Configure trunk ports on S1 and S2.

a. Configure port F0/1 on S1 as a trunk port.

```
S1(config)# interface f0/1
S1(config-if)# switchport mode trunk
```

Note: If performing this lab with a 3560 switch, the user must first enter the **switchport trunk encapsulation dot1q** command.

b. Configure port F0/1 on S2 as a trunk port.

```
S2(config)# interface f0/1
S2(config-if)# switchport mode trunk
```

c. Verify that S1 port F0/1 is in trunking mode with the **show interfaces trunk** command.

```
S1# show interfaces trunk

Port        Mode           Encapsulation  Status      Native vlan
Fa0/1       on             802.1q         trunking    1

Port        Vlans allowed on trunk
Fa0/1       1-4094

Port        Vlans allowed and active in management domain
Fa0/1       1

Port        Vlans in spanning tree forwarding state and not pruned
Fa0/1       1
```

Step 3: Change the native VLAN for the trunk ports on S1 and S2.

a. Changing the native VLAN for trunk ports to an unused VLAN helps prevent VLAN hopping attacks.

From the output of the **show interfaces trunk** command in the previous step, what is the current native VLAN for the S1 F0/1 trunk interface?

_____

b. Set the native VLAN on the S1 F0/1 trunk interface to an unused VLAN 99.

```
S1(config)# interface f0/1
S1(config-if)# switchport trunk native vlan 99
S1(config-if)# end
```

c. The following message should display after a brief period of time:

```
02:16:28: %CDP-4-NATIVE_VLAN_MISMATCH: Native VLAN mismatch discovered on
FastEthernet0/1 (99), with S2 FastEthernet0/1 (1).
```

What does the message mean?

_____

_____

_____

_____

d. Set the native VLAN on the S2 F0/1 trunk interface to VLAN 99.

```
S2(config)# interface f0/1
S2(config-if)# switchport trunk native vlan 99
S2(config-if)# end
```

Step 4: Prevent the use of DTP on S1 and S2.

Setting the trunk port to **nonegotiate** also helps to mitigate VLAN hopping by turning off the generation of DTP frames.

```
S1(config)# interface f0/1
S1(config-if)# switchport nonegotiate

S2(config)# interface f0/1
S2(config-if)# switchport nonegotiate
```

Step 5: Verify the trunking configuration on port F0/1.

```
S1# show interfaces f0/1 trunk


Port        Mode         Encapsulation  Status      Native vlan
Fa0/1       on           802.1q         trunking    99


Port        Vlans allowed on trunk
Fa0/1       1-4094


Port        Vlans allowed and active in management domain
Fa0/1       1


Port        Vlans in spanning tree forwarding state and not pruned
Fa0/1       1


S1# show interfaces f0/1 switchport

Name: Fa0/1
Switchport: Enabled
Administrative Mode: trunk
Operational Mode: trunk
Administrative Trunking Encapsulation: dot1q
Operational Trunking Encapsulation: dot1q
Negotiation of Trunking: Off
Access Mode VLAN: 1 (default)
Trunking Native Mode VLAN: 99 (Inactive)
Administrative Native VLAN tagging: enabled
Voice VLAN: none
Administrative private-vlan host-association: none
Administrative private-vlan mapping: none
Administrative private-vlan trunk native VLAN: none
Administrative private-vlan trunk Native VLAN tagging: enabled
Administrative private-vlan trunk encapsulation: dot1q
Administrative private-vlan trunk normal VLANs: none
Administrative private-vlan trunk private VLANs: none
Operational private-vlan: none
Trunking VLANs Enabled: ALL
Pruning VLANs Enabled: 2-1001
```

```
Capture Mode Disabled
Capture VLANs Allowed: ALL

Protected: false
Unknown unicast blocked: disabled
Unknown multicast blocked: disabled
Appliance trust: none
```

Step 6: Verify the configuration with the show run command.

Use the **show run** command to display the running configuration, beginning with the first line that has the text string "0/1" in it.

```
S1# show run | begin 0/1
interface FastEthernet0/1
 switchport trunk native vlan 99
 switchport mode trunk
 switchport nonegotiate

<output omitted>
```

Task 2: Secure Access Ports

Network attackers hope to spoof their system, or a rogue switch that they add to the network, as the root bridge in the topology by manipulating the STP root bridge parameters. If a port that is configured with PortFast receives a BPDU, STP can put the port into the blocking state by using a feature called BPDU guard.

Step 1: Disable trunking on S1 access ports.

a. On S1, configure Fa0/5, the port to which R1 is connected, as access mode only.

```
S1(config)# interface f0/5
S1(config-if)# switchport mode access
```

b. On S1, configure Fa0/6, the port to which PC-A is connected, as access mode only.

```
S1(config)# interface f0/6
S1(config-if)# switchport mode access
```

Step 2: Disable trunking on S2 access ports.

On S2, configure Fa0/18, the port to which PC-B is connected, as access mode only.

```
S2(config)# interface f0/18
S2(config-if)# switchport mode access
```

Task 3: Protect Against STP Attacks

The topology has only two switches and no redundant paths, but STP is still active. In this step, you will enable switch security features that can help reduce the possibility of an attacker manipulating switches via STP-related methods.

Step 1: Enable PortFast on S1 and S2 access ports.

PortFast is configured on access ports that connect to a single workstation or server, which enables them to become active more quickly.

a. Enable PortFast on the S1 Fa0/5 access port.

```
S1(config)# interface f0/5
S1(config-if)# spanning-tree portfast
%Warning: portfast should only be enabled on ports connected to a single host.
Connecting hubs, concentrators, switches, bridges, etc... to this interface when
portfast is enabled, can cause temporary bridging loops. Use with CAUTION

%Portfast has been configured on FastEthernet0/5 but will only
 have effect when the interface is in a non-trunking mode.
```

b. Enable PortFast on the S1 Fa0/6 access port.

```
S1(config)# interface f0/6
S1(config-if)# spanning-tree portfast
```

c. Enable PortFast on the S2 Fa0/18 access ports.

```
S2(config)# interface f0/18
S2(config-if)# spanning-tree portfast
```

Step 2: Enable BPDU guard on the S1 and S2 access ports.

BPDU guard is a feature that can help prevent rogue switches and spoofing on access ports.

a. Enable BPDU guard on the switch port F0/6.

```
S1(config)# interface f0/6
S1(config-if)# spanning-tree bpduguard enable

S2(config)# interface f0/18
S2(config-if)# spanning-tree bpduguard enable
```

Note: PortFast and BPDU guard can also be enabled globally with the **spanning-tree portfast default** and **spanning-tree portfast bpduguard** commands in global configuration mode.

Note: BPDU guard can be enabled on all access ports that have PortFast enabled. These ports should never receive a BPDU. BPDU guard is best deployed on user-facing ports to prevent rogue switch network extensions by an attacker. If a port is enabled with BPDU guard and receives a BPDU, it is disabled and must be manually re-enabled. An **err-disable timeout** can be configured on the port so that it can recover automatically after a specified time period.

b. Verify that BPDU guard is configured by using the **show spanning-tree interface f0/6 detail** command on S1.

```
S1# show spanning-tree interface f0/6 detail

Port 6 (FastEthernet0/6) of VLAN0001 is designated forwarding
   Port path cost 19, Port priority 128, Port Identifier 128.6.
   Designated root has priority 1, address 001d.4635.0c80
   Designated bridge has priority 1, address 001d.4635.0c80
   Designated port id is 128.6, designated path cost 0
   Timers: message age 0, forward delay 0, hold 0
   Number of transitions to forwarding state: 1
   The port is in the portfast mode
   Link type is point-to-point by default
   Bpdu guard is enabled
```

```
    BPDU: sent 3349, received 0
```

Step 3: Enable root guard.

Root guard is another option to help prevent rogue switches and spoofing. Root guard can be enabled on all ports on a switch that are not root ports. It is normally enabled only on ports connecting to edge switches where a superior BPDU should never be received. Each switch should have only one root port, which is the best path to the root switch.

a. The following command configures root guard on S2 interface Gi0/1. Normally, this is done if another switch is attached to this port. Root guard is best deployed on ports that connect to switches that should not be the root bridge. In the lab topology, S1 F0/1 would be the most logical candidate for root guard. However, S2 Gi0/1 is shown here as an example, as Gigabit ports are more commonly used for inter-switch connections.

```
S2(config)# interface g0/1
S2(config-if)# spanning-tree guard root
```

b. Issue the **show run | begin Gig** command to verify that root guard is configured.

```
S2# show run | begin Gig
interface GigabitEthernet0/1
 spanning-tree guard root
```

Note: The S2 Gi0/1 port is not currently up, so it is not participating in STP. Otherwise, you could use the **show spanning-tree interface Gi0/1 detail** command.

Note: The expression in the command **show run | begin** is case-sensitive.

c. If a port that is enabled with BPDU guard receives a superior BPDU, it enters a root-inconsistent state. Use the **show spanning-tree inconsistentports** command to determine if there are any ports currently receiving superior BPDUs that should not be.

```
S2# show spanning-tree inconsistentports

Name                  Interface             Inconsistency
-------------------   -------------------   -----------------

Number of inconsistent ports (segments) in the system : 0
```

Note: Root guard allows a connected switch to participate in STP as long as the device does not try to become the root. If root guard blocks the port, subsequent recovery is automatic. The port returns to the forwarding state if the superior BPDUs stop.

Step 4: Enable Loop Guard

The STP loop guard feature provides additional protection against Layer 2 forwarding loops (STP loops). An STP loop is created when an STP blocking port in a redundant topology erroneously transitions to the forwarding state. This usually happens because one of the ports of a physically redundant topology (not necessarily the STP blocking port) no longer receives STP BPDUs. Having all ports in forwarding state will result in forwarding loops. If a port enabled with loopguard stops hearing BPDUs from the designated port on the segment, it goes into the loop inconsistent state instead of transitioning into forwarding state. Loop inconsistent is basically blocking, and no traffic is forwarded. When the port detects BPDUs again it automatically recovers by moving back into blocking state.

a. Loop guard should be applied to non-designated ports. Therefore, the global command can be configured on non-root switches.

```
S2(config)# spanning-tree loopguard default
```

b. Verify Loopguard configuration

```
S2# show spanning-tree summary
Switch is in pvst mode

Extended system ID              is enabled
Portfast Default                is disabled
PortFast BPDU Guard Default     is disabled
Portfast BPDU Filter Default    is disabled
Loopguard Default               is enabled
EtherChannel misconfig guard    is enabled
UplinkFast                      is disabled
BackboneFast                    is disabled
Configured Pathcost method used is short


Name                 Blocking Listening Learning Forwarding STP Active
-------------------- -------- --------- -------- ---------- ----------
VLAN0001                    0         0        0          3          3
-------------------- -------- --------- -------- ---------- ---------
```

Task 4: Configure Port Security and Disable Unused Ports

Switches can be subject to a CAM table, also known as a MAC address table, overflow, MAC spoofing attacks, and unauthorized connections to switch ports. In this task, you will configure port security to limit the number of MAC addresses that can be learned on a switch port and disable the port if that number is exceeded.

Step 1: Record the R1 Fa0/0 MAC address.

From the R1 CLI, use the **show interface** command and record the MAC address of the interface.

```
R1# show interfaces g0/1
GigabitEthernet0/1 is up, line protocol is up
  Hardware is CN Gigabit Ethernet, address is fc99.4775.c3e1 (bia fc99.4775.c3e1)
  Internet address is 192.168.1.1/24
  MTU 1500 bytes, BW 100000 Kbit/sec, DLY 100 usec,
     reliability 255/255, txload 1/255, rxload 1/255
  Encapsulation ARPA, loopback not set
  Keepalive set (10 sec)
  Full Duplex, 100Mbps, media type is RJ45
<Output Omitted>
```

What is the MAC address of the R1 G0/1 interface?

_____

_____

Step 2: Configure basic port security.

This procedure should be performed on all access ports that are in use. S1 port Fa0/5 is shown here as an example.

a. From the S1 CLI, enter interface configuration mode for the port that connects to the router (Fast Ethernet 0/5).

```
S1(config)# interface f0/5
```

b. Shut down the switch port.

```
S1(config-if)# shutdown
```

c. Enable port security on the port.

```
S1(config-if)# switchport port-security
```

Note: A switch port must be configured as an access port to enable port security.

Note: Entering just the **switchport port-security** command sets the maximum MAC addresses to **1** and the violation action to **shutdown**. The **switchport port-security maximum** and **switchport port-security violation** commands can be used to change the default behavior.

d. Configure a static entry for the MAC address of R1 Fa0/1/ interface recorded in Step 1.

```
S1(config-if)# switchport port-security mac-address xxxx.xxxx.xxxx
```

Note: *xxxx.xxxx.xxxx* is the actual MAC address of the router G0/1 interface.

Note: You can also use the **switchport port-security mac-address sticky** command to add all the secure MAC addresses that are dynamically learned on a port (up to the maximum set) to the switch running configuration.

e. Enable the switch port.

```
S1(config-if)# no shutdown
```

Step 3: Verify port security on S1 Fa0/5.

a. On S1, issue the **show port-security** command to verify that port security has been configured on S1 F0/5.

```
S1# show port-security interface f0/5
Port Security                : Enabled
Port Status                  : Secure-up
Violation Mode               : Shutdown
Aging Time                   : 0 mins
Aging Type                   : Absolute
SecureStatic Address Aging   : Disabled
Maximum MAC Addresses        : 1
Total MAC Addresses          : 1
Configured MAC Addresses     : 1
Sticky MAC Addresses         : 0
Last Source Address:Vlan     : 0000.0000.0000:0
Security Violation Count     : 0
```

What is the Security Violation Count? _____

What is the status of the F0/5 port?

_____

_____

What is the Last Source Address and VLAN?

_____

_____

b. From the R1 CLI, ping PC-A to verify connectivity. This also ensures that the R1 Fa0/1 MAC address is learned by the switch.

   R1# `ping 192.168.1.10`

c. Now, violate security by changing the MAC address on the router interface. Enter interface configuration mode for the Fast Ethernet 0/1. Configure a MAC address for the interface on the interface, using **aaaa.bbbb.cccc** as the address.

   R1(config)# `interface G0/1`
   R1(config-if)# `mac-address aaaa.bbbb.cccc`
   R1(config-if)# `end`

   Note: You can also change the PC MAC address attached to S1 F0/6 and achieve similar results to those shown here.

d. From the R1 CLI, ping PC-A. Was the ping successful? Explain.

   _____

   _____

e. On S1 console, observe the messages when port F0/5 detects the violating MAC address.

   ```
   *Jan 14 01:34:39.750: %PM-4-ERR_DISABLE: psecure-violation error detected on Fa0/5,
   putting Fa0/5 in err-disable state
   *Jan 14 01:34:39.750: %PORT_SECURITY-2-PSECURE_VIOLATION: Security violation occurred,
   caused by MAC address aaaa.bbbb.cccc on port FastEthernet0/5.
   *Jan 14 01:34:40.756: %LINEPROTO-5-UPDOWN: Line protocol on Interface FastEthernet0/5,
   changed state to down
   *Jan 14 01:34:41.755: %LINK-3-UPDOWN: Interface FastEthernet0/5, changed state to down
   ```

f. On the switch, use the **show port-security** commands to verify that port security has been violated.

   ```
   S1# show port-security
   Secure Port MaxSecureAddr CurrentAddr SecurityViolation Security Action
               (Count)       (Count)     (Count)
   -------------------------------------------------------------------
       Fa0/5        1             1               1          Shutdown
   -------------------------------------------------------------------
   Total Addresses in System (excluding one mac per port)     : 0
   Max Addresses limit in System (excluding one mac per port) : 8192


   S1# show port-security interface f0/5
   Port Security              : Enabled
   Port Status                : Secure-shutdown
   Violation Mode             : Shutdown
   Aging Time                 : 0 mins
   Aging Type                 : Absolute
   SecureStatic Address Aging : Disabled
   Maximum MAC Addresses      : 1
   Total MAC Addresses        : 1
   Configured MAC Addresses   : 1
   Sticky MAC Addresses       : 0
   Last Source Address:Vlan   : aaaa.bbbb.cccc:1
   Security Violation Count   : 1
   ```

```
S1# show port-security address
Secure Mac Address Table
--------------------------------------------------------------------------
Vlan    Mac Address        Type                   Ports   Remaining Age
                                                          (mins)

----    -----------        ----                   -----   -------------
   1    fc99.4775.c3e1     SecureConfigured       Fa0/5       -
--------------------------------------------------------------------------
Total Addresses in System (excluding one mac per port)      : 0
Max Addresses limit in System (excluding one mac per port) : 8192
```

g. Remove the hard-coded MAC address from the router and re-enable the Fast Ethernet 0/1 interface.

```
R1(config)# interface g0/1
R1(config-if)# no mac-address aaaa.bbbb.cccc
```

Note: This will restore the original FastEthernet interface MAC address.

From R1, try to ping the PC-A again at 192.168.1.10. Was the ping successful? Why or why not?

_____

_____

Step 4: Clear the S1 Fa0/5 error disabled status.

a. From the S1 console, clear the error and re-enable the port using the commands shown in the example. This will change the port status from Secure-shutdown to Secure-up.

```
S1(config)# interface f0/5
S1(config-if)# shutdown
S1(config-if)# no shutdown
```

Note: This assumes the device/interface with the violating MAC address has been removed and replaced with the original device/interface configuration.

b. From R1, ping PC-A again. You should be successful this time.

```
R1# ping 192.168.1.10
```

Step 5: Remove basic port security on S1 F0/5.

From the S1 console, remove port security on Fa0/5. This procedure can also be used to re-enable the port, but **port security** commands must be reconfigured.

```
S1(config)# interface f0/5
S1(config-if)# no switchport port-security
S1(config-if)# no switchport port-security mac-address fc99.4775.c3e1
```

You can also use the following commands to reset the interface to its default settings:

```
S1(config)# default interface f0/5
S1(config)# interface f0/5
```

Note: This **default interface** command also requires that you reconfigure the port as an access port to re-enable the security commands.

Step 6: (Optional) Configure port security for VoIP.

This example shows a typical port security configuration for a voice port. Three MAC addresses are allowed and should be learned dynamically. One MAC address is for the IP phone, one is for the switch, and one is for the PC connected to the IP phone. Violations of this policy result in the port being shut down. The aging timeout for the learned MAC addresses is set to two hours.

The following example displays S2 port F0/18:

```
S2(config)# interface f0/18
S2(config-if)# switchport mode access
S2(config-if)# switchport port-security
S2(config-if)# switchport port-security maximum 3
S2(config-if)# switchport port-security violation shutdown
S2(config-if)# switchport port-security aging time 120
```

Step 7: Disable unused ports on S1 and S2.

As a further security measure, disable ports that are not being used on the switch.

a. Ports F0/1, F0/5, and F0/6 are used on S1. The remaining Fast Ethernet ports and the two Gigabit Ethernet ports will be shut down.

```
S1(config)# interface range f0/2 - 4
S1(config-if-range)# shutdown
S1(config-if-range)# interface range f0/7 - 24
S1(config-if-range)# shutdown
S1(config-if-range)# interface range g0/1 - 2
S1(config-if-range)# shutdown
```

b. Ports Fa0/1 and Fa0/18 are used on S2. The remaining Fast Ethernet ports and the Gigabit Ethernet ports will be shut down.

```
S2(config)# interface range f0/2 - 17 , f0/19 - 24 , g0/1 - 2
S2(config-if-range)# shutdown
```

Step 8: Move active ports to a VLAN other than the default VLAN 1.

As a further security measure, you can move all active end-user ports and router ports to a VLAN other than the default VLAN 1 on both switches.

a. Configure a new VLAN for users on each switch using the following commands:

```
S1(config)# vlan 20
S1(config-vlan)# name Users

S2(config)# vlan 20
S2(config-vlan)# name Users
```

b. Add the current active access (non-trunk) ports to the new VLAN.

```
S1(config)# interface f0/6
S1(config-if-range)# switchport access vlan 20

S2(config)# interface f0/18
S2(config-if)# switchport access vlan 20
```

Note: This will prevent communication between end-user hosts and the management VLAN IP address of the switch, which is currently VLAN 1. The switch can still be accessed and configured using the console connection.

Note: To provide SSH access to the switch, a specific port can be designated as the management port and added to VLAN 1 with a specific management workstation attached. A more elaborate solution is to create a new VLAN for switch management (or use the existing native trunk VLAN 99), and configure a separate subnet for the management and user VLANs. In Part 4 you will enable trunking with subinterfaces on R1 to provide communication between the management and user VLAN subnets.

Step 9: Configure a port with the PVLAN Edge feature.

Some applications require that no traffic be forwarded at Layer 2 between ports on the same switch so that one neighbor does not see the traffic generated by another neighbor. In such an environment, the use of the Private VLAN (PVLAN) Edge feature, also known as protected ports, ensures that there is no exchange of unicast, broadcast, or multicast traffic between these ports on the switch. The PVLAN Edge feature can only be implemented for ports on the same switch and is locally significant.

For example, to prevent traffic between host PC-A on S1 (port Fa0/6) and a host on another S1 port (e.g. port Fa0/7, which was previously shut down), you could use the **switchport protected** command to activate the PVLAN Edge feature on these two ports. Use the **no switchport protected** interface configuration command to disable protected port.

a. Configure the PVLAN Edge feature in interface configuration mode using the following commands:

```
S1(config)# interface f0/6
S1(config-if)# switchport protected
S1(config-if)# interface f0/7
S1(config-if)# switchport protected
S1(config-if)# no shut
S1(config-if)# end
```

b. Verify that the PVLAN Edge Feature (protected port) is enabled on Fa0/6.

```
S1# show interfaces fa0/6 switchport
Name: Fa0/6
Switchport: Enabled
Administrative Mode: dynamic auto
Operational Mode: static access
Administrative Trunking Encapsulation: dot1q
Negotiation of Trunking: On
Access Mode VLAN: 20 (Users)
Trunking Native Mode VLAN: 1 (default)
Administrative Native VLAN tagging: enabled
Voice VLAN: none
Administrative private-vlan host-association: none
Administrative private-vlan mapping: none
Administrative private-vlan trunk native VLAN: none
Administrative private-vlan trunk Native VLAN tagging: enabled
Administrative private-vlan trunk encapsulation: dot1q
Administrative private-vlan trunk normal VLANs: none
Administrative private-vlan trunk private VLANs: none
Operational private-vlan: none
Trunking VLANs Enabled: ALL
```

```
Pruning VLANs Enabled: 2-1001
Capture Mode Disabled
Capture VLANs Allowed: ALL

Protected: true
Unknown unicast blocked: disabled
Unknown multicast blocked: disabled
Appliance trust: none
```

c. Deactivate protected port on interfaces Fa0/6 and Fa0/7 using the following commands:

```
S1(config)# interface range f0/6 - 7
S1(config-if-range)# no switchport protected
```

Part 4: Configure DHCP Snooping

DHCP snooping is a Cisco Catalyst feature that determines which switch ports can respond to DHCP requests. It enables only authorized DHCP servers to respond to DHCP requests and distribute network information to clients.

Task 1: Set Up DHCP

Step 1: Set up DHCP on R1 for VLAN 1.

```
R1(config)# ip dhcp pool CCNAS
R1(dhcp-config)# network 192.168.1.0 255.255.255.0
R1(dhcp-config)# default-router 192.168.1.1
R1(config)# ip dhcp excluded-address 192.168.1.1 192.168.1.4
```

Step 2: Set up DHCP on R1 for VLAN 20.

```
R1(config)# ip dhcp pool 20Users
R1(dhcp-config)# network 192.168.20.0 255.255.255.0
R1(dhcp-config)# default-router 192.168.20.1
R1(config)# ip dhcp excluded-address 192.168.20.1
```

Task 2: Configure Inter-VLAN Communication

Step 1: Configure subinterfaces on R1.

```
R1(config)# interface g0/1
R1(config-if)# shutdown
R1(config-if)# no ip address 192.168.1.1 255.255.255.0
R1(config-if)# no shutdown
R1(config-if)# int g0/1.1
R1(config-if)# encapsulation dot1q 1
R1(config-if)# ip address 192.168.1.1 255.255.255.0
R1(config-if)# int g0/1.20
R1(config-if)# encapsulation dot1q 20
R1(config-if)# ip address 192.168.20.1 255.255.255.0
R1(config-if)# int g0/1.99
R1(config-if)# encapsulation dot1q 99
```

```
R1(config-if)# ip address 192.168.99.1 255.255.255.0
```

Step 2: Configure S1 interface f0/5 as a trunk port.

```
S1(config)# int f0/5
S1(config-if)# switchport mode trunk
S1(config-if)# switchport trunk native vlan 99
```

Step 3: Configure PC-A and PC-B to obtain an IP Address using DHCP.

Change network settings on PC-A and PC-B to obtain an IP Address automatically.

Step 4: Verify DHCP operation.

Use ipconfig at the command prompt of PC-A and PC-B.

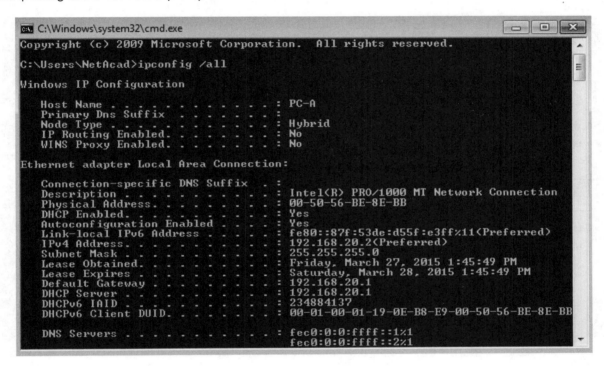

Task 3: Configure DHCP Snooping

Step 1: Enable DHCP snooping globally.

```
S1(config)# ip dhcp snooping
S1(config)# ip dhcp snooping information option
```

Step 2: Enable DHCP snooping for VLAN 1 and 20.

```
S1(config)# ip dhcp snooping vlan 1,20
```

Step 3: Limit the number of DHCP requests on an interface.

```
S1(config)# interface f0/6
S1(config-if)# ip dhcp snooping limit rate 10
```

```
S1(config-if)# exit
```

Step 4: Identify the trusted interface(s). DHCP responses are only permitted through trusted ports.

```
S1(config)# interface f0/5
S1(config-if)# description connects to DHCP server
S1(config-if)# ip dhcp snooping trust
```

Step 5: Verify DHCP snooping configuration.

```
S1# show ip dhcp snooping
```

```
DHCP snooping is configured on following VLANs:
1,20
DHCP snooping is operational on following VLANs:
1,20
DHCP snooping is configured on the following L3 Interfaces:
Insertion of option 82 is enabled
    circuit-id default format: vlan-mod-port
    remote-id: 0022.568a.3a80 (MAC)
Option 82 on untrusted port is not allowed
Verification of hwaddr field is enabled
Verification of giaddr field is enabled
DHCP snooping trust/rate is configured on the following Interfaces:
Interface                Trusted    Allow option    Rate limit (pps)
-----------------------  -------    ------------    ----------------
FastEthernet0/5          yes        yes             unlimited
FastEthernet0/6          no         no                     10
```

Router Interface Summary Table

Router Interface Summary				
Router Model	**Ethernet Interface #1**	**Ethernet Interface #2**	**Serial Interface #1**	**Serial Interface #2**
1800	Fast Ethernet 0/0 (F0/0)	Fast Ethernet 0/1 (F0/1)	Serial 0/0/0 (S0/0/0)	Serial 0/0/1 (S0/0/1)
1900	Gigabit Ethernet 0/0 (G0/0)	Gigabit Ethernet 0/1 (G0/1)	Serial 0/0/0 (S0/0/0)	Serial 0/0/1 (S0/0/1)
2801	Fast Ethernet 0/0 (F0/0)	Fast Ethernet 0/1 (F0/1)	Serial 0/1/0 (S0/1/0)	Serial 0/1/1 (S0/1/1)
2811	Fast Ethernet 0/0 (F0/0)	Fast Ethernet 0/1 (F0/1)	Serial 0/0/0 (S0/0/0)	Serial 0/0/1 (S0/0/1)
2900	Gigabit Ethernet 0/0 (G0/0)	Gigabit Ethernet 0/1 (G0/1)	Serial 0/0/0 (S0/0/0)	Serial 0/0/1 (S0/0/1)

Note: Determine how the router is configured by identifying the type of router and the number of interfaces the router has. There is no way to effectively list all the combinations of configurations for each router class. This table includes identifiers for the possible combinations of Ethernet and Serial interfaces in the device. The table does not include any other type of interface, even though a specific router may contain one. For example, an ISDN BRI interface. The string in parenthesis is the legal abbreviation that can be used in Cisco IOS commands to represent the interface.

Chapter 7: Cryptographic Systems

Lab 7.5.1.2 – Exploring Encryption Methods

Objectives

Part 1: Decipher a Pre-Encrypted Message Using the Vigenère Cipher

Use an encrypted message, a cipher key, and the Vigenère cipher square to decipher the message.

Part 2: Create a Vigenère Cipher Encrypted Message and Decrypt It

a.   Work with a lab partner and agree on a secret password.

b.   Create a secret message using the Vigenère cipher and the key.

c.   Exchange messages and decipher them using the pre-shared key.

d.   Use an interactive Vigenère decoding tool to verify decryption.

Background

The Cisco IOS password encryption service uses a Cisco-proprietary algorithm that is based on the Vigenère cipher. Vigenère is an example of a common type of cipher mechanism called polyalphabetic substitution.

Note: Students can work in teams of two for this lab.

Required Resources

End-user device with Internet access

Part 1: Decipher a Pre-Encrypted Message Using the Vigenère Cipher

In Part 1, you will analyze an encrypted message and decrypt it using a cipher key and the Vigenère cipher square.

Step 1: Review the encrypted message.

The following message has been encrypted using the Vigenère cipher:

VECIHXEJZXMA

Step 2: Review the cipher keyword.

The cipher keyword **TCPIP** was used to encrypt the message. The same keyword will be used to decrypt or decipher the message.

Step 3: Review the structure of the Vigenère square.

A standard Vigenère square or table is used with the keyword to decipher the message.

```
  |A B C D E F G H I J K L M N O P Q R S T U V W X Y Z
 A|A B C D E F G H I J K L M N O P Q R S T U V W X Y Z
 B|B C D E F G H I J K L M N O P Q R S T U V W X Y Z A
 C|C D E F G H I J K L M N O P Q R S T U V W X Y Z A B
 D|D E F G H I J K L M N O P Q R S T U V W X Y Z A B C
 E|E F G H I J K L M N O P Q R S T U V W X Y Z A B C D
 F|F G H I J K L M N O P Q R S T U V W X Y Z A B C D E
 G|G H I J K L M N O P Q R S T U V W X Y Z A B C D E F
 H|H I J K L M N O P Q R S T U V W X Y Z A B C D E F G
 I|I J K L M N O P Q R S T U V W X Y Z A B C D E F G H
 J|J K L M N O P Q R S T U V W X Y Z A B C D E F G H I
 K|K L M N O P Q R S T U V W X Y Z A B C D E F G H I J
 L|L M N O P Q R S T U V W X Y Z A B C D E F G H I J K
 M|M N O P Q R S T U V W X Y Z A B C D E F G H I J K L
 N|N O P Q R S T U V W X Y Z A B C D E F G H I J K L M
 O|O P Q R S T U V W X Y Z A B C D E F G H I J K L M N
 P|P Q R S T U V W X Y Z A B C D E F G H I J K L M N O
 Q|Q R S T U V W X Y Z A B C D E F G H I J K L M N O P
 R|R S T U V W X Y Z A B C D E F G H I J K L M N O P Q
 S|S T U V W X Y Z A B C D E F G H I J K L M N O P Q R
 T|T U V W X Y Z A B C D E F G H I J K L M N O P Q R S
 U|U V W X Y Z A B C D E F G H I J K L M N O P Q R S T
 V|V W X Y Z A B C D E F G H I J K L M N O P Q R S T U
 W|W X Y Z A B C D E F G H I J K L M N O P Q R S T U V
 X|X Y Z A B C D E F G H I J K L M N O P Q R S T U V W
 Y|Y Z A B C D E F G H I J K L M N O P Q R S T U V W X
 Z|Z A B C D E F G H I J K L M N O P Q R S T U V W X Y
```

Step 4: Decrypt the message using the keyword and Vigenère square.

a. Use the table below to help you decrypt the message. Start by entering the letters of the encrypted message in the second row of cells, from left to right.

b. Enter the keyword TCPIP in the top row, repeating the letters until there is a keyword letter for each letter of the encrypted message, even if the keyword letters at the end do not represent the complete keyword.

c. Refer to the Vigenère square or table shown in Step 3 and find the horizontal row that starts with the first letter of the keyword (the letter T). Scan across that row and locate the first letter of the encrypted message in the row (the letter V). The letter at the top of the column where the encrypted message letter appears is the first letter of the decrypted message (the letter C).

d. Continue this process until you have decrypted the entire message and enter it in row 3 of the following table.

Cipher Keyword												
Encrypted Message												
Decrypted Message												

Part 2: Create a Vigenère Cipher-Encrypted Message and Decrypt It

In Part 2, work with a lab partner and agree on a secret password to use as the pre-shared key. Each lab partner creates a secret message using the Vigenère cipher and the key. Partners exchange messages and decipher them using their pre-shared key.

Note: If you do not have a partner, you can perform the steps yourself.

Step 1: Determine the cipher keyword.

With your partner, establish a cipher keyword and enter it here.

_____

_____

Step 2: Create a plain text message and encrypt it (both partners).

a. Create a plain text (decrypted) message to be encrypted by your partner.

_____

_____

b. You can use the following table to help you encrypt the message. You can enter the unencrypted message and cipher keyword here, but do not let your partner see it.

c. In the Vigenère table, locate the row that starts with the first letter of the cipher keyword. Next locate the first letter to be encrypted at the top of the column in the table. The point (cell) at which the table row (key letter) and column (message letter) intersect is the first letter of the encrypted message. Continue this process until you have encrypted the entire message.

Note: This table is limited to messages of 12 characters. You can create longer messages if desired. Message encryption and decryption are not case-sensitive.

Cipher Keyword												
Encrypted Message												
Decrypted Message												

Step 3: Decrypt the message from your partner.

a. You can use the following table to help you decrypt your partner's encrypted message. Enter the encrypted message from your partner and the cipher keyword.

b. Use the same procedure described in Part 1, Step 4.

   Note: This table is limited to messages of 12 characters. You can create longer messages if desired.

Cipher Keyword												
Encrypted Message												
Decrypted Message												

Step 4: Use an interactive decryption tool to confirm decryption.

a. An Internet search for "Vigenère decode" shows that various cipher encryption and decryption tools are available. Many of these are interactive.

b. One interactive tool is located at http://sharkysoft.com/vigenere/1.0/. At this site, enter the encrypted message from your partner in the top part of the screen and the cipher key in the middle. Click **Decode** to see the clear text version of the message. You can also use this tool to encrypt messages.

c. The following example uses Sharky's Vigenère Cipher tool to decode the encrypted message from Part 1.

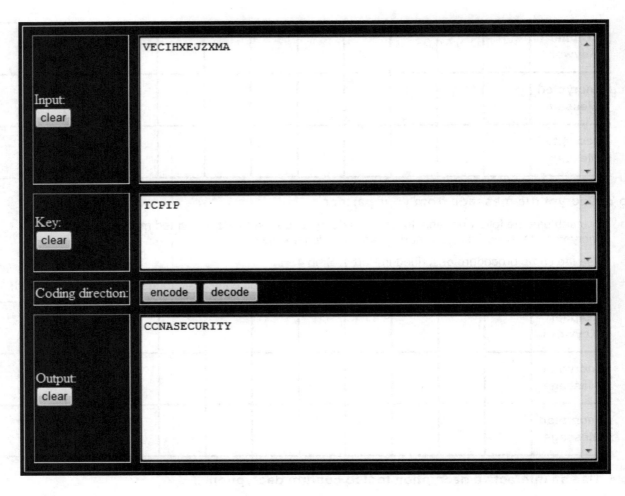

Reflection

1. Could the Vigenère cipher be used to decode messages in the field without a computer?

    _____

    _____

    _____

    _____

2. Search the Internet for Vigenère cipher cracking tools. Is the Vigenère cipher considered a strong encryption system that is difficult to crack?

    _____

    _____

    _____

    _____

Chapter 8: Implementing Virtual Private Networks

Lab 8.4.1.3 – Configure Site-to-Site VPN using CLI

Topology

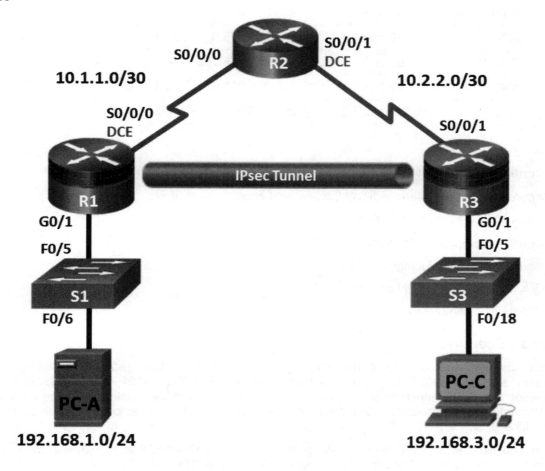

Note: ISR G1 devices use FastEthernet interfaces instead of GigabitEthernet interfaces.

IP Addressing Table

Device	Interface	IP Address	Subnet Mask	Default Gateway	Switch Port
R1	G0/1	192.168.1.1	255.255.255.0	N/A	S1 F0/5
	S0/0/0 (DCE)	10.1.1.1	255.255.255.252	N/A	N/A
R2	S0/0/0	10.1.1.2	255.255.255.252	N/A	N/A
	S0/0/1 (DCE)	10.2.2.2	255.255.255.252	N/A	N/A
R3	G0/1	192.168.3.1	255.255.255.0	N/A	S3 F0/5
	S0/0/1	10.2.2.1	255.255.255.252	N/A	N/A
PC-A	NIC	192.168.1.3	255.255.255.0	192.168.1.1	S1 F0/6
PC-C	NIC	192.168.3.3	255.255.255.0	192.168.3.1	S3 F0/18

Objectives

Part 1: Configure Basic Device Settings

- Configure hostnames, interface IP addresses, and access passwords.
- Configure the OSPF dynamic routing protocol.

Part 2: Configure a Site-to-Site VPN Using Cisco IOS

- Configure IPsec VPN settings on R1 and R3.
- Verify site-to-site IPsec VPN configuration.
- Test IPsec VPN operation.

Background / Scenario

VPNs can provide a secure method of transmitting data over a public network, such as the Internet. VPN connections can help reduce the costs associated with leased lines. Site-to-Site VPNs typically provide a secure (IPsec or other) tunnel between a branch office and a central office. Another common implementation of VPN technology is remote access to a corporate office from a telecommuter location, such as a small office or home office.

In this lab, you will build and configure a multi-router network, use Cisco IOS to configure a site-to-site IPsec VPN, and then test the VPN. The IPsec VPN tunnel is from R1 to R3 via R2. R2 acts as a pass-through and has no knowledge of the VPN. IPsec provides secure transmission of sensitive information over unprotected networks, such as the Internet. IPsec acts at the network layer and protecting and authenticating IP packets between participating IPsec devices (peers), such as Cisco routers.

Note: The router commands and output in this lab are from a Cisco 1941 router with Cisco IOS Release 15.4(3)M2 (with a Security Technology Package license). Other routers and Cisco IOS versions can be used. See the Router Interface Summary Table at the end of the lab to determine which interface identifiers to use based on the equipment in the lab. Depending on the router model and Cisco IOS version, the commands available and output produced might vary from what is shown in this lab.

Note: Before beginning, ensure that the routers and the switches have been erased and have no startup configurations.

Required Resources

- 3 routers (Cisco 1941 with Cisco IOS Release 15.4(3)M2 image with a Security Technology package license)
- 2 switches (Cisco 2960 or comparable) (not required)
- 2 PCs (Windows 7 or Windows 8.1, SSH Client, and WinRadius)
- Serial and Ethernet cables, as shown in the topology
- Console cables to configure Cisco networking devices

Part 1: Configure Basic Device Settings

In Part 1, you will set up the network topology and configure basic settings, such as the interface IP addresses, dynamic routing, device access, and passwords.

Note: All tasks should be performed on R1, R2, and R3. The procedure for R1 is shown here as an example.

Step 1: Cable the network as shown in the topology.

Attach the devices as shown in the topology diagram and cable as necessary.

Step 2: Configure basic settings for each router.

a. Configure hostnames, as shown in the topology.

b. Configure the interface IP addresses, as shown in the IP Addressing Table.

c. Configure a clock rate of 64000 for the serial router interfaces with a DCE serial cable attached.

Step 3: Disable DNS lookup.

Disable DNS lookup to prevent the router from attempting to translate incorrectly entered commands.

Step 4: Configure the OSPF routing protocol on R1, R2, and R3.

a. On R1, use the following commands:

```
R1(config)# router ospf 101
R1(config-router)# network 192.168.1.0 0.0.0.255 area 0
R1(config-router)# network 10.1.1.0 0.0.0.3 area 0
```

b. On R2, use the following commands:

```
R2(config)# router ospf 101
R2(config-router)# network 10.1.1.0 0.0.0.3 area 0
R2(config-router)# network 10.2.2.0 0.0.0.3 area 0
```

c. On R3, use the following commands:

```
R3(config)# router ospf 101
R3(config-router)# network 192.168.3.0 0.0.0.255 area 0
R3(config-router)# network 10.2.2.0 0.0.0.3 area 0
```

Step 5: Configure PC host IP settings.

a.   Configure a static IP address, subnet mask, and default gateway for PC-A, as shown in the IP Addressing Table.

b.   Configure a static IP address, subnet mask, and default gateway for PC-C, as shown in the IP Addressing Table.

Step 6: Verify basic network connectivity.

a.   Ping from R1 to the R3 Fa0/1 interface at IP address 192.168.3.1.

If the pings are unsuccessful, troubleshoot the basic device configurations before continuing.

b.   Ping from PC-A on the R1 LAN to PC-C on the R3 LAN.

If the pings are unsuccessful, troubleshoot the basic device configurations before continuing.

Note: If you can ping from PC-A to PC-C, you have demonstrated that the OSPF routing protocol is configured and functioning correctly. If you cannot ping, but the device interfaces are up and IP addresses are correct, use the **show run** and **show ip route** commands to help identify routing protocol-related problems.

Step 7: Configure and encrypt passwords.

Note: Passwords in this task are set to a minimum of 10 characters but are relatively simple for the benefit of performing the lab. More complex passwords are recommended in a production network.

Configure the same settings for R1 and R3. R1 is shown here as an example.

a.   Configure a minimum password length.

Use the **security passwords** command to set a minimum password length of 10 characters.

b.   Configure the enable secret password on both routers with a password of **cisco12345**. Use the type 9 (SCRYPT) hashing algorithm.

c.   Create a local **admin01** account using **admin01pass** for the password. Use the type 9 (SCRYPT) hashing algorithm.

Step 8: Configure the console line.

Configure the console to use the local database for login. For additional security, configure the line to log out after five minutes of inactivity. Issue the **logging synchronous** command to prevent console messages from interrupting command entry.

Step 9: Configure SSH Server.

a.   Configure a domain name **ccnasecurity.com**.

b.   Configure the RSA keys with **1024** for the number of modulus bits.

c.   Issue the command to force the use of SSH version 2.

d.   Configure the vty lines on R1 and R3 to use the local database for login. Remote access to the routers should only be allowed using SSH. Configure the vty lines to logout after five minutes of inactivity.

Step 10: Save the basic running configuration for all three routers.

Save the running configuration to the startup configuration from the privileged EXEC mode prompt on R1, R2, and R3.

```
R1# copy running-config startup-config
```

Part 2: Configure a Site-to-Site VPN with Cisco IOS

In Part 2 of this lab, you will configure an IPsec VPN tunnel between R1 and R3 that passes through R2. You will configure R1 and R3 using the Cisco IOS CLI. You will then review and test the resulting configuration.

Task 1: Configure IPsec VPN Settings on R1 and R3.

Step 1: Verify connectivity from the R1 LAN to the R3 LAN.

In this task, you will verify that PC-A on the R1 LAN can ping PC-C on the R3 LAN with no tunnel in place.

Ping the PC-C IP address of **192.168.3.3** from PC-A.

```
PC-A:\> ping 192.168.3.3
```

If the pings are unsuccessful, troubleshoot the basic device configurations before continuing.

Step 2: Enable IKE policies on R1 and R3.

IPsec is an open framework that allows for the exchange of security protocols as new technologies, and encryption algorithms as they are developed.

There are two central configuration elements in the implementation of an IPsec VPN:

- Implement Internet Key Exchange (IKE) parameters
- Implement IPsec parameters

a. Verify that IKE is supported and enabled.

IKE Phase 1 defines the key exchange method used to pass and validate IKE policies between peers. In IKE Phase 2, the peers exchange and match IPsec policies for the authentication and encryption of data traffic.

IKE must be enabled for IPsec to function. IKE is enabled, by default, on IOS images with cryptographic feature sets. If it is disabled, you can enable it with the **crypto isakmp enable** command. Use this command to verify that the router IOS supports IKE and that it is enabled.

```
R1(config)# crypto isakmp enable
```

```
R3(config)# crypto isakmp enable
```

Note: If you cannot execute this command on the router, you must upgrade to the IOS image that includes the Cisco cryptographic services.

b. Establish an ISAKMP policy and view the available options.

To allow IKE Phase 1 negotiation, you must create an ISAKMP policy and configure a peer association involving that ISAKMP policy. An ISAKMP policy defines the authentication and encryption algorithms and the hash function used to send control traffic between the two VPN endpoints. When an ISAKMP security association has been accepted by the IKE peers, IKE Phase 1 has been completed. IKE Phase 2 parameters will be configured later.

Issue the **crypto isakmp policy number** global configuration mode command on R1 for policy 10.

```
R1(config)# crypto isakmp policy 10
```

c. View the various IKE parameters available using Cisco IOS help by typing a question mark (**?**).

```
R1(config-isakmp)# ?
ISAKMP commands:
   authentication  Set authentication method for protection suite
```

```
default          Set a command to its defaults
encryption       Set encryption algorithm for protection suite
exit             Exit from ISAKMP protection suite configuration mode
group            Set the Diffie-Hellman group
hash             Set hash algorithm for protection suite
lifetime         Set lifetime for ISAKMP security association
no               Negate a command or set its defaults
```

Step 3: Configure the IKE Phase 1 ISAKMP policy on R1 and R3.

Your choice of an encryption algorithm determines how confidential the control channel between the endpoints is. The hash algorithm controls data integrity, ensuring that the data received from a peer has not been tampered with in transit. The authentication type ensures that the packet was sent and signed by the remote peer. The Diffie-Hellman group is used to create a secret key shared by the peers that has not been sent across the network.

a. Configure an ISAKMP policy with a priority of **10**. Use **pre-shared key** as the authentication type, **aes 256** for the encryption algorithm, **sha** as the hash algorithm, and the Diffie-Hellman group **14** key exchange. Give the policy a lifetime of **3600** seconds (one hour).

   Note: Older versions of Cisco IOS do not support AES 256 encryption and SHA as a hash algorithm. Substitute whatever encryption and hashing algorithm your router supports. Ensure that the same changes are made on R3 in order to be in sync.

```
R1(config)# crypto isakmp policy 10
R1(config-isakmp)# hash sha
R1(config-isakmp)# authentication pre-share
R1(config-isakmp)# group 14
R1(config-isakmp)# lifetime 3600
R1(config-isakmp)# encryption aes 256
R1(config-isakmp)# end
```

b. Configure the same policy on R3.

```
R3(config)# crypto isakmp policy 10
R3(config-isakmp)# hash sha
R3(config-isakmp)# authentication pre-share
R3(config-isakmp)# group 14
R3(config-isakmp)# lifetime 3600
R3(config-isakmp)# encryption aes 256
R3(config-isakmp)# end
```

c. Verify the IKE policy with the **show crypto isakmp policy** command.

```
R1# show crypto isakmp policy
Global IKE policy
Protection suite of priority 10
        encryption algorithm:   AES - Advanced Encryption Standard (256 bit keys).
        hash algorithm:         Secure Hash Standard
        authentication method:  Pre-Shared Key
        Diffie-Hellman group:   #14 (2048 bit)
        lifetime:               3600 seconds, no volume limit
```

Step 4: Configure pre-shared keys.

Because pre-shared keys are used as the authentication method in the IKE policy, a key must be configured on each router that points to the other VPN endpoint. These keys must match for authentication to be successful. The global configuration mode **crypto isakmp key <key-string> address <ip-address>** command is used to enter a pre-shared key. Use the IP address of the remote peer, which is the remote interface that the peer would use to route traffic to the local router.

Which IP addresses should you use to configure the IKE peers, given the topology diagram and IP addressing table?

_____

_____

_____

a. Each IP address that is used to configure the IKE peers is also referred to as the IP address of the remote VPN endpoint. Configure the pre-shared key of **cisco123** on router R1. Production networks should use a complex key. This command points to the remote peer R3 S0/0/1 IP address.

```
R1(config)# crypto isakmp key cisco123 address 10.2.2.1
```

b. Configure the pre-shared key **cisco123** on router R3. The command for R3 points to the R1 S0/0/0 IP address.

```
R3(config)# crypto isakmp key cisco123 address 10.1.1.1
```

Step 5: Configure the IPsec transform set and lifetime.

a. The IPsec transform set is another crypto configuration parameter that routers negotiate to form a security association. To create an IPsec transform set, use the **crypto ipsec transform-set <tag>** command. Use **?** to see which parameters are available.

```
R1(config)# crypto ipsec transform-set 50 ?
  ah-md5-hmac    AH-HMAC-MD5 transform
  ah-sha-hmac    AH-HMAC-SHA transform
  comp-lzs       IP Compression using the LZS compression algorithm
  esp-3des       ESP transform using 3DES(EDE) cipher (168 bits)
  esp-aes        ESP transform using AES cipher
  esp-des        ESP transform using DES cipher (56 bits)
  esp-md5-hmac   ESP transform using HMAC-MD5 auth
  esp-null       ESP transform w/o cipher
  esp-seal       ESP transform using SEAL cipher (160 bits)
  esp-sha-hmac   ESP transform using HMAC-SHA auth
```

b. On R1 and R3, create a transform set with tag 50 and use an ESP transform with an AES 256 cipher with ESP and the SHA hash function. The transform sets must match.

```
R1(config)# crypto ipsec transform-set 50 esp-aes 256 esp-sha-hmac
R1(cfg-crypto-trans)# exit

R3(config)# crypto ipsec transform-set 50 esp-aes 256 esp-sha-hmac
R3(cfg-crypto-trans)# exit
```

What is the function of the IPsec transform set?

_____

_____

_____

_____

c. You can also change the IPsec security association lifetime from the default of 3600 seconds. On R1 and R3, set the IPsec security association lifetime to 30 minutes, or 1800 seconds.

```
R1(config)# crypto ipsec security-association lifetime seconds 1800
```

```
R3(config)# crypto ipsec security-association lifetime seconds 1800
```

Step 6: Define interesting traffic.

To make use of the IPsec encryption with the VPN, it is necessary to define extended access lists to tell the router which traffic to encrypt. A packet that is permitted by an access list used for defining IPsec traffic is encrypted if the IPsec session is configured correctly. A packet that is denied by one of these access lists is not dropped it is sent unencrypted. Also, like any other access list, there is an implicit deny at the end, which means the default action is to not encrypt traffic. If there is no IPsec security association correctly configured, no traffic is encrypted and traffic is forwarded unencrypted.

In this scenario, from the perspective of R1, the traffic you want to encrypt is traffic going from R1's Ethernet LAN to R3's Ethernet LAN or vice versa from the perspective of R3. These access lists are used outbound on the VPN endpoint interfaces and must mirror each other.

a. Configure the IPsec VPN interesting traffic ACL on R1.

```
R1(config)# access-list 101 permit ip 192.168.1.0 0.0.0.255 192.168.3.0 0.0.0.255
```

b. Configure the IPsec VPN interesting traffic ACL on R3.

```
R3(config)# access-list 101 permit ip 192.168.3.0 0.0.0.255 192.168.1.0 0.0.0.255
```

Does IPsec evaluate whether the access lists are mirrored as a requirement to negotiate its security association?

_____

_____

_____

Step 7: Create and apply a crypto map.

A crypto map associates traffic that matches an access list to a peer and various IKE and IPsec settings. After the crypto map is created, it can be applied to one or more interfaces. The interfaces that it is applied to should be the ones facing the IPsec peer.

To create a crypto map, use **crypto map <name> <sequence-num> <type>** command in global configuration mode to enter crypto map configuration mode for that sequence number. Multiple crypto map statements can belong to the same crypto map and are evaluated in ascending numerical order. Enter crypto map configuration mode on R1. Use a type of ipsec-isakmp, which means IKE is used to establish IPsec security associations.

a. Create the crypto map on R1, name it **CMAP**, and use **10** as the sequence number. A message displays after the command is issued.

```
R1(config)# crypto map CMAP 10 ipsec-isakmp
% NOTE: This new crypto map will remain disabled until a peer
and a valid access list have been configured.
```

b. Use the **match address <access-list>** command to specify which access list defines which traffic to encrypt.

```
R1(config-crypto-map)# match address 101
```

c. To view the list of possible **set** commands that you can do with a crypto map, use the help function.

```
R1(config-crypto-map)# set ?
  identity              Identity restriction.
  ip                    Interface Internet Protocol config commands
  isakmp-profile        Specify isakmp Profile
  nat                   Set NAT translation
  peer                  Allowed Encryption/Decryption peer.
  pfs                   Specify pfs settings
  reverse-route         Reverse Route Injection.
  security-association  Security association parameters
  transform-set         Specify list of transform sets in priority order
```

d. Setting a peer IP or hostname is required. Set it to R3's remote VPN endpoint interface using the following command.

```
R1(config-crypto-map)# set peer 10.2.2.1
```

e. Use the **set transform-set <tag>** command to hard code the transform set to be used with this peer. Set the perfect forwarding secrecy type using the **set pfs <type>** command, and modify the default IPsec security association life time with the **set security-association lifetime seconds <seconds>** command.

```
R1(config-crypto-map)# set pfs group14
R1(config-crypto-map)# set transform-set 50
R1(config-crypto-map)# set security-association lifetime seconds 900
R1(config-crypto-map)# exit
```

f. Create a mirrored matching crypto map on R3.

```
R3(config)# crypto map CMAP 10 ipsec-isakmp
R3(config-crypto-map)# match address 101
R3(config-crypto-map)# set peer 10.1.1.1
R3(config-crypto-map)# set pfs group14
R3(config-crypto-map)# set transform-set 50
R3(config-crypto-map)# set security-association lifetime seconds 900
R3(config-crypto-map)# exit
```

g. Apply the crypto map to interfaces.

Note: The SAs are not established until the crypto map has been activated by interesting traffic. The router generates a notification that crypto is now on.

Apply the crypto maps to the appropriate interfaces on R1 and R3.

```
R1(config)# interface S0/0/0
R1(config-if)# crypto map CMAP
*Jan 28 04:09:09.150: %CRYPTO-6-ISAKMP_ON_OFF: ISAKMP is ON
R1(config)# end

R3(config)# interface S0/0/1
R3(config-if)# crypto map CMAP
```

```
*Jan 28 04:10:54.138: %CRYPTO-6-ISAKMP_ON_OFF: ISAKMP is ON
R3(config)# end
```

Task 2: Verify the Site-to-Site IPsec VPN Configuration.

Step 1: Verify the IPsec configuration on R1 and R3.

a. Previously, you used the **show crypto isakmp policy** command to display the configured ISAKMP policies on the router. The **show crypto ipsec transform-set** command displays the configured IPsec policies in the form of the transform sets.

```
R1# show crypto ipsec transform-set
Transform set 50: { esp-256-aes esp-sha-hmac  }
   will negotiate = { Tunnel,  },

Transform set #$!default_transform_set_1: { esp-aes esp-sha-hmac  }
   will negotiate = { Transport,  },

Transform set #$!default_transform_set_0: { esp-3des esp-sha-hmac  }
   will negotiate = { Transport,  },

R3# show crypto ipsec transform-set
Transform set 50: { esp-256-aes esp-sha-hmac  }
   will negotiate = { Tunnel,  },

Transform set #$!default_transform_set_1: { esp-aes esp-sha-hmac  }
   will negotiate = { Transport,  },

Transform set #$!default_transform_set_0: { esp-3des esp-sha-hmac  }
   will negotiate = { Transport,  },
```

b. Use the **show crypto map** command to display the crypto maps that will be applied to the router.

```
R1# show crypto map
Crypto Map "CMAP" 10 ipsec-isakmp
        Peer = 10.2.2.1
        Extended IP access list 101
            access-list 101 permit ip 192.168.1.0 0.0.0.255 192.168.3.0 0.0.0.255
        Current peer: 10.2.2.1
        Security association lifetime: 4608000 kilobytes/900 seconds
        Responder-Only (Y/N): N
        PFS (Y/N): Y
        DH group:  group14
        Transform sets={
                50:  { esp-256-aes esp-sha-hmac  } ,
        }
        Interfaces using crypto map CMAP:
                Serial0/0/0

R3# show crypto map
Crypto Map "CMAP" 10 ipsec-isakmp
```

```
        Peer = 10.1.1.1
        Extended IP access list 101
            access-list 101 permit ip 192.168.3.0 0.0.0.255 192.168.1.0 0.0.0.255
        Current peer: 10.1.1.1
        Security association lifetime: 4608000 kilobytes/900 seconds
        Responder-Only (Y/N): N
        PFS (Y/N): Y
        DH group:  group14
        Transform sets={
                50:  { esp-256-aes esp-sha-hmac  } ,
        }
        Interfaces using crypto map CMAP:
                Serial0/0/1
```

Note: The output of these **show** commands does not change if interesting traffic goes across the connection. You test various types of traffic in the next task.

Task 3: Verify the IPsec VPN Operation.

Step 1: Display ISAKMP security associations.

The **show crypto isakmp sa** command reveals that no IKE SAs exist yet. When interesting traffic is sent, this command output will change.

```
R1# show crypto isakmp sa
IPv4 Crypto ISAKMP SA
dst             src             state           conn-id status

IPv6 Crypto ISAKMP SA
```

Step 2: Display IPsec security associations.

The **show crypto ipsec sa** command shows the unused SA between R1 and R3.

Note: The number of packets sent across is zero, and there is a lack of any security associations listed toward the bottom of the output. The output for R1 is shown here.

```
R1# show crypto ipsec sa

interface: Serial0/0/0
    Crypto map tag: CMAP, local addr 10.1.1.1

   protected vrf: (none)
   local  ident (addr/mask/prot/port): (192.168.1.0/255.255.255.0/0/0)
   remote ident (addr/mask/prot/port): (192.168.3.0/255.255.255.0/0/0)
   current_peer 10.2.2.1 port 500
     PERMIT, flags={origin_is_acl,}
    #pkts encaps: 0, #pkts encrypt: 0, #pkts digest: 0
    #pkts decaps: 0, #pkts decrypt: 0, #pkts verify: 0
    #pkts compressed: 0, #pkts decompressed: 0
    #pkts not compressed: 0, #pkts compr. failed: 0
    #pkts not decompressed: 0, #pkts decompress failed: 0
    #send errors 0, #recv errors 0
```

```
          local crypto endpt.: 10.1.1.1, remote crypto endpt.: 10.2.2.1
          path mtu 1500, ip mtu 1500, ip mtu idb Serial0/0/0
          current outbound spi: 0x0(0)
          PFS (Y/N): N, DH group: none

          inbound esp sas:

          inbound ah sas:

          inbound pcp sas:

          outbound esp sas:

          outbound ah sas:

          outbound pcp sas:
```

Why haven't any SAs been negotiated?

_____

_____

_____

Step 3: Generate some uninteresting test traffic and observe the results.

   a.   Ping from R1 to the R3 S0/0/1 interface IP address **10.2.2.1**. These pings should be successful.

   b.   Issue the **show crypto isakmp sa** command.

   c.   Ping from R1 to the R3 G0/1 interface IP address **192.168.3.1**. These pings should be successful.

   d.   Issue the **show crypto isakmp sa** command again. Was an SA created for these pings? Explain.

_____

_____

   e.   Issue the **debug ip ospf hello** command. You should see OSPF hello packets passing between R1 and R3.

```
R1# debug ip ospf hello
OSPF hello events debugging is on
R1#
*Apr  7 18:04:46.467: OSPF: Send hello to 224.0.0.5 area 0 on GigabitEthernet0/1 from
192.168.1.1
*Apr  7 18:04:50.055: OSPF: Send hello to 224.0.0.5 area 0 on Serial0/0/0 from
10.1.1.1
*Apr  7 18:04:52.463: OSPF: Rcv hello from 10.2.2.2 area 0 from Serial0/0/0 10.1.1.2
*Apr  7 18:04:52.463: OSPF: End of hello processing
*Apr  7 18:04:55.675: OSPF: Send hello to 224.0.0.5 area 0 on GigabitEthernet0/1 from
192.168.1.1
*Apr  7 18:04:59.387: OSPF: Send hello to 224.0.0.5 area 0 on Serial0/0/0 from
10.1.1.1
```

```
*Apr  7 18:05:02.431: OSPF: Rcv hello from 10.2.2.2 area 0 from Serial0/0/0 10.1.1.2
*Apr  7 18:05:02.431: OSPF: End of hello processing
```

f. Turn off debugging with the **no debug ip ospf hello** or **undebug all** command.

g. Re-issue the **show crypto isakmp sa** command. Was an SA created between R1 and R3? Explain.

_____

_____

_____

Step 4: Generate some interesting test traffic and observe the results.

a. Use an extended ping from R1 to the R3 G0/1 interface IP address **192.168.3.1**. Extended ping allows you to control the source address of the packets. Respond as shown in the following example. Press **Enter** to accept the defaults, except where a specific response is indicated.

```
R1# ping
Protocol [ip]:
Target IP address: 192.168.3.1
Repeat count [5]:
Datagram size [100]:
Timeout in seconds [2]:
Extended commands [n]: y
Source address or interface: 192.168.1.1
Type of service [0]:
Set DF bit in IP header? [no]:
Validate reply data? [no]:
Data pattern [0xABCD]:
Loose, Strict, Record, Timestamp, Verbose[none]:
Sweep range of sizes [n]:
Type escape sequence to abort.
Sending 5, 100-byte ICMP Echos to 192.168.3.1, timeout is 2 seconds:

Packet sent with a source address of 192.168.1.1
..!!!
Success rate is 100 percent (3/5), round-trip min/avg/max = 92/92/92 ms
```

b. Re-issue the **show crypto isakmp sa** command.

```
R1# show crypto isakmp sa
IPv4 Crypto ISAKMP SA
dst             src             state           conn-id status
10.2.2.1        10.1.1.1        QM_IDLE            1001 ACTIVE


IPv6 Crypto ISAKMP SA
```

Why was an SA created between R1 and R3 this time?

_____

_____

_____

What are the endpoints of the IPsec VPN tunnel?

_____

_____

_____

c. Ping from PC-A to PC-C. If the pings were successful, issue the **show crypto ipsec sa** command. How many packets have been transformed between R1 and R3?

_____

_____

_____

```
R1# show crypto ipsec sa

interface: Serial0/0/0
    Crypto map tag: CMAP, local addr 10.1.1.1

   protected vrf: (none)
   local  ident (addr/mask/prot/port): (192.168.1.0/255.255.255.0/0/0)
   remote ident (addr/mask/prot/port): (192.168.3.0/255.255.255.0/0/0)
   current_peer 10.2.2.1 port 500
     PERMIT, flags={origin_is_acl,}
    #pkts encaps: 7, #pkts encrypt: 7, #pkts digest: 7
    #pkts decaps: 7, #pkts decrypt: 7, #pkts verify: 7
    #pkts compressed: 0, #pkts decompressed: 0
    #pkts not compressed: 0, #pkts compr. failed: 0
    #pkts not decompressed: 0, #pkts decompress failed: 0
    #send errors 2, #recv errors 0

     local crypto endpt.: 10.1.1.1, remote crypto endpt.: 10.2.2.1
     path mtu 1500, ip mtu 1500, ip mtu idb Serial0/0/0
     current outbound spi: 0xC1DD058(203280472)

     inbound esp sas:
      spi: 0xDF57120F(3747025423)
        transform: esp-256-aes esp-sha-hmac ,
        in use settings ={Tunnel, }
        conn id: 2005, flow_id: FPGA:5, crypto map: CMAP
        sa timing: remaining key lifetime (k/sec): (4485195/877)
        IV size: 16 bytes
        replay detection support: Y
        Status: ACTIVE

     inbound ah sas:

     inbound pcp sas:
```

```
outbound esp sas:
 spi: 0xC1DD058(203280472)
    transform: esp-256-aes esp-sha-hmac ,
    in use settings ={Tunnel, }
    conn id: 2006, flow_id: FPGA:6, crypto map: CMAP
    sa timing: remaining key lifetime (k/sec): (4485195/877)
    IV size: 16 bytes
    replay detection support: Y
    Status: ACTIVE

outbound ah sas:

outbound pcp sas:
```

d. The previous example used pings to generate interesting traffic. What other types of traffic would result in an SA forming and tunnel establishment?

_____

_____

_____

_____

_____

_____

Reflection

1. Would traffic on the Gigabit Ethernet link between PC-A and the R1 G0/0 interface be encrypted by the site-to-site IPsec VPN tunnel? Explain.

_____

_____

_____

Router Interface Summary Table

Router Interface Summary				
Router Model	Ethernet Interface #1	Ethernet Interface #2	Serial Interface #1	Serial Interface #2
1800	Fast Ethernet 0/0 (Fa0/0)	Fast Ethernet 0/1 (Fa0/1)	Serial 0/0/0 (S0/0/0)	Serial 0/0/1 (S0/0/1)
1900	Gigabit Ethernet 0/0 (G0/0)	Gigabit Ethernet 0/1 (G0/1)	Serial 0/0/0 (S0/0/0)	Serial 0/0/1 (S0/0/1)
2801	Fast Ethernet 0/0 (Fa0/0)	Fast Ethernet 0/1 (Fa0/1)	Serial 0/1/0 (S0/1/0)	Serial 0/1/1 (S0/1/1)
2811	Fast Ethernet 0/0 (Fa0/0)	Fast Ethernet 0/1 (Fa0/1)	Serial 0/0/0 (S0/0/0)	Serial 0/0/1 (S0/0/1)
2900	Gigabit Ethernet 0/0 (G0/0)	Gigabit Ethernet 0/1 (G0/1)	Serial 0/0/0 (S0/0/0)	Serial 0/0/1 (S0/0/1)

Note: To find out how the router is configured, look at the interfaces to identify the type of router and how many interfaces the router has. There is no way to effectively list all the combinations of configurations for each router class. This table includes identifiers for the possible combinations of Ethernet and Serial interfaces in the device. This table does not include any other type of interface, even though a specific router may contain one. An example of this might be an ISDN BRI interface. The string in parenthesis is the legal abbreviation that can be used in Cisco IOS commands to represent the interface.

Chapter 9: Implementing the Cisco Adaptive Security Appliance

Lab 9.3.1.2 – Configure ASA Basic Settings and Firewall Using CLI

Topology

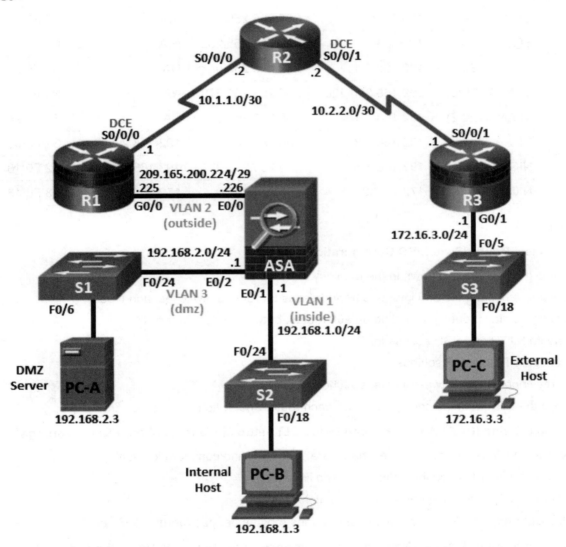

Note: ISR G2 devices use GigabitEthernet interfaces instead of FastEthernet interfaces.

IP Addressing Table

Device	Interface	IP Address	Subnet Mask	Default Gateway	Switch Port
R1	G0/0	209.165.200.225	255.255.255.248	N/A	ASA E0/0
	S0/0/0 (DCE)	10.1.1.1	255.255.255.252	N/A	N/A
R2	S0/0/0	10.1.1.2	255.255.255.252	N/A	N/A
	S0/0/1 (DCE)	10.2.2.2	255.255.255.252	N/A	N/A
R3	G0/1	172.16.3.1	255.255.255.0	N/A	S3 F0/5
	S0/0/1	10.2.2.1	255.255.255.252	N/A	N/A
ASA	VLAN 1 (E0/1)	192.168.1.1	255.255.255.0	NA	S2 F0/24
ASA	VLAN 2 (E0/0)	209.165.200.226	255.255.255.248	NA	R1 G0/0
ASA	VLAN 3 (E0/2)	192.168.2.1	255.255.255.0	NA	S1 F0/24
PC-A	NIC	192.168.2.3	255.255.255.0	192.168.2.1	S1 F0/6
PC-B	NIC	192.168.1.3	255.255.255.0	192.168.1.1	S2 F0/18
PC-C	NIC	172.16.3.3	255.255.255.0	172.16.3.1	S3 F0/18

Objectives

Part 1: Basic Router/Switch/PC Configuration

- Cable the network as shown in the topology.
- Configure hostnames and interface IP addresses for routers, switches, and PCs.
- Configure static routing, including default routes, between R1, R2, and R3.
- Enable HTTP and SSH access for R1.
- Configure PC host IP settings.
- Verify connectivity between hosts, switches, and routers.
- Save the basic running configuration for each router and switch.

Part 2: Accessing the ASA Console and Using CLI Setup Mode to Configure Basic Settings

- Access the ASA console and view hardware, software, and configuration settings.
- Determine the ASA version, interfaces, and license.
- Determine the file system and contents of flash memory.
- Use CLI Setup mode to configure basic settings (hostname, passwords, clock, etc.).

Part 3: Configuring Basic ASA Settings and Interface Security Levels Using the CLI.

- Configure the hostname and domain name.
- Configure the login and enable passwords.
- Set the date and time.
- Configure the inside and outside interfaces.
- Test connectivity to the ASA.

- Configure SSH access to the ASA.
- Configure HTTPS access on the ASA for ASDM.

Part 4: Configuring Routing, Address Translation, and Inspection Policy Using the CLI

- Configure a static default route for the ASA.
- Configure PAT and network objects.
- Modify the MPF application inspection global service policy.

Part 5: Configuring DHCP, AAA, and SSH

- Configure the ASA as a DHCP server/client.
- Configure Local AAA user authentication.
- Configure SSH remote access to the AAA.

Part 6: Configuring DMZ, Static NAT, and ACLs

- Configure the DMZ interface VLAN 3 on the ASA.
- Configure static NAT for the DMZ server using a network object.
- Configure an ACL to allow access to the DMZ for Internet users.
- Verify access to the DMZ server for external and internal users.

Background/Scenario

The Cisco Adaptive Security Appliance (ASA) is an advanced network security device that integrates a stateful firewall, VPN, and other capabilities. This lab employs an ASA 5505 to create a firewall and protect an internal corporate network from external intruders while allowing internal hosts access to the Internet. The ASA creates three security interfaces: Outside, Inside, and DMZ. It provides outside users limited access to the DMZ and no access to inside resources. Inside users can access the DMZ and outside resources.

The focus of this lab is the configuration of the ASA as a basic firewall. Other devices will receive minimal configuration to support the ASA portion of this lab. This lab uses the ASA CLI, which is similar to the IOS CLI, to configure basic device and security settings.

In Part 1 of this lab, you will configure the topology and non-ASA devices. In Parts 2 through 4 you will configure basic ASA settings and the firewall between the inside and outside networks. In part 5 you will configure the ASA for additional services, such as DHCP, AAA, and SSH. In Part 6, you will configure a DMZ on the ASA and provide access to a server in the DMZ.

Your company has one location connected to an ISP. R1 represents a CPE device managed by the ISP. R2 represents an intermediate Internet router. R3 represents an ISP that connects an administrator from a network management company, who has been hired to remotely manage your network. The ASA is an edge security device that connects the internal corporate network and DMZ to the ISP while providing NAT and DHCP services to inside hosts. The ASA will be configured for management by an administrator on the internal network and by the remote administrator. Layer 3 VLAN interfaces provide access to the three areas created in the lab: Inside, Outside, and DMZ. The ISP has assigned the public IP address space of 209.165.200.224/29, which will be used for address translation on the ASA.

Note: The router commands and output in this lab are from a Cisco 1941 with Cisco IOS Release 15.4(3)M2 image with a Security Technology license. Other routers and Cisco IOS versions can be used. See the Router Interface Summary Table at the end of this lab to determine which interface identifiers to use based on the equipment in your class. Depending on the router model and Cisco IOS version, the available commands and output produced might vary from what is shown in this lab.

The ASA used with this lab is a Cisco model 5505 with an 8-port integrated switch, running OS version 9.2(3), Adaptive Security Device Manager (ASDM) version 7.4(1), and comes with a Base license that allows a maximum of three VLANs.

Note: Ensure that the routers and switches have been erased and have no startup configurations.

Required Resources

- 3 Routers (Cisco 1941 with Cisco IOS Release 15.4(3)M2 image with a Security Technology Package license)
- 3 Switches (Cisco 2960 with cryptography IOS image for SSH support – Release 15.0(2)SE7 or comparable)
- 1 ASA 5505 (OS version 9.2(3) and ASDM version 7.4(1) and Base license or comparable)
- 3 PCs (Windows 7 or Windows 8 with SSH client software)
- Serial and Ethernet cables as shown in the topology
- Console cables to configure Cisco networking devices

Part 1: Basic Router/Switch/PC Configuration

In Part 1 of this lab, you will set up the network topology and configure basic settings on the routers, such as interface IP addresses and static routing.

Note: Do not configure ASA settings at this time.

Step 1: Cable the network and clear previous device settings.

Attach the devices that are shown in the topology diagram and cable as necessary. Make sure that the routers and switches have been erased and have no startup configurations.

Step 2: Configure basic settings for routers and switches.

a.   Configure hostnames as shown in the topology for each router.

b.   Configure router interface IP addresses as shown in the IP Addressing Table.

c.   Configure a clock rate for routers with a DCE serial cable attached to their serial interface. R1 is shown here as an example.

```
R1(config)# interface S0/0/0
R1(config-if)# clock rate 64000
```

d.   Configure the host name for the switches. Other than the host name, the switches can be left in their default configuration state. Configuring the VLAN management IP address for the switches is optional.

Step 3: Configure static routing on the routers.

a.   Configure a static default route from R1 to R2 and from R3 to R2.

```
R1(config)# ip route 0.0.0.0 0.0.0.0 Serial0/0/0
R3(config)# ip route 0.0.0.0 0.0.0.0 Serial0/0/1
```

b.   Configure a static route from R2 to the R1 G0/0 subnet (connected to ASA interface E0/0) and a static route from R2 to the R3 LAN.

```
R2(config)# ip route 209.165.200.224 255.255.255.248 Serial0/0/0
R2(config)# ip route 172.16.3.0 255.255.255.0 Serial0/0/1
```

Step 4: Enable the HTTP server and configure a user account, encrypted passwords, and crypto keys for SSH.

Note: Passwords in this task are set to a minimum of 10 characters but are relatively simple for the purposes of this lab. More complex passwords are recommended in a production network.

a. Enable HTTP access to R1 using the **ip http server** command in global config mode. Set the console and VTY passwords to cisco. This will provide web and SSH targets for testing later in the lab.

```
R1(config)# ip http server
```

b. Configure a minimum password length of 10 characters using the **security passwords** command.

```
R1(config)# security passwords min-length 10
```

c. Configure a domain name.

```
R1(config)# ip domain-name ccnasecurity.com
```

d. Configure crypto keys for SSH.

```
R1(config)# crypto key generate rsa general-keys modulus 1024
```

e. Configure an admin01 user account using algorithm-type scrypt for encryption and a password of cisco12345.

```
R1(config)# username admin01 algorithm-type scrypt secret cisco12345
```

f. Configure line console 0 to use the local user database for logins. For additional security, the **exec-timeout** command causes the line to log out after five minutes of inactivity. The **logging synchronous** command prevents console messages from interrupting command entry.

Note: To avoid repetitive logins during this lab, the **exec-timeout** command can be set to 0 0, which prevents it from expiring. However, this is not considered to be a good security practice.

```
R1(config)# line console 0
R1(config-line)# login local
R1(config-line)# exec-timeout 5 0
R1(config-line)# logging synchronous
```

g. Configure line vty 0 4 to use the local user database for logins and restrict access to only SSH connections.

```
R1(config)# line vty 0 4
R1(config-line)# login local
R1(config-line)# transport input ssh
R1(config-line)# exec-timeout 5 0
```

h. Configure the enable password with strong encryption.

```
R1(config)# enable algorithm-type scrypt secret class12345
```

Step 5: Configure PC host IP settings.

Configure a static IP address, subnet mask, and default gateway for PC-A, PC-B, and PC-C as shown in the IP Addressing Table.

Step 6: Verify connectivity.

Because the ASA is the focal point for the network zones, and it has not yet been configured, there will be no connectivity between devices that are connected to it. However, PC-C should be able to ping the R1 interface. From PC-C, ping the R1 G0/0 IP address (209.165.200.225). If these pings are not successful, troubleshoot the basic device configurations before continuing.

Note: If you can ping from PC-C to R1 G0/0 and S0/0/0 you have demonstrated that static routing is configured and functioning correctly.

Step 7: Save the basic running configuration for each router and switch.

Part 2: Accessing the ASA Console and Using CLI Setup to Configure Basic Settings

In Part 2 of this lab, you will access the ASA via the console and use various **show** commands to determine hardware, software, and configuration settings. You will clear the current configuration and use the CLI interactive setup utility to configure basic ASA settings.

Note: Do not configure ASA settings at this time.

Step 1: Access the ASA console.

a. Accessing the ASA via the console port is the same as with a Cisco router or switch. Connect to the ASA console port with a rollover cable.

b. Use a terminal emulation program, such as TeraTerm or PuTTy to access the CLI. Then use the serial port settings of 9600 baud, eight data bits, no parity, one stop bit, and no flow control.

c. Enter privileged mode with the **enable** command and password (if a password has been set). The password is blank by default. Press **Enter**. If the password has been changed to what is specified in this lab, enter the word **class**. The default ASA hostname and prompt is ciscoasa>.

```
ciscoasa> enable
Password: class (or press Enter if none set)
```

Step 2: Determine the ASA version, interfaces, and license.

The ASA 5505 comes with an integrated eight-port Ethernet switch. Ports E0/0 to E0/5 are normal Fast Ethernet ports and ports E0/6 and E0/7 are PoE ports for use with PoE devices, such as IP phones or network cameras.

Use the **show version** command to determine various aspects of this ASA device.

```
ciscoasa# show version

Cisco Adaptive Security Appliance Software Version 9.2(3)
Device Manager Version 7.4(1)

Compiled on Mon 15-Dec-14 18:17 by builders
System image file is "disk0:/asa923-k8.bin"
Config file at boot was "startup-config"

ciscoasa up 23 hours 0 mins

Hardware:  ASA5505, 512 MB RAM, CPU Geode 500 MHz
Internal ATA Compact Flash, 128MB
BIOS Flash M50FW016 @ 0xfff00000, 2048KB

Encryption hardware device : Cisco ASA-5505 on-board accelerator (revision 0x0)
                            Boot microcode      : CN1000-MC-BOOT-2.00
                            SSL/IKE microcode   : CNLite-MC-SSLm-PLUS-2.03
```

```
                        IPSec microcode       : CNlite-MC-IPSECm-MAIN-2.06
                        Number of accelerators: 1

     0: Int: Internal-Data0/0  : address is 0007.7dbf.5645, irq 11
     1: Ext: Ethernet0/0       : address is 0007.7dbf.563d, irq 255
     2: Ext: Ethernet0/1       : address is 0007.7dbf.563e, irq 255

     <output omitted>
```

What software version is this ASA running?

_____

What is the name of the system image file and from where was it loaded?

_____

_____

The ASA can be managed using a built-in GUI known as ASDM. What version of ASDM is this ASA running?

_____

How much RAM does this ASA have?

_____

How much flash memory does this ASA have?

_____

How many Ethernet ports does this ASA have?

_____

What type of license does this ASA have?

_____

How many VLANs can be created with this license?

_____

Step 3: Determine the file system and contents of flash memory.

a. Display the ASA file system using the **show file system** command. Determine what prefixes are supported.

```
ciscoasa# show file system

File Systems:

        Size(b)        Free(b)      Type     Flags    Prefixes
  * 128573440       55664640       disk     rw        disk0: flash:
                -              -    network  rw        tftp:
                -              -    opaque   rw        system:
                -              -    network  ro        http:
                -              -    network  ro        https:
                -              -    network  rw        ftp:
                -              -    network  rw        smb:
```

What is another name for flash:?_____

b. Display the contents of flash memory using one of these commands: **show flash**, **show disk0**, **dir flash:**, or **dir disk0:**.

```
ciscoasa# show flash
--#--   --length--   -----date/time------   path
  168   25159680     Aug 29 2011 13:00:52   asa923-k8.bin
  122   0            Aug 29 2011 13:09:32   nat_ident_migrate
   13   2048         Aug 29 2011 13:02:14   coredumpinfo
   14   59           Aug 29 2011 13:02:14   coredumpinfo/coredump.cfg
  169   16280544     Aug 29 2011 13:02:58   asdm-741.bin
    3   2048         Aug 29 2011 13:04:42   log
    6   2048         Aug 29 2011 13:05:00   crypto_archive
  171   34816        Jan 01 1980 00:00:00   FSCK0000.REC
  173   36864        Jan 01 1980 00:00:00   FSCK0001.REC
  174   12998641     Aug 29 2011 13:09:22   csd_3.5.2008-k9.pkg
  175   2048         Aug 29 2011 13:09:24   sdesktop
  211   0            Aug 29 2011 13:09:24   sdesktop/data.xml
  176   6487517      Aug 29 2011 13:09:26   anyconnect-macosx-i386-2.5.2014-k9.pkg
  177   6689498      Aug 29 2011 13:09:30   anyconnect-linux-2.5.2014-k9.pkg
  178   4678691      Aug 29 2011 13:09:32   anyconnect-win-2.5.2014-k9.pkg
<output omitted>
```

c. What is the name of the ASDM file in flash:? _____

Step 4: Determine the current running configuration.

The ASA 5505 is commonly used as an edge security device that connects a small business or teleworker to an ISP device, such as a DSL or cable modem, for access to the Internet. The default factory configuration for the ASA 5505 includes the following:

*   An inside VLAN 1 interface is configured that includes the Ethernet 0/1 through 0/7 switch ports. The VLAN 1 IP address and mask are 192.168.1.1 and 255.255.255.0.

*   An outside VLAN 2 interface is configured that includes the Ethernet 0/0 switch port. VLAN 2 derives its IP address from the ISP using DHCP by default.

*   The default route is derived from the DHCP default gateway.

*   All inside IP addresses are translated when accessing the outside, using interface PAT on the VLAN 2 interface.

*   By default, inside users can access the outside with an access list and outside users are prevented from accessing the inside.

*   The DHCP server is enabled on the security appliance, so a PC connecting to the VLAN 1 interface receives an address between 192.168.1.5 and 192.168.1.36 (base license) though the actual range may vary.

*   The HTTP server is enabled for ASDM and is accessible to users on the 192.168.1.0/24 network.

*   No console or enable passwords are required, and the default hostname is ciscoasa.

Note: In this lab, you will manually configure settings similar to those listed above, as well as some additional settings, using the ASA CLI.

a. Display the current running configuration using the **show running-config** command.

```
ciscoasa# show running-config
: Saved
:
ASA Version 9.2(3)
!
hostname ciscoasa
enable password 8Ry2YjIyt7RRXU24 encrypted
names
!
interface Ethernet0/0
 switchport access vlan 2
!
interface Ethernet0/1
!
interface Ethernet0/2
```

Note: To stop the output from a command using the CLI, press **Q**.

If you see VLANs 1 and 2 and other settings as described previously, the device is most likely configured with the default factory configuration. You may also see other security features, such as a global policy that inspects selected application traffic, which the ASA inserts by default if the original startup configuration has been erased. The actual output varies depending on the ASA model, version, and configuration status.

b. You can restore the ASA to its factory default settings by using the **configure factory-default** command.

```
ciscoasa# conf t
ciscoasa(config)# configure factory-default

WARNING: The boot system configuration will be cleared.
The first image found in disk0:/ will be used to boot the
system on the next reload.
Verify there is a valid image on disk0:/ or the system will
not boot.

Begin to apply factory-default configuration:
Clear all configuration
WARNING: DHCPD bindings cleared on interface 'inside', address pool removed
Executing command: interface Ethernet 0/0
Executing command: switchport access vlan 2
Executing command: no shutdown
Executing command: exit
Executing command: interface Ethernet 0/1
Executing command: switchport access vlan 1
Executing command: no shutdown
Executing command: exit
```

c. Review this output and pay particular attention to the VLAN interfaces, NAT-related, and DHCP-related sections. These will be configured later in this lab using the CLI.

d. You may want to capture and print the factory-default configuration as a reference. Use the terminal emulation program to copy it from the ASA and paste it into a text document. You can then edit this file if desired, so that it contains only valid commands. You should remove password commands and enter the **no shut** command to bring up the desired interfaces.

Step 5: Clear the previous ASA configuration settings.

a. Use the **write erase** command to remove the startup-config file from flash memory.

```
ciscoasa# write erase
Erase configuration in flash memory? [confirm]
[OK]
ciscoasa#

ciscoasa# show start
No Configuration
```

Note: The IOS command **erase startup-config** is not supported on the ASA.

b. Use the **reload** command to restart the ASA. This causes the ASA to come up in CLI Setup mode. If prompted that the config has been modified and needs to be saved, respond with **N**, and then press **Enter** to proceed with the reload.

```
ciscoasa# reload
Proceed with reload? [confirm]
ciscoasa#
***
*** --- START GRACEFUL SHUTDOWN ---
Shutting down isakmp
Shutting down File system
***
*** --- SHUTDOWN NOW ---
Process shutdown finished
Rebooting.....
CISCO SYSTEMS
Embedded BIOS Version 1.0(12)13 08/28/08 15:50:37.45
<output omitted>
```

Step 6: Use the Setup interactive CLI mode to configure basic settings.

When the ASA completes the reload process, it should detect that the startup-config file is missing and present a series of interactive prompts to configure basic ASA settings. If it does not come up in this mode, repeat Step 5. As an alternative, you can run the **setup** command at the global configuration mode prompt, but you must first create a VLAN interface (VLAN 1), name the VLAN management (using the **nameif** command), and assign the VLAN an IP address.

Note: The interactive prompt mode does not configure the ASA with factory defaults as described in Step 4. This mode can be used to configure minimal basic settings, such as hostname, clock, and passwords. You can also go directly to the CLI to configure the ASA settings, as described in Part 3.

a. Respond to the Setup interactive prompts as shown here, after the ASA reloads.

```
Pre-configure Firewall now through interactive prompts [yes]? <Enter>
```

```
Firewall Mode [Routed]: <Enter>
Enable password [<use current password>]: class
Allow password recovery [yes]? <Enter>
Clock (UTC):
  Year [2015]: <Enter>
  Month [Apr]: <Enter>
  Day [19]: <Enter>
  Time [23:32:19]: <Enter>
Management IP address: 192.168.1.1
Management network mask: 255.255.255.0
Host name: ASA-Init
Domain name: generic.com
IP address of host running Device Manager: <Enter>

The following configuration will be used:
Enable password: cisco
Allow password recovery: yes
Clock (UTC): 23:32:19 Apr 19 2015
Firewall Mode: Routed
Management IP address: 192.168.1.1
Management network mask: 255.255.255.0
Host name: ASA-Init
Domain name: generic.com


Use this configuration and save to flash? [yes] yes
INFO: Security level for "management" set to 0 by default.
Cryptochecksum: c8a535f0 e273d49e 5bddfd19 e12566b1

2070 bytes copied in 0.940 secs
Type help or '?' for a list of available commands.
ASA-Init>
```

Note: In the above configuration, the IP address of the host running ASDM was left blank. It is not necessary to install ASDM on a host. It can be run from the flash memory of the ASA device itself using the browser of the host.

Note: The responses to the prompts are automatically stored in the startup-config and the running config. However, additional security-related commands, such as a global default inspection service policy, are inserted into the running-config by the ASA OS.

b. Enter privileged EXEC mode with the **enable** command. Enter **class** for the password.

c. Issue the **show run** command to see the additional security-related configuration commands that are inserted by the ASA.

d. Issue the **copy run start** command to capture the additional security-related commands in the startup-config file.

Part 3: Configuring ASA Settings and Interface Security Using the CLI

In Part 3, you will configure basic settings by using the ASA CLI, even though some of them were already configured using the Setup mode interactive prompts in Part 2. In this part, you will start with the settings configured in Part 2 and then add to or modify them to create a complete basic configuration.

Tip: Many ASA CLI commands are similar to, if not the same, as those used with the Cisco IOS CLI. In addition, the process of moving between configuration modes and sub-modes is essentially the same.

Note: You must complete Part 2 before beginning Part 3.

Step 1: Configure the hostname and domain name.

a. Enter global configuration mode using the **config t** command. The first time you enter configuration mode after running Setup, you will be prompted to enable anonymous reporting. Respond with no.

```
ASA-Init# config t
ASA-Init(config)#


**************************** NOTICE ****************************


Help to improve the ASA platform by enabling anonymous reporting,
which allows Cisco to securely receive minimal error and health
information from the device. To learn more about this feature,
please visit: http://www.cisco.com/go/smartcall


Would you like to enable anonymous error reporting to help improve
the product? [Y]es, [N]o, [A]sk later: n


In the future, if you would like to enable this feature,
issue the command "call-home reporting anonymous".


Please remember to save your configuration.
```

b. Configure the ASA hostname using the **hostname** command.

```
ASA-Init(config)# hostname CCNAS-ASA
```

c. Configure the domain name using the **domain-name** command.

```
CCNAS-ASA(config)# domain-name ccnasecurity.com
```

Step 2: Configure the login and enable mode passwords.

a. The login password isused for Telnet connections (and SSH prior to ASA version 8.4). By default, it is set to cisco, but since the default startup configuration was erased you have the option to configure the login password using the **passwd** or **password** command. This command is optional because later in the lab we will configure the ASA for SSH, and not Telnet access.

```
CCNAS-ASA(config)# passwd cisco
```

b. Configure the privileged EXEC mode (enable) password using the **enable password** command.

```
CCNAS-ASA(config)# enable password class
```

Step 3: Set the date and time.

The date and time can be set manually using the **clock set** command. The syntax for the **clock set** command is **clock set** *hh:mm:ss {month day | day month} year*. The following example shows how to set the date and time using a 24-hour clock:

```
CCNAS-ASA(config)# clock set 19:09:00 april 19 2015
```

Step 4: Configure the inside and outside interfaces.

ASA 5505 interface notes:

The 5505 is different from the other 5500 series ASA models. With other ASAs, the physical port can be assigned a Layer 3 IP address directly, much like a Cisco router. With the ASA 5505, the eight integrated switch ports are Layer 2 ports. To assign Layer 3 parameters, you must create a switch virtual interface (SVI) or logical VLAN interface and then assign one or more of the physical Layer 2 ports to it. All eight switch ports are initially assigned to VLAN 1, unless the factory default configuration is present, in which case, port E0/0 is assigned to VLAN 2. In this step, you will create internal and external VLAN interfaces, name them, assign IP addresses, and set the interface security level.

If you completed the initial configuration Setup utility, interface VLAN 1 is configured as the management VLAN with an IP address of 192.168.1.1. You will configure it as the inside interface for this lab. You will only configure the VLAN 1 (inside) and VLAN 2 (outside) interfaces at this time. The VLAN 3 (dmz) interface will be configured in Part 6 of the lab.

a. Configure a logical VLAN 1 interface for the inside network (192.168.1.0/24) and set the security level to the highest setting of 100.

```
CCNAS-ASA(config)# interface vlan 1
CCNAS-ASA(config-if)# nameif inside
CCNAS-ASA(config-if)# ip address 192.168.1.1 255.255.255.0
CCNAS-ASA(config-if)# security-level 100
```

b. Create a logical VLAN 2 interface for the outside network (209.165.200.224/29), set the security level to the lowest setting of 0, and access the VLAN 2 interface.

```
CCNAS-ASA(config-if)# interface vlan 2
CCNAS-ASA(config-if)# nameif outside
INFO: Security level for "outside" set to 0 by default.

CCNAS-ASA(config-if)# ip address 209.165.200.226 255.255.255.248
CCNAS-ASA(config-if)# no shutdown
```

Interface security-level notes:

You may receive a message that the security level for the inside interface was set automatically to 100, and the outside interface was set to 0. The ASA uses interface security levels from 0 to 100 to enforce the security policy. Security level 100 (inside) is the most secure and level 0 (outside) is the least secure.

By default, the ASA applies a policy where traffic from a higher security level interface to one with a lower level is permitted and traffic from a lower security level interface to one with a higher security level is denied. The ASA default security policy permits outbound traffic, which is inspected, by default. Returning traffic is allowed due to stateful packet inspection. This default "routed mode" firewall behavior of the ASA allows packets to be routed from the inside network to the outside network, but not vice-versa. In Part 4 of this lab, you will configure NAT to increase the firewall protection.

c. Use the **show interface** command to ensure that ASA Layer 2 ports E0/0 (for VLAN 2) and E0/1 (for VLAN 1) are both up. An example is shown for E0/0. If either port is shown as down/down, check the physical connections. If either port is administratively down, bring it up with the **no shutdown** command.

```
CCNAS-ASA# show interface e0/0
Interface Ethernet0/0 "", is administratively down, line protocol is up
   Hardware is 88E6095, BW 100 Mbps, DLY 100 usec
         Auto-Duplex(Full-duplex), Auto-Speed(100 Mbps)
<output omitted>
```

d. Assign ASA Layer 2 port E0/1 to VLAN 1 and port E0/0 to VLAN 2. Use the **no shutdown** command to ensure they are up.

```
CCNAS-ASA(config)# interface e0/1
CCNAS-ASA(config-if)# switchport access vlan 1
CCNAS-ASA(config-if)# no shutdown
CCNAS-ASA(config-if)# interface e0/0
CCNAS-ASA(config-if)# switchport access vlan 2
CCNAS-ASA(config-if)# no shutdown
```

Note: Even though E0/1 is in VLAN 1 by default, the commands are provided above.

e. Display the status for all ASA interfaces using the **show interface ip brief** command.

Note: This command is different from the **show ip interface brief** IOS command. If any of the physical or logical interfaces previously configured are not up/up, troubleshoot as necessary before continuing.

Tip: Most ASA **show** commands, as well as **ping**, **copy**, and others, can be issued from within any configuration mode prompt without the **do** command that is required with IOS.

```
CCNAS-ASA(config)# show interface ip brief
Interface                IP-Address       OK? Method Status          Protocol
Ethernet0/0              unassigned       YES unset  up              up
Ethernet0/1              unassigned       YES unset  up              up
Ethernet0/2              unassigned       YES unset  up              up
Ethernet0/3              unassigned       YES unset  down            down
Ethernet0/4              unassigned       YES unset  down            down
Ethernet0/5              unassigned       YES unset  down            down
Ethernet0/6              unassigned       YES unset  down            down
Ethernet0/7              unassigned       YES unset  down            down
Internal-Data0/0         unassigned       YES unset  up              up
Internal-Data0/1         unassigned       YES unset  up              up
Vlan1                    192.168.1.1      YES manual up              up
Vlan2                    209.165.200.226  YES manual up              up
Virtual0                 127.0.0.1        YES unset  up              up
```

f. Display the information for the Layer 3 VLAN interfaces using the **show ip address** command.

```
CCNAS-ASA(config)# show ip address
System IP Addresses:
Interface       Name       IP address        Subnet mask       Method
Vlan1           inside     192.168.1.1       255.255.255.0     manual
Vlan2           outside    209.165.200.226   255.255.255.248   manual

Current IP Addresses:
Interface       Name       IP address        Subnet mask       Method
Vlan1           inside     192.168.1.1       255.255.255.0     manual
Vlan2           outside    209.165.200.226   255.255.255.248   manual
```

g. Use the **show switch vlan** command to display the inside and outside VLANs configured on the ASA and to display the assigned ports.

```
CCNAS-ASA# show switch vlan
VLAN Name                            Status    Ports
---- ------------------------------  --------- ------------------------------
1    inside                          up        Et0/1, Et0/2, Et0/3, Et0/4
                                               Et0/5, Et0/6, Et0/7
2    outside                         up        Et0/0
```

h. You may also use the **show running-config interface type/number** command to display the configuration for a particular interface from the running configuration.

```
CCNAS-ASA# show run interface vlan 1
!
interface Vlan1
 nameif inside
 security-level 100
 ip address 192.168.1.1 255.255.255.0
```

Step 5: Test connectivity to the ASA.

a. Ensure that PC-B has a static IP address of 192.168.1.3, a subnet mask of 255.255.255.0, and a default gateway of 192.168.1.1 (the IP address of ASA VLAN 1 inside interface).

b. You should be able to ping from PC-B to the ASA inside interface address and ping from the ASA to PC-B. If the pings fail, troubleshoot the configuration as necessary.

```
CCNAS-ASA# ping 192.168.1.3
Type escape sequence to abort.
Sending 5, 100-byte ICMP Echos to 192.168.1.3, timeout is 2 seconds:
!!!!!
Success rate is 100 percent (5/5), round-trip min/avg/max = 1/1/1 ms
```

c. From PC-C, ping the VLAN 2 (outside) interface at IP address 209.165.200.226. You should not be able to ping this address.

Step 6: Configure ASDM access to the ASA.

a. You can configure the ASA to accept HTTPS connections using the **http** command. This allows access to the ASA GUI (ASDM). Configure the ASA to allow HTTPS connections from any host on the inside network (192.168.1.0/24).

```
CCNAS-ASA(config)# http server enable
CCNAS-ASA(config)# http 192.168.1.0 255.255.255.0 inside
```

b. Open a browser on PC-B and test the HTTPS access to the ASA by entering **https://192.168.1.1**. You will be prompted with a security certificate warning. Click **Continue**. Click **Yes** for the other security warnings. You should see the Cisco ASDM Welcome screen that allows you to: Install ASDM Launcher and Run ASDM, Run ASDM, or Run Startup Wizard.

Note: If you are unable to launch ASDM, the IP address must be added to the allowed list of IP addresses in Java.

1) Access the Windows Control Panel and click **Java**.

2) In the Java Control Panel, select **Security** tab. Click **Edit Site List**.

3) In the Exception Site list, click **Add**. In the Location field, type **https://192.168.1.1**.

4) Click **OK** to add the IP address.

5) Verify that the IP address has been added. Click **OK** to accept the changes.

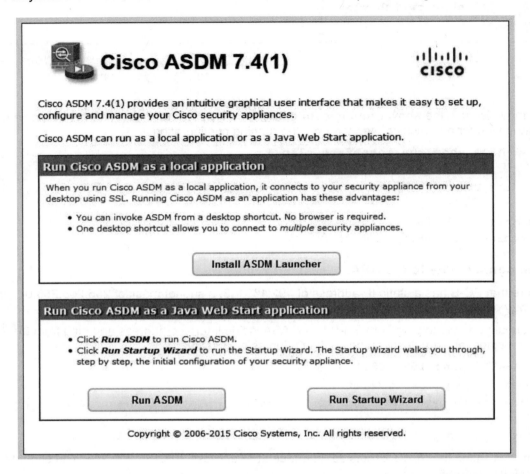

c.   Close the browser. In the next lab, you will use ASDM extensively to configure the ASA. The objective here is not to use the ASDM configuration screens, but to verify HTTP/ASDM connectivity to the ASA. If you are unable to access ASDM, check your configurations. If the configurations are correct contact your instructor for further assistance.

Part 4: Configuring Routing, Address Translation, and Inspection Policy Using the CLI

In Part 4 of this lab, you will provide a default route for the ASA to reach external networks. You will configure address translation using network objects to enhance firewall security. You will then modify the default application inspection policy to allow specific traffic.

Note: You must complete Part 3 before proceeding to Part 4.

Step 1: Configure a static default route for the ASA.

In Part 3, you configured the ASA outside interface with a static IP address and subnet mask. However, the ASA does not have a gateway of last resort defined. To enable the ASA to reach external networks, you will configure a default static route on the ASA outside interface.

Note: If the ASA outside interface was configured as a DHCP client, it could obtain a default gateway IP address from the ISP. However, in this lab, the outside interface is configured with a static address.

a. Ping from the ASA to R1 G0/0 at IP address 209.165.200.225. Was the ping successful?

_____

_____

b. Ping from the ASA to R1 S0/0/0 at IP address 10.1.1.1. Was the ping successful?

_____

_____

c. Create a "quad zero" default route using the **route** command, associate it with the ASA outside interface, and point to the R1 G0/0 at IP address 209.165.200.225 as the gateway of last resort. The default administrative distance is one by default.

```
CCNAS-ASA(config)# route outside 0.0.0.0 0.0.0.0 209.165.200.225
```

d. Issue the **show route** command to display the ASA routing table and the static default route you just created.

```
CCNAS-ASA# show route
Codes: L - local, C - connected, S - static, R - RIP, M - mobile, B - BGP
       D - EIGRP, EX - EIGRP external, O - OSPF, IA - OSPF inter area
       N1 - OSPF NSSA external type 1, N2 - OSPF NSSA external type 2
       E1 - OSPF external type 1, E2 - OSPF external type 2
       i - IS-IS, su - IS-IS summary, L1 - IS-IS level-1, L2 - IS-IS level-2
       ia - IS-IS inter area, * - candidate default, U - per-user static route
       o - ODR, P - periodic downloaded static route, + - replicated route

Gateway of last resort is 209.165.200.225 to network 0.0.0.0

S*    0.0.0.0 0.0.0.0 [1/0] via 209.165.200.225, outside
C        192.168.1.0 255.255.255.0 is directly connected, inside
L        192.168.1.1 255.255.255.255 is directly connected, inside
C        209.165.200.224 255.255.255.248 is directly connected, outside
L        209.165.200.226 255.255.255.255 is directly connected, outside
```

e. Ping from the ASA to R1 S0/0/0 IP address 10.1.1.1. Was the ping successful?

_____

_____

Step 2: Configure address translation using PAT and network objects.

Note: Beginning with ASA version 8.3, network objects are used to configure all forms of NAT. A network object is created, and it is within this object that NAT is configured. In Step 2a, the network object **INSIDE-NET** is used to translate the inside network addresses (192.168.10.0/24) to the global address of the outside ASA interface. This type of object configuration is called Auto-NAT.

a. Create the network object **INSIDE-NET** and assign attributes to it using the **subnet** and **nat** commands.

```
CCNAS-ASA(config)# object network INSIDE-NET
CCNAS-ASA(config-network-object)# subnet 192.168.1.0 255.255.255.0
CCNAS-ASA(config-network-object)# nat (inside,outside) dynamic interface
CCNAS-ASA(config-network-object)# end
```

b. The ASA splits the configuration into the object portion that defines the network to be translated and the actual **nat** command parameters. These appear in two different places in the running configuration. Display the NAT object configuration using the **show run object** and **show run nat** commands.

```
CCNAS-ASA# show run object
object network INSIDE-NET
 subnet 192.168.1.0 255.255.255.0


CCNAS-ASA# show run nat
!
object network INSIDE-NET
 nat (inside,outside) dynamic interface
```

c. From PC-B, attempt to ping the R1 G0/0 interface at IP address **209.165.200.225**. Were the pings successful? _____

d. Issue the **show nat** command on the ASA to see the translated and untranslated hits. Notice that, of the pings from PC-B, four were translated and four were not because ICMP is not being inspected by the global inspection policy. The outgoing pings (echoes) were translated, and the returning echo replies were blocked by the firewall policy. You will configure the default inspection policy to allow ICMP in the next step. **Note:** Depending on the processes and daemons running on the particular computer used as PC-B, you may see more translated and untranslated hits than the four echo requests and echo replies.

```
CCNAS-ASA# show nat


Auto NAT Policies (Section 2)
1 (inside) to (outside) source dynamic INSIDE-NET interface
    translate_hits = 4, untranslate_hits = 4
```

e. Ping from PC-B to R1 again and quickly issue the **show xlate** command to see the addresses being translated.

```
CCNAS-ASA# show xlate
1 in use, 28 most used
Flags: D - DNS, i - dynamic, r - portmap, s - static, I - identity, T - twice

ICMP PAT from inside:192.168.1.3/512 to outside:209.165.200.226/21469 flags ri idle
0:00:03 timeout 0:00:30
```

Note: The flags (r and i) indicate that the translation was based on a port map (r) and was done dynamically (i).

f. Open a browser on PC-B and enter the IP address of R1 G0/0 (209.165.200.225). In a pop-up window, you should be prompted by R1 that authentication is required. TCP-based HTTP traffic is permitted, by default, by the firewall inspection policy.

g. On the ASA, reissue the **show nat** and **show xlate** commands to see the hits and addresses being translated for the HTTP connection.

Step 3: Modify the default MPF application inspection global service policy.

For application layer inspection, as well as other advanced options, the Cisco MPF is available on ASAs. Cisco MPF uses three configuration objects to define modular, object-oriented, and hierarchical policies:

*   **Class maps** - Define a match criterion.

*   **Policy maps** - Associate actions to the match criteria.

*   **Service policies** - Attach the policy map to an interface, or globally to all interfaces of the appliance.

a. Display the default MPF policy map that performs the inspection on inside-to-outside traffic. Only traffic that was initiated from the inside is allowed back in to the outside interface. Notice that the ICMP protocol is missing.

```
CCNAS-ASA# show run | begin class
class-map inspection_default
 match default-inspection-traffic
!
policy-map type inspect dns preset_dns_map
 parameters
  message-length maximum client auto
  message-length maximum 512

policy-map global_policy
 class inspection_default
  inspect dns preset_dns_map
  inspect ftp
  inspect h323 h225
  inspect h323 ras
  inspect ip-options
  inspect netbios
  inspect rsh
  inspect rtsp
  inspect skinny
  inspect esmtp
  inspect sqlnet
  inspect sunrpc
  inspect tftp
  inspect sip
  inspect xdmcp
!
service-policy global_policy global
<output omitted>
```

b. Add the inspection of ICMP traffic to the policy map list using the following commands:

```
CCNAS-ASA(config)# policy-map global_policy
CCNAS-ASA(config-pmap)# class inspection_default
CCNAS-ASA(config-pmap-c)# inspect icmp
```

c. Display the default MPF policy map to verify ICMP is now listed in the inspection rules.

```
CCNAS-ASA(config-pmap-c)# show run policy-map
!
policy-map type inspect dns preset_dns_map
 parameters
  message-length maximum client auto
  message-length maximum 512
policy-map global_policy
 class inspection_default
  inspect dns preset_dns_map
  inspect ftp
```

```
      inspect h323 h225
      inspect h323 ras
      inspect ip-options
      inspect netbios
      inspect rsh
      inspect rtsp
      inspect skinny
      inspect esmtp
      inspect sqlnet
      inspect sunrpc
      inspect tftp
      inspect sip
      inspect xdmcp
      inspect icmp
   !
```

d. From PC-B, attempt to ping the R1 G0/0 interface at IP address 209.165.200.225. The pings should be successful this time because ICMP traffic is now being inspected and legitimate return traffic is being allowed.

Part 5: Configuring DHCP, AAA, and SSH

In Part 5, you will configure ASA features, such as DHCP and enhanced login security, using AAA and SSH.

Note: You must complete Part 4 before beginning Part 5.

Step 1: Configure the ASA as a DHCP server.

The ASA can be both a DHCP server and a DHCP client. In this step, you will configure the ASA as a DHCP server to dynamically assign IP addresses for DHCP clients on the inside network.

a. Configure a DHCP address pool and enable it on the ASA inside interface. This is the range of addresses to be assigned to inside DHCP clients. Attempt to set the range from 192.168.1.5 through 192.168.1.100.

```
CCNAS-ASA(config)# dhcpd address 192.168.1.5-192.168.1.100 inside
Warning, DHCP pool range is limited to 32 addresses, set address range as:
192.168.1.5-192.168.1.36
```

Were you able to do this on this ASA?

_____

_____

b. Repeat the **dhcpd** command and specify the pool as **192.168.1.5-192.168.1.36**

```
CNAS-ASA(config)# dhcpd address 192.168.1.5-192.168.1.36 inside
```

c. (Optional) Specify the IP address of the DNS server to be given to clients.

```
CCNAS-ASA(config)# dhcpd dns 209.165.201.2
```

Note: Other parameters can be specified for clients, such as WINS server, lease length, and domain name. By default, the ASA sets its own IP address as the DHCP default gateway, so there is no need to configure it. However, to manually configure the default gateway, or set it to a different networking device's IP address, use the following command:

```
CCNAS-ASA(config)# dhcpd option 3 ip 192.168.1.1
```

d. Enable the DHCP daemon within the ASA to listen for DHCP client requests on the enabled interface (inside).

```
CCNAS-ASA(config)# dhcpd enable inside
```

e. Verify the DHCP daemon configuration by using the **show run dhcpd** command.

```
CCNAS-ASA(config)# show run dhcpd
dhcpd dns 209.165.201.2
!
dhcpd address 192.168.1.5-192.168.1.36 inside
dhcpd enable inside
```

f. Access the Network Connection IP Properties for PC-B, and change it from a static IP address to a DHCP client so that it obtains an IP address automatically from the ASA DHCP server. The procedure to do this varies depending on the PC operating system. It may be necessary to issue the **ipconfig /renew** command on PC-B to force it to obtain a new IP address from the ASA.

Step 2: Configure AAA to use the local database for authentication.

a. Define a local user named admin by entering the **username** command. Specify a password of **cisco12345**.

```
CCNAS-ASA(config)# username admin password cisco12345
```

b. Configure AAA to use the local ASA database for SSH user authentication.

```
CCNAS-ASA(config)# aaa authentication ssh console LOCAL
```

Note: For added security, starting with ASA version 8.4(2), configure AAA authentication to support SSH connections. The Telnet/SSH default login is not supported. You can no longer connect to the ASA using SSH with the default username and the login password.

Step 3: Configure SSH remote access to the ASA.

You can configure the ASA to accept SSH connections from a single host or a range of hosts on the inside or outside network.

a. Generate an **RSA** key pair, which is required to support SSH connections. The modulus (in bits) can be 512, 768, 1024, or 2048. The larger the key modulus size you specify, the longer it takes to generate an RSA. Specify a modulus of **1024** using the **crypto key** command.

```
CCNAS-ASA(config)# crypto key generate rsa modulus 1024
INFO: The name for the keys will be: <Default-RSA-Key>
Keypair generation process begin. Please wait...
```

Note: You may receive a message that a RSA key pair is already defined. To replace the RSA key pair enter **yes** at the prompt.

b. Save the RSA keys to persistent flash memory using either the **copy run start** or **write mem** command.

```
CCNAS-ASA# write mem
Building configuration...
Cryptochecksum: 3c845d0f b6b8839a f9e43be0 33feb4ef
3270 bytes copied in 0.890 secs
[OK]
```

c. Configure the ASA to allow SSH connections from any host on the inside network (192.168.1.0/24) and from the remote management host at the branch office (172.16.3.3) on the outside network. Set the SSH timeout to **10** minutes (the default is 5 minutes).

```
CCNAS-ASA(config)# ssh 192.168.1.0 255.255.255.0 inside
```

```
CCNAS-ASA(config)# ssh 172.16.3.3 255.255.255.255 outside
CCNAS-ASA(config)# ssh timeout 10
```

d. On PC-C, use an SSH client (such as PuTTY) to connect to the ASA outside interface at the IP address **209.165.200.226**. The first time you connect you may be prompted by the SSH client to accept the RSA host key of the ASA SSH server. Log in as user **admin** and provide the password **cisco12345**. You can also connect to the ASA inside interface from a PC-B SSH client using the IP address **192.168.1.1**.

Part 6: Configuring DMZ, Static NAT, and ACLs

Previously, you configured address translation using PAT for the inside network. In this part of the lab, you will create a DMZ on the ASA, configure static NAT to a DMZ server, and apply ACLs to control access to the server.

To accommodate the addition of a DMZ and a web server, you will use another address from the ISP range assigned 209.165.200.224/29 (.224-.231). Router R1 G0/0 and the ASA outside interface are already using 209.165.200.225 and .226. You will use the public address 209.165.200.227 and static NAT to provide address translation access to the server.

Step 1: Configure the DMZ interface VLAN 3 on the ASA.

a. Configure DMZ VLAN **3**, which is where the public access web server will reside. Assign VLAN 3 IP address **192.168.2.1/24**, name it **dmz**, and assign a security level of **70**.

Note: If you are working with the ASA 5505 Base license, you will see the error message shown in the output below. The ASA 5505 Base license allows for the creation of up to three named VLAN interfaces. However, you must disable communication between the third interface and one of the other interfaces using the **no forward** command. This is not an issue if the ASA has a Security Plus license, which allows 20 named VLANs.

Because the server does not need to initiate communication with the inside users, disable forwarding to interface VLAN 1.

```
CCNAS-ASA(config)# interface vlan 3
CCNAS-ASA(config-if)# ip address 192.168.2.1 255.255.255.0
CCNAS-ASA(config-if)# nameif dmz
ERROR: This license does not allow configuring more than 2 interfaces with
nameif and without a "no forward" command on this interface or on 1 interface(s)
with nameif already configured.

CCNAS-ASA(config-if)# no forward interface vlan 1
CCNAS-ASA(config-if)# nameif dmz
INFO: Security level for "dmz" set to 0 by default.

CCNAS-ASA(config-if)# security-level 70
CCNAS-ASA(config-if)# no shut
```

b. Assign ASA physical interface E0/2 to DMZ VLAN 3 and enable the interface.

```
CCNAS-ASA(config-if)# interface Ethernet0/2
CCNAS-ASA(config-if)# switchport access vlan 3
CCNAS-ASA(config-if)# no shut
```

c. Display the status for all ASA interfaces using the **show interface ip brief** command.

```
CCNAS-ASA # show interface ip brief
```

```
Interface                IP-Address       OK? Method Status        Protocol
Ethernet0/0              unassigned       YES unset  up            up
Ethernet0/1              unassigned       YES unset  up            up
Ethernet0/2              unassigned       YES unset  up            up
Ethernet0/3              unassigned       YES unset  down          down
Ethernet0/4              unassigned       YES unset  down          down
Ethernet0/5              unassigned       YES unset  down          down
Ethernet0/6              unassigned       YES unset  down          down
Ethernet0/7              unassigned       YES unset  down          down
Internal-Data0/0         unassigned       YES unset  up            up
Internal-Data0/1         unassigned       YES unset  up            up
Vlan1                    192.168.1.1      YES manual up            up
Vlan2                    209.165.200.226  YES manual up            up
Vlan3                    192.168.2.1      YES manual up            up
Virtual0                 127.0.0.1        YES unset  up            up
```

d. Display the information for the Layer 3 VLAN interfaces using the **show ip address** command.

```
CCNAS-ASA # show ip address
System IP Addresses:
Interface       Name       IP address        Subnet mask        Method
Vlan1           inside     192.168.1.1       255.255.255.0      manual
Vlan2           outside    209.165.200.226   255.255.255.248    manual
Vlan3           dmz        192.168.2.1       255.255.255.0      manual
<output omitted>
```

e. Display the VLANs and port assignments on the ASA using the **show switch vlan** command.

```
CCNAS-ASA(config)# show switch vlan
VLAN Name                           Status     Ports
---- ------------------------------ ---------  ------------------------------
1    inside                         up         Et0/1, Et0/3, Et0/4, Et0/5
                                               Et0/6, Et0/7
2    outside                        up         Et0/0
3    dmz                            up         Et0/2
```

Step 2: Configure static NAT to the DMZ server using a network object.

Configure a network object named **dmz-server** and assign it the static IP address of the DMZ server (**192.168.2.3**). While in object definition mode, use the **nat** command to specify that this object is used to translate a DMZ address to an outside address using static NAT, and specify a public translated address of **209.165.200.227**.

```
CCNAS-ASA(config)# object network dmz-server
CCNAS-ASA(config-network-object)# host 192.168.2.3
CCNAS-ASA(config-network-object)# nat (dmz,outside) static 209.165.200.227
```

Step 3: Configure an ACL to allow access to the DMZ server from the Internet.

Configure a named access list (**OUTSIDE-DMZ**) that permits any IP protocol from any external host to the internal IP address of the DMZ server. Apply the access list to the ASA outside interface in the **IN** direction.

```
CCNAS-ASA(config)# access-list OUTSIDE-DMZ permit ip any host 192.168.2.3
```

```
CCNAS-ASA(config)# access-group OUTSIDE-DMZ in interface outside
```

Note: Unlike IOS ACLs, the ASA ACL **permit** statement must permit access to the internal private DMZ address. External hosts access the server using its public static NAT address, the ASA translates it to the internal host IP address, and then applies the ACL.

You can modify this ACL to allow only services that you want to be exposed to external hosts, such as web (HTTP) or file transfer (FTP).

Step 4: Test access to the DMZ server.

a. Create a loopback 0 interface on Internet R2 representing an external host. Assign **Lo0** IP address **172.30.1.1** and a mask of **255.255.255.0**. Ping the DMZ server public address from R2 using the loopback interface as the source of the ping. The pings should be successful.

```
R2(config-if)# interface lo0
R2(config-if)# ip address 172.30.1.1 255.255.255.0
R2(config-if)# end
R2# ping 209.165.200.227 source lo0

Type escape sequence to abort.
Sending 5, 100-byte ICMP Echos to 209.165.200.227, timeout is 2 seconds:
Packet sent with a source address of 172.30.1.1
!!!!!
Success rate is 100 percent (5/5), round-trip min/avg/max = 1/2/4 ms
```

b. Clear the NAT counters using the **clear nat counters** command.

```
CCNAS-ASA# clear nat counters
```

c. Ping from PC-C to the DMZ server at the public address **209.165.200.227**. The pings should be successful.

d. Issue the **show nat** and **show xlate** commands on the ASA to see the effect of the pings. Both the PAT (inside to outside) and static NAT (dmz to outside) policies are shown.

```
CCNAS-ASA# show nat

Auto NAT Policies (Section 2)
1 (dmz) to (outside) source static dmz-server 209.165.200.227
    translate_hits = 0, untranslate_hits = 4

2 (inside) to (outside) source dynamic INSIDE-NET interface
    translate_hits = 4, untranslate_hits = 0
```

Note: Pings from inside to outside are translated hits. Pings from outside host PC-C to the DMZ are considered untranslated hits.

```
CCNAS-ASA# show xlate
1 in use, 3 most used
Flags: D - DNS, i - dynamic, r - portmap, s - static, I - identity, T - twice
NAT from dmz:192.168.2.3 to outside:209.165.200.227
    flags s idle 0:22:58 timeout 0:00:00
```

Note: This time the flag is "**s**", which indicates a static translation.

e. You can also access the DMZ server from a host on the inside network because the ASA inside interface (VLAN 1) is set to security level of 100 (the highest) and the DMZ interface (VLAN 3) is set to 70. The

ASA acts like a router between the two networks. Ping the DMZ server (PC-A) internal address (**192.168.2.3**) from inside network host PC-B (192.168.1.X). The pings should be successful because of the interface security level and the fact that ICMP is being inspected on the inside interface by the global inspection policy. The pings from PC-B to PC-A will not affect the NAT translation counts because both PC-B and PC-A are behind the firewall, and no translation takes place.

f. The DMZ server cannot ping PC-B on the inside network because the DMZ interface VLAN 3 has a lower security level and because the **no forward** command was specified when the VLAN 3 interface was created. Try to ping from the DMZ server PC-A to PC-B at IP address **192.168.1.3**. The pings should not be successful.

g. Use the **show run** command to display the configuration for VLAN 3.

```
CCNAS-ASA# show run interface vlan 3
!
interface Vlan3
 no forward interface Vlan1
 nameif dmz
 security-level 70
 ip address 192.168.2.1 255.255.255.0
```

Note: An access list can be applied to the inside interface to control the type of access to be permitted or denied to the DMZ server from inside hosts.

Reflection

1. How does the configuration of the ASA firewall differ from that of an ISR?

_____

_____

_____

_____

2. What does the ASA use to define address translation and what is the benefit?

_____

_____

_____

_____

3. How does the ASA 5505 use logical and physical interfaces to manage security and how does this differ from other ASA models?

_____

_____

_____

_____

Router Interface Summary Table

Router Interface Summary				
Router Model	**Ethernet Interface #1**	**Ethernet Interface #2**	**Serial Interface #1**	**Serial Interface #2**
1800	Fast Ethernet 0/0 (F0/0)	Fast Ethernet 0/1 (F0/1)	Serial 0/0/0 (S0/0/0)	Serial 0/0/1 (S0/0/1)
1900	Gigabit Ethernet 0/0 (G0/0)	Gigabit Ethernet 0/1 (G0/1)	Serial 0/0/0 (S0/0/0)	Serial 0/0/1 (S0/0/1)
2801	Fast Ethernet 0/0 (F0/0)	Fast Ethernet 0/1 (F0/1)	Serial 0/1/0 (S0/1/0)	Serial 0/1/1 (S0/1/1)
2811	Fast Ethernet 0/0 (F0/0)	Fast Ethernet 0/1 (F0/1)	Serial 0/0/0 (S0/0/0)	Serial 0/0/1 (S0/0/1)
2900	Gigabit Ethernet 0/0 (G0/0)	Gigabit Ethernet 0/1 (G0/1)	Serial 0/0/0 (S0/0/0)	Serial 0/0/1 (S0/0/1)

Note: To find out how the router is configured, look at the interfaces to identify the type of router and how many interfaces the router has. There is no way to effectively list all the combinations of configurations for each router class. This table includes identifiers for the possible combinations of Ethernet and Serial interfaces in the device. The table does not include any other type of interface, even though a specific router may contain one. An example of this might be an ISDN BRI interface. The string in parenthesis is the legal abbreviation that can be used in Cisco IOS commands to represent the interface.

Chapter 10: Advanced Cisco Adaptive Security Appliance

Lab A 10.1.4.8 – Configure ASA Basic Settings and Firewall Using ASDM

Topology

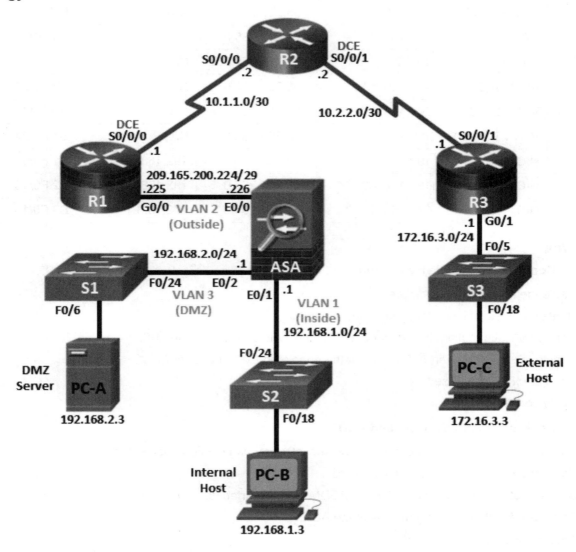

Note: ISR G1 devices use FastEthernet interfaces instead of GigabitEthernet interfaces.

IP Addressing Table

Device	Interface	IP Address	Subnet Mask	Default Gateway	Switch Port
R1	G0/0	209.165.200.225	255.255.255.248	N/A	ASA E0/0
	S0/0/0 (DCE)	10.1.1.1	255.255.255.252	N/A	N/A
R2	S0/0/0	10.1.1.2	255.255.255.252	N/A	N/A
	S0/0/1 (DCE)	10.2.2.2	255.255.255.252	N/A	N/A
R3	G0/1	172.16.3.1	255.255.255.0	N/A	S3 F0/5
	S0/0/1	10.2.2.1	255.255.255.252	N/A	N/A
ASA	VLAN 1 (E0/1)	192.168.1.1	255.255.255.0	NA	S2 F0/24
	VLAN 2 (E0/0)	209.165.200.226	255.255.255.248	NA	R1 G0/0
	VLAN 3 (E0/2)	192.168.2.1	255.255.255.0	NA	S1 F0/24
PC-A	NIC	192.168.2.3	255.255.255.0	192.168.2.1	S1 F0/6
PC-B	NIC	192.168.1.3	255.255.255.0	192.168.1.1	S2 F0/18
PC-C	NIC	172.16.3.3	255.255.255.0	172.16.3.1	S3 F0/18

Objectives

Part 1: Configure Basic Device Settings

- Cable the network and clear previous device settings.
- Configure basic settings for routers and switches.
- Configure static routing, including default routes, between R1, R2, and R3.
- Enable the HTTP server on R1 and set the enable and VTY passwords.
- Configure PC host IP settings.
- Verify connectivity.

Part 2: Access the ASA Console and ASDM

- Access the ASA console and view hardware, software, and configuration settings.
- Clear previous ASA configuration settings.
- Bypass Setup mode and configure the ASDM VLAN interfaces.
- Configure ASDM and verify access to the ASA.
- Access ASDM and explore the GUI.

Part 3: Configure ASA Settings and Firewall Using the ASDM Startup Wizard

- Access the Configuration menu and launch the Startup wizard.
- Configure the hostname, domain name, and enable the password.
- Configure the inside and outside VLAN interfaces.
- Configure DHCP, address translation, and administrative access.
- Review the summary and deliver the commands to the ASA.

- Test access to an external website from PC-B.
- Test access to an external website using the ASDM Packet Tracer utility.

Part 4: Configure ASA Settings from the ASDM Configuration Menu

- Set the ASA date and time.
- Configure a static default route for the ASA.
- Configure AAA user authentication using the local ASA database.
- Test SSH access to the ASA.
- Test connectivity using ASDM Ping and Traceroute.
- Modify the MPF application inspection policy.

Part 5: Configure DMZ, Static NAT, and ACLs

- Configure the ASA DMZ VLAN 3 interface.
- Configure the DMZ server and static NAT.
- View the DMZ Access Rule generated by ASDM.
- Test access to the DMZ server from the outside network.

Background/Scenario

The Cisco Adaptive Security Appliance (ASA) is an advanced network security device that integrates a stateful firewall, a VPN, and other capabilities. This lab employs an ASA 5505 to create a firewall and protect an internal corporate network from external intruders while allowing internal hosts access to the Internet. The ASA creates three security interfaces: Outside, Inside, and DMZ. It provides outside users with limited access to the DMZ and no access to internal resources. Inside users can access the DMZ and outside resources.

The focus of this lab is the configuration of the ASA as a basic firewall. Other devices will receive minimal configuration to support the ASA portion of the lab. This lab uses the ASA GUI interface ASDM to configure basic device and security settings.

In Part 1 of this lab, you will configure the topology and non-ASA devices. In Part 2, you will prepare the ASA for Adaptive Security Device Manager (ASDM) access. In Part 3, you will use the ASDM Startup wizard to configure basic ASA settings and the firewall between the inside and outside networks. In Part 4, you will configure additional settings via the ASDM configuration menu. In Part 5, you will configure a DMZ on the ASA and provide access to a server in the DMZ.

Your company has one location connected to an ISP. R1 represents a customer-premise equipment (CPE) device managed by the ISP. R2 represents an intermediate Internet router. R3 connects an administrator from a network management company, who has been hired to remotely manage your network. The ASA is an edge security device that connects the internal corporate network and DMZ to the ISP while providing NAT and DHCP services to inside hosts. The ASA will be configured for management by an administrator on the internal network and the remote administrator. Layer 3 VLAN interfaces provide access to the three areas created in the lab: Inside, Outside, and DMZ. The ISP has assigned the public IP address space of 209.165.200.224/29, which will be used for address translation on the ASA.

Note: The router commands and output in this lab are from a Cisco 1941 router with Cisco IOS Release 15.4(3)M2 (with a Security Technology Package license). Other routers and Cisco IOS versions can be used. See the Router Interface Summary Table at the end of the lab to determine which interface identifiers to use based on the equipment in the lab. Depending on the router model and Cisco IOS version, the commands available and the output produced might vary from what is shown in this lab.

The ASA used with this lab is a Cisco model 5505 with an eight-port integrated switch, running OS version 9.2(3) and ASDM version 7.4(1), and comes with a Base license that allows a maximum of three VLANs.

Note: Before beginning, ensure that the routers and switches have been erased and have no startup configurations.

Required Resources

- 1 ASA 5505 (OS version 9.2(3) and ASDM version 7.4(1) and Base license or comparable)
- 3 routers (Cisco 1941 with Cisco IOS Release 15.4(3)M2 image with a Security Technology package license)
- 3 switches (Cisco 2960 or comparable) (not required)
- 3 PCs (Windows 7 or Windows 8.1, SSH Client, and WinRadius)
- Serial and Ethernet cables, as shown in the topology
- Console cables to configure Cisco networking devices

Part 1: Configure Basic Device Settings

In Part 1, you will set up the network topology and configure basic settings on the routers, such as interface IP addresses and static routing.

Note: Do not configure ASA settings at this time.

Step 1: Cable the network and clear previous device settings.

Attach the devices shown in the topology diagram and cable as necessary. Ensure that the routers and switches have been erased and have no startup configurations.

Step 2: Configure basic settings for routers and switches.

a. Configure hostnames, as shown in the topology, for each router.

b. Configure router interface IP addresses, as shown in the IP Addressing table.

c. Configure a clock rate for routers with a DCE serial cable attached to the serial interface. R1 is shown here as an example.

```
R1(config)# interface S0/0/0
R1(config-if)# clock rate 64000
```

d. Configure the hostname for the switches. With the exception of the hostname, the switches can be left in their default configuration state. Configuring the VLAN management IP address for the switches is optional.

Step 3: Configure static routing on the routers.

a. Configure a static default route from R1 to R2 and from R3 to R2.

```
R1(config)# ip route 0.0.0.0 0.0.0.0 10.1.1.2

R3(config)# ip route 0.0.0.0 0.0.0.0 10.2.2.2
```

b. Configure a static route from R2 to the R1 Fa0/0 subnet (connected to ASA interface E0/0) and a static route from R2 to the R3 LAN.

```
R2(config)# ip route 209.165.200.224 255.255.255.248 10.1.1.1
R2(config)# ip route 172.16.3.0 255.255.255.0 10.2.2.1
```

Step 4: Configure and encrypt passwords on R1.

Note: Passwords in this task are set to a minimum of 10 characters and are relatively simple for the purposes of performing the lab. More complex passwords are recommended in a production network.

a. Configure a minimum password length. Use the **security passwords** command to set a minimum password length of 10 characters.

b. Configure the enable secret password on both routers with a password of **cisco12345**. Use the type 9 (SCRYPT) hashing algorithm.

c. Create a local **admin01** account using **admin01pass** for the password. Use the type 9 (SCRYPT) hashing algorithm and set privilege level to 15

d. Configure the Console and VTY lines to use the local database for login. For additional security, configure the lines to log out after five minutes of inactivity. Issue the **logging synchronous** command to prevent console messages from interrupting command entry.

e. Enable HTTP server access on R1. Use the local database for HTTP authentication.

    Note: HTTP server access will be used to demonstrate ASDM tools in Part 3.

Step 5: Configure PC host IP settings.

Configure a static IP address, subnet mask, and default gateway for PC-A, PC-B, and PC-C as shown in the IP Addressing table.

Step 6: Verify connectivity.

There will be no connectivity between devices that are connected to the ASA because the ASA is the focal point for the network zones and it has not been configured. However, PC-C should be able to ping the R1 interface G0/0. From PC-C, ping the R1 G0/0 IP address (**209.165.200.225**). If these pings are unsuccessful, troubleshoot the basic device configurations before continuing.

Note: If you can ping from PC-C to R1 G0/0 and S0/0/0, you have demonstrated that addressing has been configured properly, and static routing is configured and functioning correctly.

Step 7: Save the basic running configuration for each router and switch.

Part 2: Access the ASA Console and ASDM

In Part 2, you will access the ASA via the console and use various **show** commands to determine hardware, software, and configuration settings. You will prepare the ASA for ASDM access and explore ASDM screens and options.

Step 1: Access the ASA console.

a. Accessing the ASA via the console port is the same as accessing it with a Cisco router or switch. Connect to the ASA console port with a rollover cable.

b. Use a terminal emulation program to access the CLI. Use the serial port settings of 9600 baud, 8 data bits, no parity, one stop bit, and no flow control.

c. If prompted to enter Interactive Firewall configuration (Setup mode), answer **no**.

d. Enter privileged mode with the **enable** command and password (if set). The password is blank by default, so press **Enter**. If the password has been changed to one that is specific to this lab, enter the password **cisco12345**. The default ASA hostname and prompt is **ciscoasa>**.

```
ciscoasa> enable
Password: cisco12345 (or press Enter if no password is set)
```

Step 2: Clear previous ASA configuration settings.

a. Use the **write erase** command to remove the **startup-config** file from flash memory.

```
ciscoasa# write erase
Erase configuration in flash memory? [confirm]
[OK]
ciscoasa#

ciscoasa# show start
No Configuration
```

Note: The **erase startup-config** IOS command is not supported on the ASA.

b. Use the **reload** command to restart the ASA. This causes the ASA to come up in CLI Setup mode. If you see the message: "System config has been modified. Save? [Y]es/[N]o:" Type **n** and then press **Enter**.

```
ciscoasa# reload
Proceed with reload? [confirm] <Enter>
ciscoasa#
***
*** --- START GRACEFUL SHUTDOWN ---
Shutting down isakmp
Shutting down File system
***
*** --- SHUTDOWN NOW ---
Process shutdown finished
Rebooting.....
CISCO SYSTEMS
Embedded BIOS Version 1.0(12)13 08/28/08 15:50:37.45
<output omitted>
```

Step 3: Bypass Setup mode and configure the ASDM VLAN interfaces.

When the ASA completes the reload process, it should detect that the **startup-config** file is missing and present a series of interactive prompts to configure basic ASA settings. If it does not come up in this mode, repeat Step 2.

a. When prompted to pre-configure the firewall through interactive prompts (Setup mode), respond with **no**.

```
Pre-configure Firewall now through interactive prompts [yes]? no
```

b. Enter privileged EXEC mode with the **enable** command. The password should be blank (no password) at this point.

c. Enter global configuration mode using the **conf t** command. The first time you enter configuration mode after reloading, you will be prompted to enable anonymous reporting. Respond with **no**.

d. Configure the inside interface VLAN 1 to prepare for ASDM access. The Security Level should be automatically set to the highest level of **100**. The VLAN 1 logical interface will be used by PC-B to access ASDM on ASA physical interface E0/1.

```
ciscoasa(config)# interface vlan 1
ciscoasa(config-if)# nameif inside
INFO: Security level for "inside" set to 100 by default.
ciscoasa(config-if)# ip address 192.168.1.1 255.255.255.0
```

```
ciscoasa(config-if)# security-level 100
ciscoasa(config-if)# exit
```

PC-B is connected to switch S2. Switch S2 is connected to ASA port E0/1. Why is it unnecessary to add physical interface E0/1 to this VLAN?

_____

_____

ASA 5505 interface notes:

The 5505 is different from the other 5500 series ASA models. On the other ASAs, like a Cisco router, the physical port can be directly assigned a Layer 3 IP address. The ASA 5505 has eight integrated switch ports that are Layer 2 ports. To assign Layer 3 parameters, you must create a switch virtual interface (SVI) or logical VLAN interface and then assign one or more of the physical Layer 2 ports to it.

By default, all ASA physical interfaces are administratively down unless the Setup utility has been run, or the factory defaults have been reset. Because no physical interface in VLAN 1 has been enabled, the VLAN 1 status is down/down. Use the **show interface ip brief** command to verify this.

```
ciscoasa(config)# show interface ip brief
Interface        IP-Address    OK? Method Status                Protocol
Ethernet0/0      unassigned    YES unset  administratively down up
Ethernet0/1      unassigned    YES unset  administratively down up
Ethernet0/2      unassigned    YES unset  administratively down up
Ethernet0/3      unassigned    YES unset  administratively down up
Ethernet0/4      unassigned    YES unset  administratively down down
Ethernet0/5      unassigned    YES unset  administratively down down
Ethernet0/6      unassigned    YES unset  administratively down down
Ethernet0/7      unassigned    YES unset  administratively down down
Internal-Data0/0 unassigned    YES unset  up                    up
Internal-Data0/1 unassigned    YES unset  up                    up
Vlan1            192.168.1.1   YES manual down                  down
Virtual0         127.0.0.1     YES unset  up                    up
```

e. Enable the E0/1 interface using the **no shutdown** command and verify the E0/1 and VLAN 1 interface status. The status and protocol for interface E0/1 and VLAN 1 should be up/up.

```
ciscoasa(config)# interface e0/1
ciscoasa(config-if)# no shut
ciscoasa(config-if)# exit

ciscoasa(config)# show interface ip brief
Interface        IP-Address    OK? Method Status                Protocol
Ethernet0/0      unassigned    YES unset  administratively down up
Ethernet0/1      unassigned    YES unset  up                    up
Ethernet0/2      unassigned    YES unset  administratively down up
Ethernet0/3      unassigned    YES unset  administratively down up
Ethernet0/4      unassigned    YES unset  administratively down down
Ethernet0/5      unassigned    YES unset  administratively down down
Ethernet0/6      unassigned    YES unset  administratively down down
Ethernet0/7      unassigned    YES unset  administratively down down
```

```
Internal-Data0/0  unassigned      YES unset  up                    up
Internal-Data0/1  unassigned      YES unset  up                    up
Vlan1             192.168.1.1     YES manual up                    up
Virtual0          127.0.0.1       YES unset  up                    up
```

f. Pre-configure outside interface VLAN 2, add physical interface E0/0 to VLAN 2 and bring up the E0/0 interface. You will assign the IP address using ASDM.

```
ciscoasa(config)# interface vlan 2
ciscoasa(config-if)# nameif outside
INFO: Security level for "outside" set to 0 by default.
ciscoasa(config-if)# security-level 0
ciscoasa(config-if)# interface e0/0
ciscoasa(config-if)# switchport access vlan 2
ciscoasa(config-if)# no shut
ciscoasa(config-if)# exit
```

g. Test connectivity to the ASA by pinging from PC-B to ASA interface VLAN 1 IP address **192.168.1.1**. The pings should be successful.

Step 4: Configure ASDM and verify access to the ASA.

a. Configure the ASA to accept HTTPS connections by using the **http** command to allow access to ASDM from any host on the inside network 192.168.1.0/24.

```
ciscoasa(config)# http server enable
ciscoasa(config)# http 192.168.1.0 255.255.255.0 inside
```

b. Open a browser on PC-B and test the HTTPS access to the ASA by entering **https://192.168.1.1**.

Note: Be sure to specify the HTTPS protocol in the URL.

Step 5: Access ASDM and explore the GUI.

a. After entering the URL above, you should see a security warning about the website security certificate. Click **Continue to this website**. The ASDM Welcome page will display. From this screen, you can run ASDM as a local application on the PC (installs ASDM on the PC), run ASDM as a browser-based Java applet directly from the ASA, or run the Startup wizard.

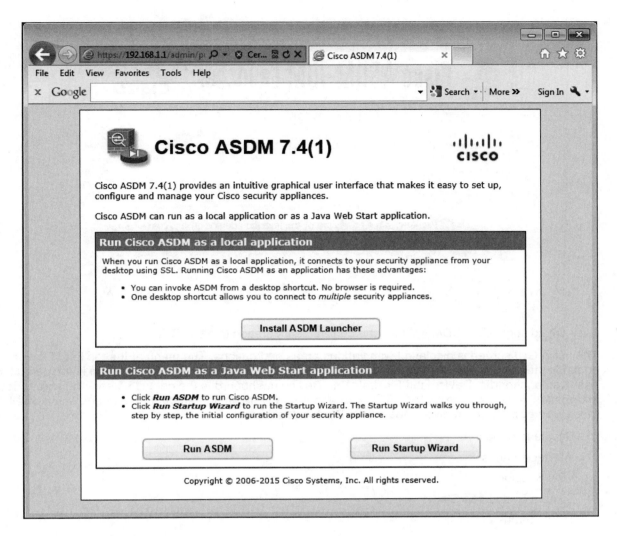

b. Click **Run ASDM**.

c. Click **Yes** in response to any other security warnings. You should see the **Cisco ASDM-IDM Launcher** dialog box within which you can enter a username and password. Leave these fields blank as they have not yet been configured.

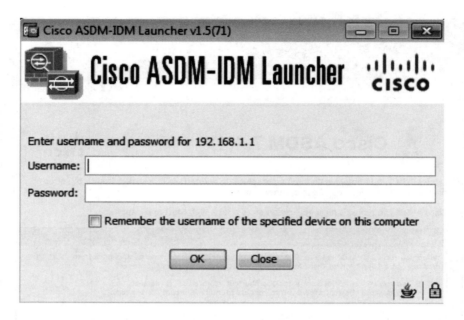

d.   Click **OK** to continue. ASDM will load the current configuration into the GUI.

e.   The initial GUI screen is displayed with various areas and options. The menu at the top left of the screen contains three main sections: Home, Configuration, and Monitoring. The Home section is the default and has two dashboards: Device and Firewall. The Device dashboard is the default screen and shows device information, such as Type (ASA 5505), ASA and ASDM version, the amount of memory, and firewall mode (routed). There are five areas on the Device dashboard:

o   Device Information

o   Interface Status

o   VPN Sessions

o   System Resources Status

o   Traffic Status

Note: If the Cisco Smart Call Home window appears, click **Do not enable Smart Call Home** and click **OK**.

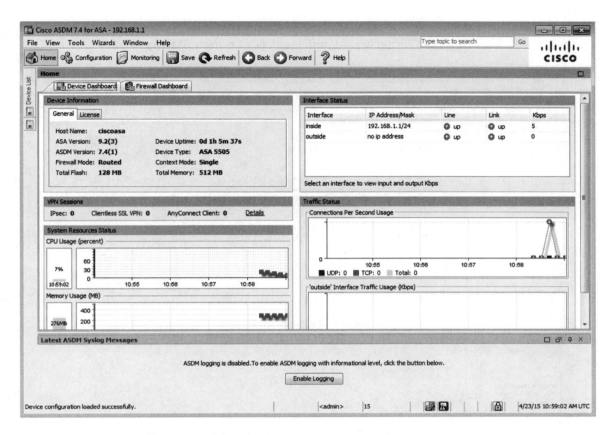

f. Click the **Configuration** and **Monitoring** buttons to become familiar with their layout and to see what options are available.

Part 3: Configure Basic ASA Settings and Firewall Using the ASDM Startup Wizard

Step 1: Access the Configuration menu and launch the Startup wizard.

a. On the menu bar, click **Configuration**. There are five main configuration areas:

- o   Device Setup
- o   Firewall
- o   Remote Access VPN
- o   Site-to-Site VPN
- o   Device Management

b. The Device Setup Startup wizard is the first option available and displays by default. Read through the on-screen text describing the Startup wizard, and then click **Launch Startup Wizard**.

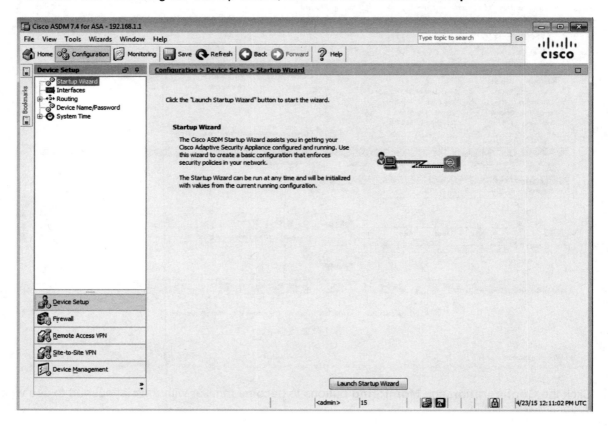

Step 2: Configure hostname, domain name, and the enable password.

a. On the first Startup Wizard screen, modify the existing configuration or reset the ASA to the factory defaults. Ensure that the **Modify Existing Configuration** option is selected, and click **Next** to continue.

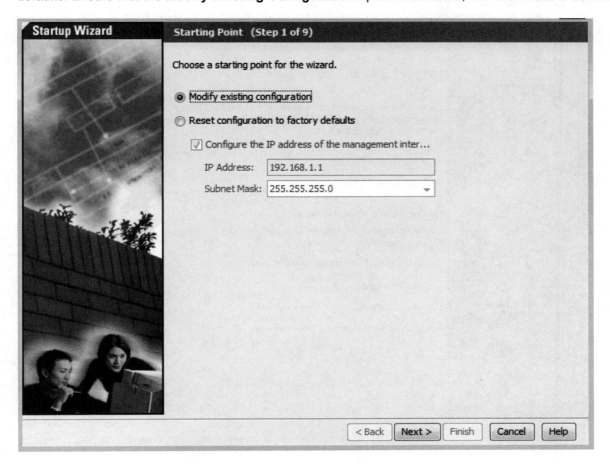

b. On the Startup Wizard Step 2 screen, configure the ASA hostname **CCNAS-ASA** and domain name **ccnasecurity.com**. Click the check box for changing the enable mode password, change it from blank (no password) to **cisco12345**, and enter it again to confirm. When the entries are completed, click **Next** to continue.

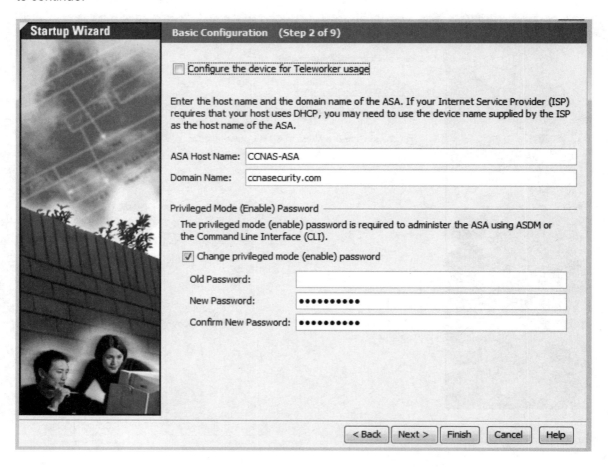

Step 3: Configure the inside and outside VLAN interfaces.

a. On the Startup Wizard Step 3 screen for the Outside and Inside VLANs, do not change the current settings because these were previously defined using the CLI. The inside VLAN is named **inside,** and the security level is set to 100 (highest). The Outside VLAN interface is named **outside,** and the security level is set to 0 (lowest). Click **Next** to continue.

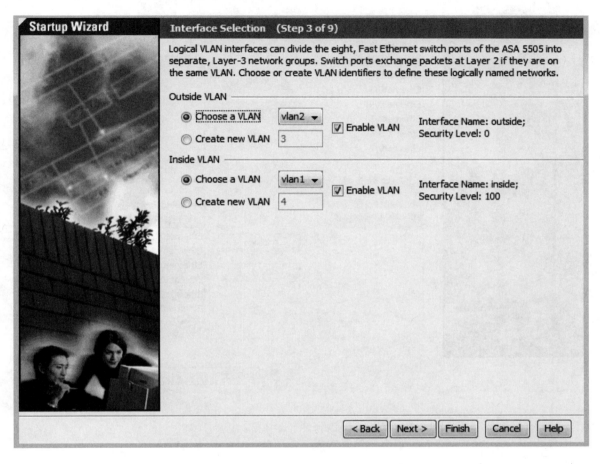

b. On the Startup Wizard Step 4 screen – Switch Port Allocation, verify that port **Ethernet0/1** is allocated for Inside VLAN 1 and that port **Ethernet0/0** is allocated for Outside VLAN 2. Click **Next** to continue.

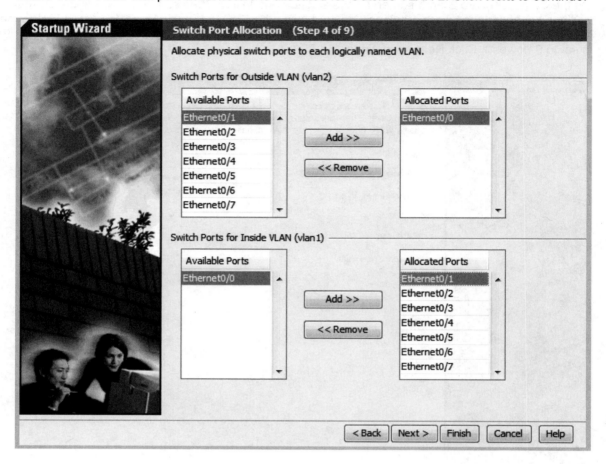

c.   On the Startup Wizard Step 5 screen – Interface IP Address Configuration, enter an Outside IP Address of **209.165.200.226** and a Mask of **255.255.255.248**. You can use the pull-down menu to select the mask. Leave the inside interface IP address as **192.168.1.1** with a mask of **255.255.255.0**. Click **Next** to continue.

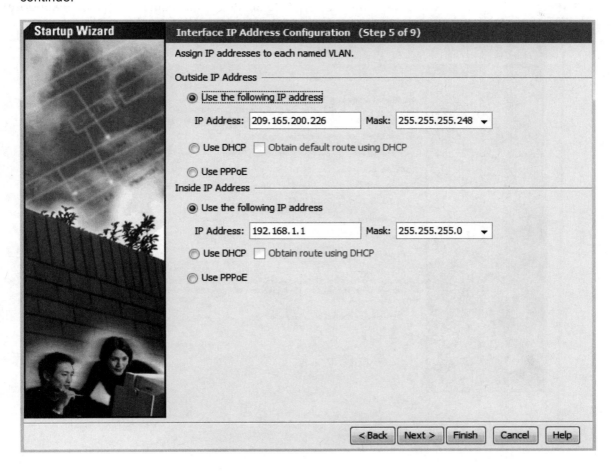

Step 4: Configure DHCP, address translation, and administrative access.

a. On the Startup Wizard Step 6 screen – DHCP Server, click the **Enable DHCP server on the inside interface** check box. Enter a Starting IP Address of **192.168.1.31** and an Ending IP Address of **192.168.1.39**. Enter the DNS Server 1 address of **10.20.30.40** and the Domain Name **ccnasecurity.com**. Do **NOT** check the box to Enable auto-configuration from interface. Click **Next** to continue.

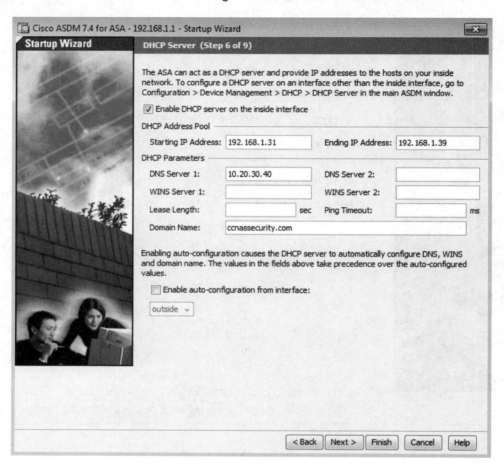

b. On the Startup Wizard Step 7 screen – Address Translation (NAT/PAT), click **Use Port Address Translation (PAT)**. The default is to use the IP address of the outside interface.

   Note: You can also specify a particular IP address for PAT or a range of addresses with NAT. Click **Next** to continue.

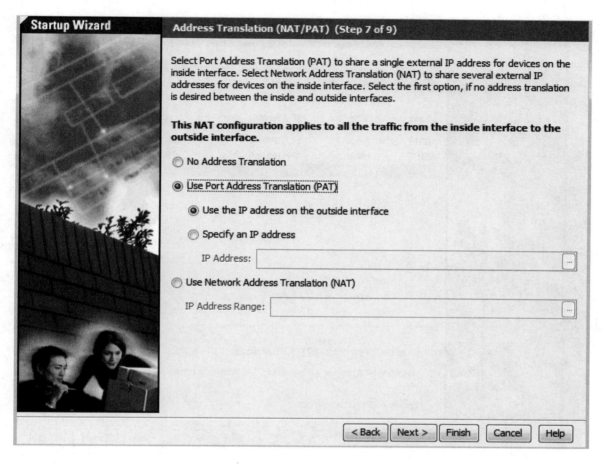

c. On the Startup Wizard Step 8 screen – Administrative Access, HTTPS/ASDM access is currently configured for hosts on the inside network 192.168.1.0/24. Add **SSH** access to the ASA for the inside network **192.168.1.0** with a subnet mask of **255.255.255.0**. Add **SSH** access to the ASA from host **172.16.3.3** on the outside network. Ensure that the **Enable HTTP server for HTTPS/ASDM access** check box is selected. Click **Next** to continue.

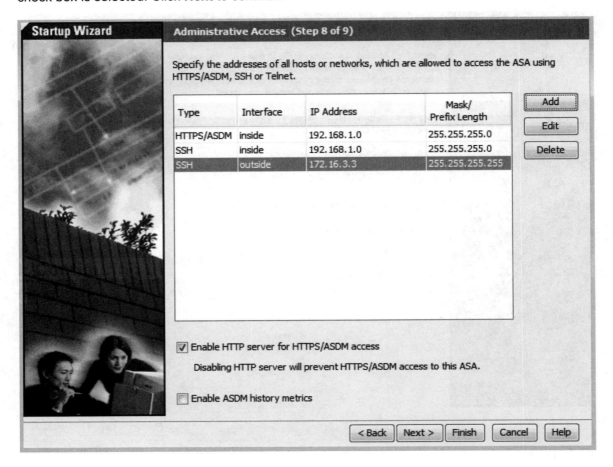

Step 5: Review the summary and deliver the commands to the ASA.

a. On the Startup Wizard Step 9 screen – Startup Wizard Summary, review the **Configuration Summary** and click **Finish**. ASDM will deliver the commands to the ASA device and then reload the modified configuration.

    Note: If the GUI dialogue box stops responding during the reload process, close it, exit ASDM, and restart the browser and ASDM. If prompted to save the configuration to flash memory, respond with **Yes**. Even though ASDM may not appear to have reloaded the configuration, the commands were delivered. If there are errors encountered as ASDM delivers the commands, you will be notified with a list of commands that succeeded and the commands that failed.

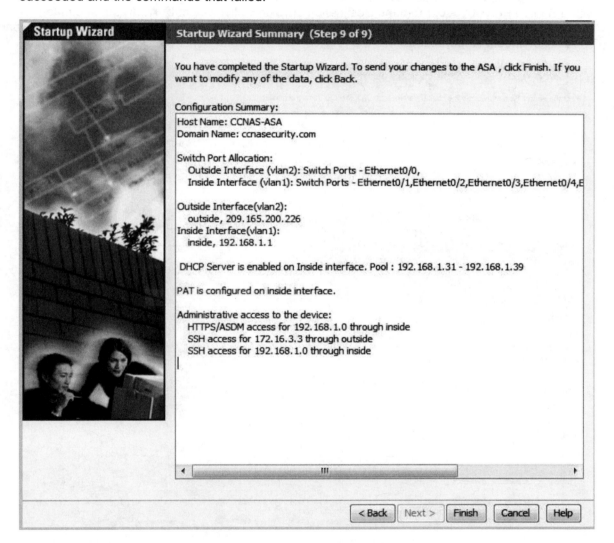

b. Restart ASDM and provide the new enable password **cisco12345** with no username. Return to the Device dashboard and check the Interface Status window. You should see the inside and outside interfaces with IP address and status. The inside interface should show a number of Kb/s. The Traffic Status window may show the ASDM access as TCP traffic spike.

Step 6: Test access to an external website from PC-B.

a. Open a browser on PC-B and enter the IP address of the R1 G0/0 interface (**209.165.200.225**) to simulate access to an external website.

b.   The R1 HTTP server was enabled in Part 1. You should be prompted with a user authentication login dialog box from the R1 GUI device manger. Enter the username **admin01** and the password **admin01pass**. Exit the browser. You should see TCP activity in the ASDM Device dashboard Traffic Status window on the Home page.

Step 7: Test access to an external website using the ASDM Packet Tracer utility.

a.   Click **Tools** > **Packet Tracer**.

b.   Select the **inside** interface from the Interface drop-down list and click **TCP** from the Packet Type radio buttons. From the Source drop-down list, select **IP Address** and enter the address **192.168.1.3** (PC-B) with a Source Port of **1500**. From the Destination drop-down list, select **IP Address**, and enter **209.165.200.225** (R1 Fa0/0) with a Destination Port of **HTTP**. Click **Start** to begin the trace of the packet. The packet should be permitted.

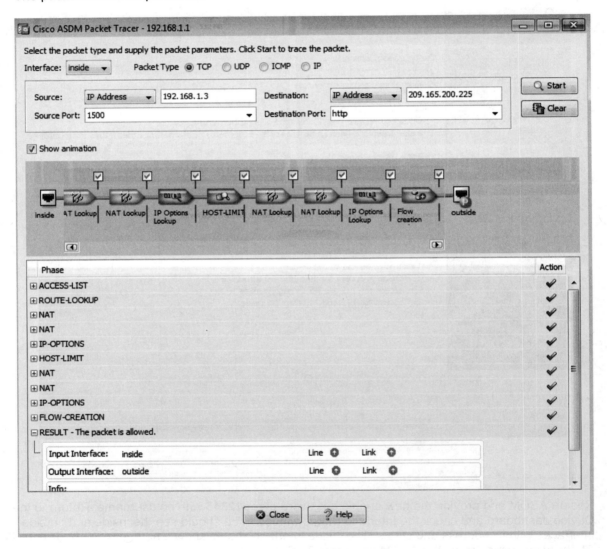

c.   Click **Clear** to reset the entries. Try another trace and select **outside** from the **Interface** drop-down list and leave **TCP** as the packet type. From the **Sources** drop-down list, select **IP Address**, and enter **209.165.200.225** (R1 G0/0) and a Source Port of 1500. From the **Destination** drop-down list, select **IP Address** and enter the address **209.165.200.226** (ASA outside interface) with a Destination Port of

telnet. Click **Start** to begin the trace of the packet. The packet should be dropped. Click **Close** to continue.

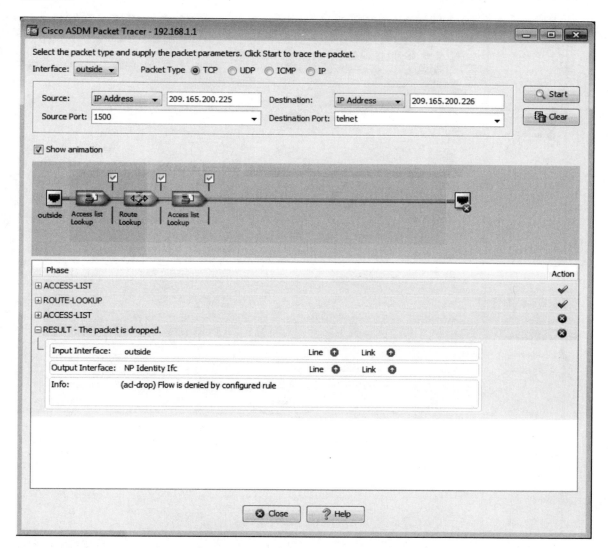

Part 4: Configure ASA Settings from the ASDM Configuration Menu

In Part 4, you will set the ASA clock, configure a default route, test connectivity using the ASDM tools ping and traceroute, configure local AAA user authentication, test SSH access, and modify the MPF application inspection policy.

Step 1: Set the ASA date and time.

a.   On the **Configuration** screen > **Device Setup** menu, click **System Time** > **Clock**.

b. Select your **Time Zone** from the drop-down list and enter the current date and time in the fields provided. (The clock is a 24-hour clock.) Click **Apply** to send the commands to the ASA.

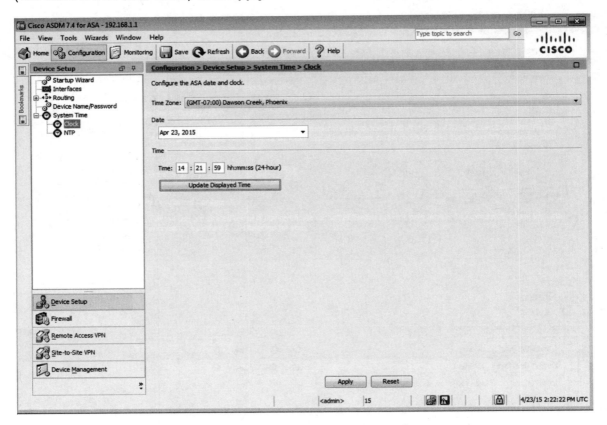

Step 2: Configure a static default route for the ASA.

a. On the **ASDM Tools** menu, select **Ping** and enter the IP address of router R1 S0/0/0 (**10.1.1.1**). The ASA does not have a default route to unknown external networks. The ping should fail because the ASA does not have a route to 10.1.1.1. Click **Close** to continue.

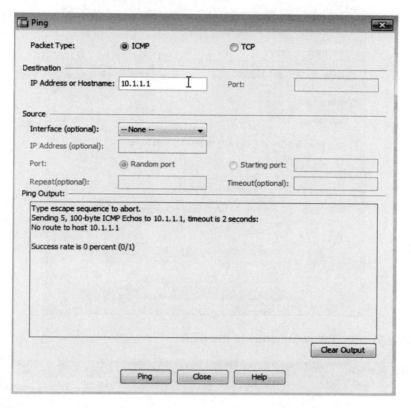

b. From the **Configuration** screen > **Device Setup** menu, click **Routing** > **Static Routes**. Click **IPv4 Only** and click **Add** to add a new static route.

c. On the Add Static Route dialog box, select the **outside** interface from the drop-down list. Click the ellipsis button to the right of **Network,** select **any4** from the list of network objects, and click **OK**. The selection of **any4** translates to a "quad zero" route. For the Gateway IP, enter **209.165.200.225** (R1 G0/0).

d. Click **OK** > **Apply** to send the commands to the ASA.

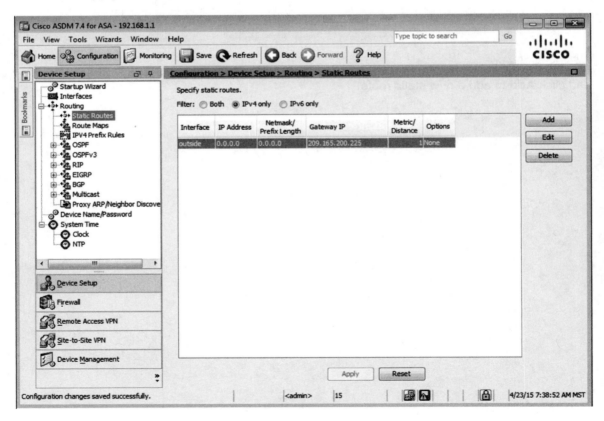

e. On the ASDM **Tools** menu, select **Ping** and enter the IP address of router R1 S0/0/0 (**10.1.1.1**). The ping should succeed this time. Click **Close** to continue.

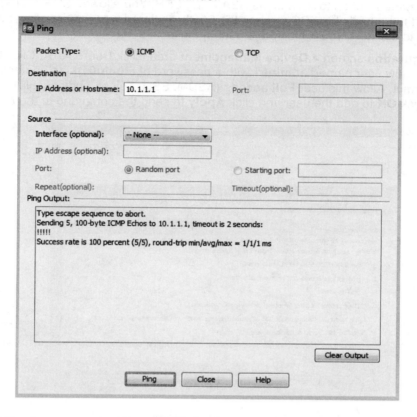

f. On the ASDM **Tools** menu, select **Traceroute** and enter the IP address of external host PC-C (**172.16.3.3**). Click **Trace Route**. The traceroute should succeed and show the hops from the ASA through R1, R2, and R3 to host PC-C. Click **Close** to continue.

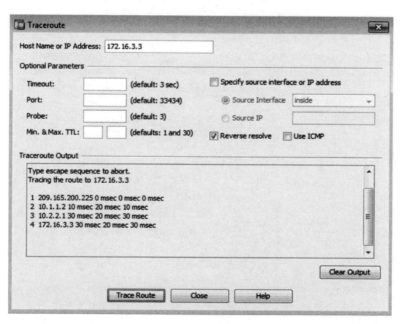

Step 3: Configure AAA user authentication using the ASA local database.

Enable AAA user authentication to access the ASA using SSH. You allowed SSH access to the ASA from the inside network and the outside host PC-C when the **Startup wizard** was run. To allow the administrator to have SSH access to the ASA, you will create a user in the local database.

a. On the **Configuration** screen > **Device Management** area, click **Users/AAA**. Click **User Accounts** > **Add**. Create a new user named **admin01** with a password of **admin01pass** and enter the password again to confirm it. Allow this user **Full access** (ASDM, SSH, Telnet, and console) and set the privilege level to **15**. Click **OK** to add the user and click **Apply** to send the command to the ASA.

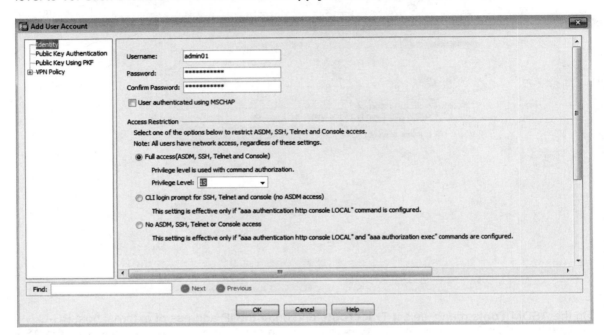

b. On the **Configuration** screen > **Device Management** area, click **Users/AAA**. Click **AAA Access**. On the **Authentication** tab, click the check box to require authentication for **HTTP/ASDM** and **SSH** connections and specify the **LOCAL** server group for each connection type. Click **Apply** to send the commands to the ASA.

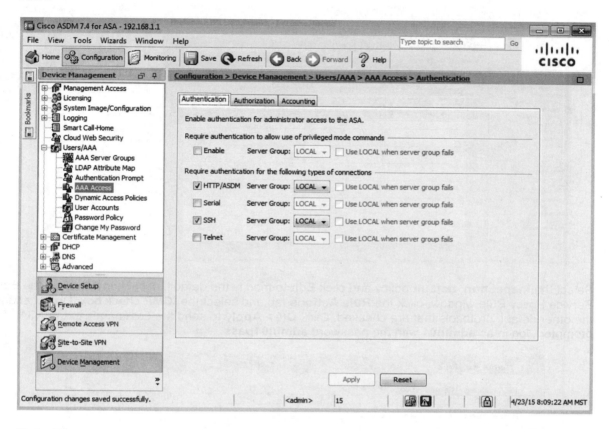

Note: The next action you attempt within ASDM will require that you log in as **admin01** with the password **admin01pass**.

Step 4: Test SSH access to the ASA.

a. Open a SSH client on PC-B, such as PuTTY, and connect to the ASA inside interface at IP address **192.168.1.1**. When prompted to log in, enter the user name **admin01** and the password **admin01pass**.

b. From **PC-C**, open an SSH client, such as PuTTY, and attempt to access the ASA outside interface at **209.165.200.226**. When prompted to log in, enter the user name **admin01** and the password **admin01pass**.

c. After logging in to the ASA using SSH, enter the **enable** command and provide the password **cisco12345**. Issue the **show run** command to display the current configuration that you have created using ASDM.

    Note: The default timeout for SSH is five minutes. You can change this setting by using the CLI **logging synchronous** command or go to ASDM **Device Management** > **Management Access** > **ASDM/HTTP/Telnet/SSH**.

Step 5: Modify the MPF application inspection policy.

For application layer inspection, and other advanced options, the Cisco Modular Policy Framework (MPF) is available on ASAs.

a.   The default global inspection policy does not inspect ICMP. To enable hosts on the internal network to ping external hosts and receive replies, ICMP traffic must be inspected. On the **Configuration** screen > **Firewall** area menu, click **Service Policy Rules**.

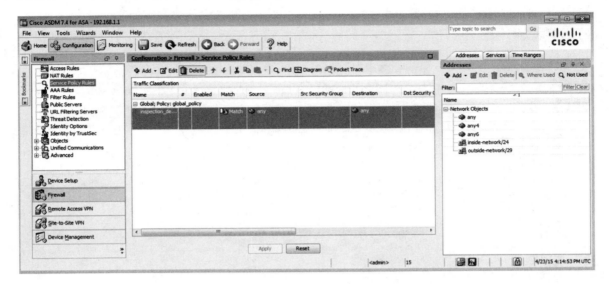

b.   Select the **inspection_default** policy and click **Edit** to modify the default inspection rules. On the Edit Service Policy Rule window, click the **Rule Actions** tab and select the **ICMP** check box. Do not change the other default protocols that are checked. Click **OK** > **Apply** to send the commands to the ASA. If prompted, log in as **admin01** with the password **admin01pass**.

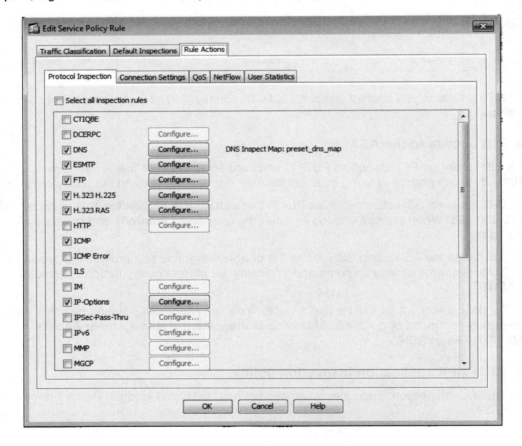

c. From PC-B, **ping** the external interface of R1 S0/0/0 (**10.1.1.1**). The pings should be successful.

Part 5: Configure DMZ, Static NAT, and ACLs

In Part 3, you configured address translation using PAT for the inside network. In this part, you will create a DMZ on the ASA, configure static NAT to a DMZ server, and apply an ACL to control access to the server.

Step 1: Configure the ASA DMZ VLAN 3 interface.

In this step, you will create a new interface VLAN 3 named **dmz**, assign physical interface E0/2 to the VLAN, set the security level to **70**, and limit communication from this interface to the inside (VLAN1) interface.

a. On the **Configuration** screen > **Device Setup** menu, click **Interfaces**. The Interface tab is displayed by default and the currently defined inside (VLAN 1, E0/1) and outside (VLAN 2, E0/0) interfaces are listed. Click **Add** to create a new interface.

b. In the Add Interface dialog box, select port **Ethernet0/2** and click **Add**. You will be prompted to change the interface from the inside network. Click **OK** on the message to remove the port from the inside interface and add it to this new interface. In the Interface Name box, name the interface **dmz**, assign it a security level of **70**, and make sure the **Enable Interface** checkbox is checked.

c. Ensure that the **Use Static IP** option is selected and enter an IP address of **192.168.2.1** with a subnet mask of **255.255.255.0**. Do NOT click **OK** at this time.

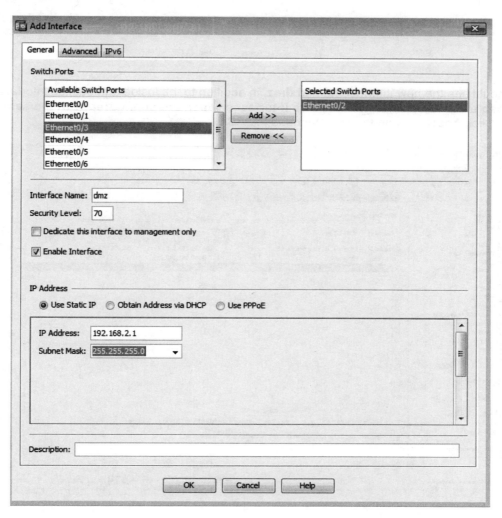

d. ASDM will configure this interface as VLAN ID 12 by default. Before clicking **OK** to add the interface, click the **Advanced** tab and specify this interface as VLAN ID **3**.

Note: If you are working with the ASA 5505 Base license, you are allowed to create up to three named interfaces. However, you must disable communication between the third interface and one of the other interfaces. Because the DMZ server does not need to initiate communication with the inside users, you can disable forwarding to interfaces VLAN 1.

e. On the Advanced tab, you need to block traffic from this interface VLAN 3 (dmz) to the VLAN 1 (inside) interface. In the Block Traffic area, select **vlan1 (inside)** from the drop-down list. Click **OK** to return to the Interfaces window.

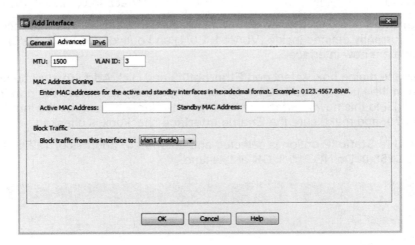

f. You should see the new interface named **dmz**, in addition to the inside and outside interfaces. Check the box **Enable traffic between two or more interfaces which are configured with the same security levels**. Click **Apply** to send the commands to the ASA.

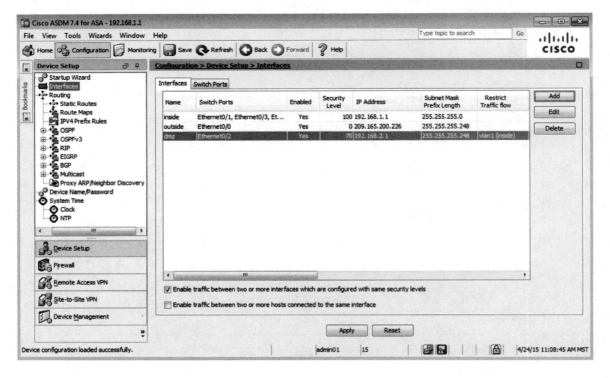

Note: If an **Error in sending command** window appears when you apply the dmz interface configuration to the ASA, you will need to manually configure the **security-level 70** command to VLAN 3 on the ASA. Close the **Error in sending command** window. Using the ASA CLI, add the **security-level 70** command to VLAN 3.

```
CCNA-ASA(config)# interface vlan 3
CCNA-ASA(config-if)# security-level 70
CCNA-ASA(config-if)# exit
```

After entering the CLI commands, ASDM will prompt you to refresh the screen. After you refresh, **70** should appear in the Security Level column for the dmz interface.

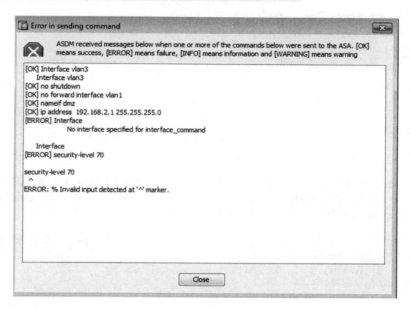

Step 2: Configure the DMZ server and static NAT.

To accommodate the addition of a DMZ and a web server, you will use another address from the ISP range assigned, 209.165.200.224/29 (.224-.231). R1 G0/0 and the ASA outside interface are already using 209.165.200.225 and .226. You will use public address **209.165.200.227** and static NAT to provide address translation access to the server.

a. On the **Firewall** menu, click the **Public Servers** option and click **Add** to define the DMZ server and services offered. In the Add Public Server dialog box, specify the Private Interface as **dmz**, the Public Interface as **outside**, and the Public IP address as **209.165.200.227**.

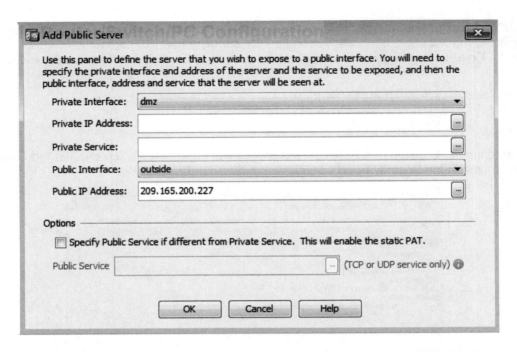

b. Click the ellipsis button to the right of Private IP Address. In the Browse Private IP Address window, click **Add** to define the server as a **Network Object**. Enter the name **DMZ-Server**, select **Host** from the Type pull-down menu, enter the IP Address **192.168.2.3**, and a Description of **PC-A**.

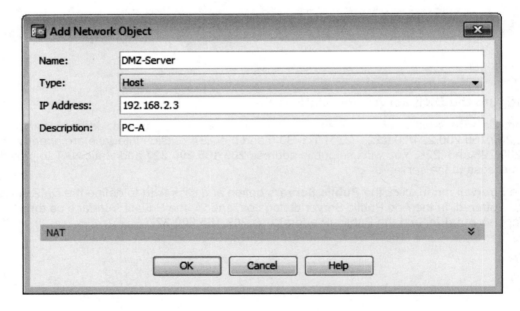

c. From the Browse Private IP Address window, verify that the DMZ-Server appears in the Selected Private IP Address field and click **OK**. You will return to the Add Public Server dialog box.

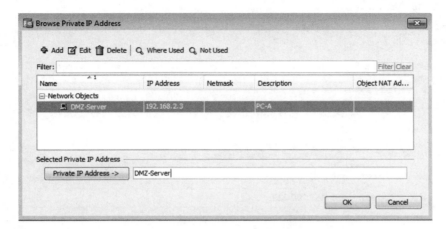

d. In the Add Public Server dialog, click the ellipsis button to the right of Private Service. In the Browse Private Service window, double-click to select the following services: **tcp/ftp**, **tcp/http**, **icmp/echo,** and **icmp/echo-reply** (scroll down to see all services). Click **OK** to continue and return to the Add Public Server dialog.

Note: You can specify Public services if they are different from the Private services, using the option on this screen.

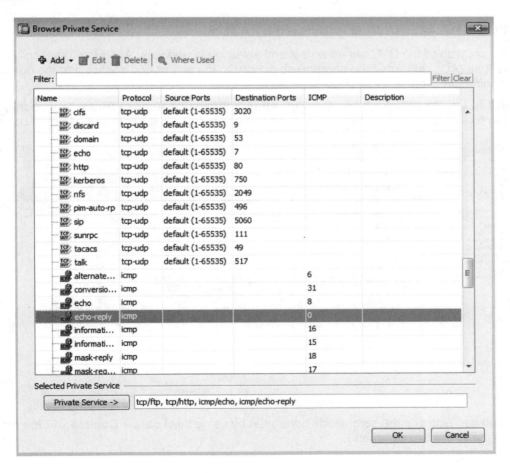

e. When you have completed all the information in the Add Public Server dialog box, it should look like the one shown below. Click **OK** to add the server. Click **Apply** at the Public Servers screen to send the commands to the ASA.

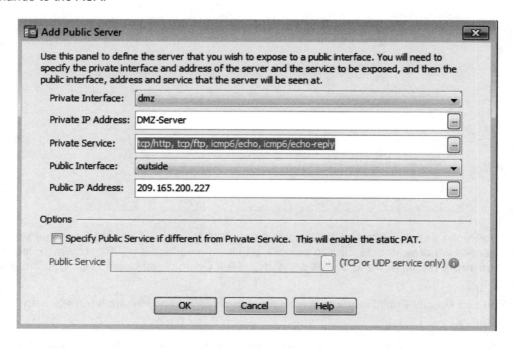

Step 3: View the DMZ Access Rule generated by ASDM.

a. After the creation of the DMZ server object and selection of services, ASDM automatically generates an Access Rule (ACL) to permit the appropriate access to the server and applies it to the outside interface in the incoming direction.

b. View this ACL in ASDM by clicking **Configuration** > **Firewall** > **Access Rules**. It appears as an outside incoming rule. You can select the rule and use the horizontal scroll bar to see all of the components.

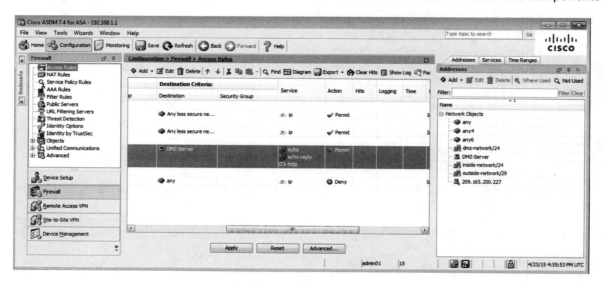

Note: You can also see the commands generated by using the **Tools** > **Command Line Interface** and entering the **show run** command.

Step 4: Test access to the DMZ server from the outside network.

a. From PC-C, ping the IP address of the static NAT public server address (**209.165.200.227**). The pings should be successful.

b. Because the ASA inside interface (VLAN 1) is set to security level 100 (the highest) and the DMZ interface (VLAN 3) is set to 70, you can also access the DMZ server from a host on the inside network. The ASA acts like a router between the two networks. Ping the DMZ server (PC-A) internal address (**192.168.2.3**) from inside network host PC-B (192.168.1.X). The pings should be successful due to the interface security level and the fact that ICMP is being inspected on the inside interface by the global inspection policy.

c. The DMZ server cannot ping PC-B on the inside network. This is because the DMZ interface VLAN 3 has a lower security level and the fact that, when the VLAN 3 interface was created, it was necessary to specify the **no forward** command. Try to ping from the DMZ server PC-A to PC-B at the IP address 192.168.1.X. The pings should not be successful.

Step 5: Use ASDM Monitoring to graph packet activity.

There are a number of aspects of the ASA that can be monitored using the **Monitoring** screen. The main categories on this screen are **Interfaces**, **VPN**, **Routing**, **Properties**, and **Logging**. In this step, you will create a graph to monitor packet activity for the outside interface.

a. On the **Monitoring** screen > **Interfaces** menu, click **Interface Graphs** > **outside**. Select **Packet Counts** and click **Add** to add the graph. The exhibit below shows Packet Counts added.

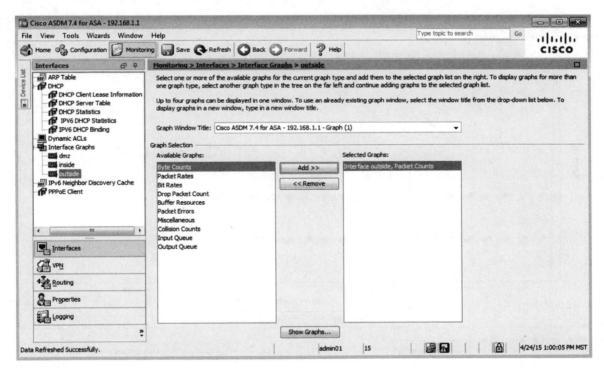

b. Click **Show Graphs** to display the graph. Initially, there is no traffic displayed.

c. From a privileged mode command prompt on R2, simulate Internet traffic to the ASA by pinging the DMZ server's public address with a repeat count of **1000**. You can increase the number of pings if desired.

```
R2# ping 209.165.200.227 repeat 1000
```

```
Type escape sequence to abort.
Sending 1000, 100-byte ICMP Echos to 209.165.200.227, timeout is 2 seconds:
!!!!!!!!!!!!!!!!!!!!!!!!!!!!!!!!!!!!!!!!!!!!!!!!!!!!!!!!!!!!!!!!!!!!!!!!!!!!!
!!!!!!!!!!!!!!!!!!!!!!!!!!!!!!!!!!!!!!!!!!!!!!!!!!!!!!!!!!!!!!!!!!!!!!!!!!!!!
<output omitted>
!!!!!!!!!!!!!!!!!!!!!!!!!!!!!!!!!!!!!!!!!!!!!!!!!!!!!!!!!!!!!!!!!!!!!!!!!!!!!
!!!!!!!!!!!!!!!!!!!!!
Success rate is 100 percent (1000/1000), round-trip min/avg/max = 1/2/12 ms
```

d. You should see the results of the pings from R2 on the graph as an Input Packet Count. The scale of the graph is automatically adjusted depending on the volume of traffic. You can also view the data in tabular form by clicking the **Table** tab. Notice that the **View** selected at the bottom left of the Graph screen is Real-time, data every 10 seconds. Click the pull-down list to see the other available options.

e. Ping from PC-B to R1 S0/0/0 at **10.1.1.1** using the **–n** option (number of packets) to specify **100** packets.

    `C:>\ ping 10.1.1.1 –n 100`

    Note: The response from the PC is relatively slow, and it may take a while to show up on the graph as Output Packet Count. The graph below shows an additional 4000 input packets and both input and output packet counts.

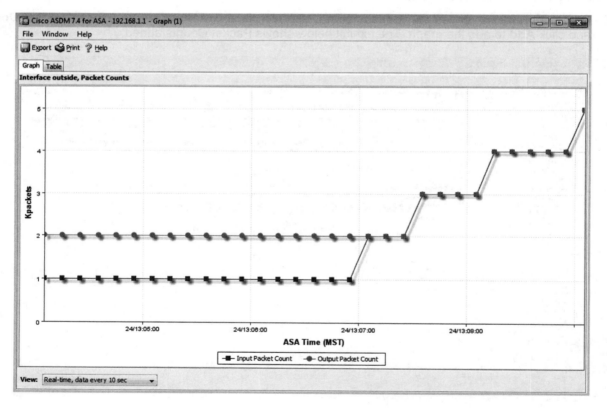

Reflection

1. What are some of the benefits of using ASDM over the CLI?

    _____

    _____

    _____

_____

_____

_____

2. What are some of the benefits of using the CLI over ASDM?

_____

_____

_____

_____

_____

_____

Router Interface Summary Table

Router Interface Summary				
Router Model	Ethernet Interface #1	Ethernet Interface #2	Serial Interface #1	Serial Interface #2
1800	Fast Ethernet 0/0 (F0/0)	Fast Ethernet 0/1 (F0/1)	Serial 0/0/0 (S0/0/0)	Serial 0/0/1 (S0/0/1)
1900	Gigabit Ethernet 0/0 (G0/0)	Gigabit Ethernet 0/1 (G0/1)	Serial 0/0/0 (S0/0/0)	Serial 0/0/1 (S0/0/1)
2801	Fast Ethernet 0/0 (F0/0)	Fast Ethernet 0/1 (F0/1)	Serial 0/1/0 (S0/1/0)	Serial 0/1/1 (S0/1/1)
2811	Fast Ethernet 0/0 (F0/0)	Fast Ethernet 0/1 (F0/1)	Serial 0/0/0 (S0/0/0)	Serial 0/0/1 (S0/0/1)
2900	Gigabit Ethernet 0/0 (G0/0)	Gigabit Ethernet 0/1 (G0/1)	Serial 0/0/0 (S0/0/0)	Serial 0/0/1 (S0/0/1)

Note: To find out how the router is configured, look at the interfaces to identify the type of router and how many interfaces the router has. There is no way to effectively list all the combinations of configurations for each router class. This table includes identifiers for the possible combinations of Ethernet and Serial interfaces in the device. The table does not include any other type of interface, even though a specific router may contain one. An example of this might be an ISDN BRI interface. The string in parenthesis is the legal abbreviation that can be used in Cisco IOS commands to represent the interface.

Lab B 10.2.1.9 – Configure a Site-to-Site IPsec VPN Using ISR CLI and ASA ASDM

Topology

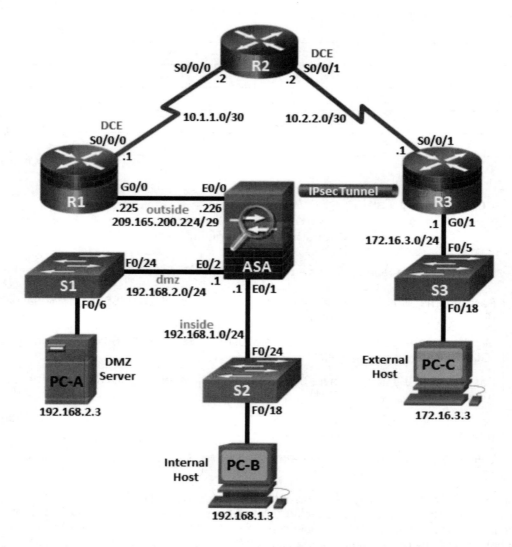

Note: ISR G2 devices use GigabitEthernet interfaces instead of FastEthernet interfaces.

IP Addressing Table

Device	Interface	IP Address	Subnet Mask	Default Gateway	Switch Port
R1	G0/0	209.165.200.225	255.255.255.248	N/A	ASA E0/0
	S0/0/0 (DCE)	10.1.1.1	255.255.255.252	N/A	N/A
R2	S0/0/0	10.1.1.2	255.255.255.252	N/A	N/A
	S0/0/1 (DCE)	10.2.2.2	255.255.255.252	N/A	N/A
R3	G0/1	172.16.3.1	255.255.255.0	N/A	S3 F0/5
	S0/0/1	10.2.2.1	255.255.255.252	N/A	N/A
ASA	VLAN 1 (E0/1)	192.168.1.1	255.255.255.0	NA	S2 Fa0/24
	VLAN 2 (E0/0)	209.165.200.226	255.255.255.248	NA	R1 F0/0
	VLAN 3 (E0/2)	192.168.2.1	255.255.255.0	NA	S1 F0/24
PC-A	NIC	192.168.2.3	255.255.255.0	192.168.2.1	S1 F0/6
PC-B	NIC	192.168.1.3	255.255.255.0	192.168.1.1	S2 F0/18
PC-C	NIC	172.16.3.3	255.255.255.0	172.16.3.1	S3 F0/18

Objectives

Part 1: Basic Router/Switch/PC Configuration

- Cable the network and clear previous device settings, as shown in the topology.
- Configure basic settings for routers.
- Configure PC host IP settings.
- Verify connectivity.
- Save the basic running configuration for each router and switch.

Part 2: Accessing the ASA Console and ASDM

- Access the ASA console.
- Clear the previous ASA configuration settings.
- Bypass Setup mode.
- Use the CLI command script to configure the ASA.
- Verify HTTP ASDM access.

Part 3: Configuring the ISR as a Site-to-Site IPsec VPN Endpoint Using the CLI

- Configure basic VPN connection information settings.
- Specify IKE policy parameters.
- Configure a transform set.
- Specify traffic to protect.
- Review the summary of the configuration.
- Review the site-to-site VPN tunnel configuration.

Part 4: Configuring the ASA as a Site-to-Site IPsec VPN Endpoint Using ASDM

- Access ASDM.

- Review the ASDM Home screen.

- Start the VPN wizard.

- Configure peer device identification.

- Specify the traffic to protect.

- Configure authentication.

- Configure miscellaneous settings.

- Review the configuration summary and deliver the commands to the ASA.

- Verify the ASDM VPN connection profile.

- Test the VPN configuration from R3.

- Use ASDM monitoring to verify the tunnel.

Background/Scenario

In addition to acting as a remote access VPN concentrator, the ASA can provide site-to-site IPsec VPN tunneling. The tunnel can be configured between two ASAs or between an ASA and another IPsec VPN-capable device, such as an ISR, as is the case with this lab.

Your company has two locations connected to an ISP. R1 represents a customer-premise equipment (CPE) device managed by the ISP. R2 represents an intermediate Internet router. R3 connects users at the remote branch office to the ISP. The ASA is an edge security device that connects the internal corporate network and DMZ to the ISP while providing NAT services to inside hosts.

Management has asked you to provide a dedicated site-to-site IPsec VPN tunnel between the ISR router at the remote branch office and the ASA device at the corporate site. This tunnel will protect traffic between the branch office LAN and the corporate LAN, as it passes through the Internet. The site-to-site VPN does not require a VPN client on the remote or corporate site host computers. Traffic from either LAN to other Internet destinations is routed by the ISP and is not protected by the VPN tunnel. The VPN tunnel will pass through R1 and R2; both routers are not aware of the tunnel's existence.

In Part 1 of this lab, you will configure the topology and non-ASA devices. In Part 2, you will prepare the ASA for ASDM access. In Part 3, you will use the CLI to configure the R3 ISR as a site-to-site IPsec VPN endpoint. In Part 4, you will configure the ASA as a site-to-site IPsec VPN endpoint using the ASDM VPN wizard.

Note: The router commands and output in this lab are from a Cisco 1941 router with Cisco IOS Release 15.4(3)M2 (with a Security Technology Package license). Other routers and Cisco IOS versions can be used. See the Router Interface Summary Table at the end of this lab to determine which interface identifiers to use based on the equipment in the lab. Depending on the router model and Cisco IOS version, the commands available and the output produced might vary from what is shown in this lab.

The ASA used with this lab is a Cisco model 5505 with an 8-port integrated switch, running OS version 9.2(3) and ASDM version 7.4(1) and comes with a Base license that allows a maximum of three VLANs.

Note: Before beginning, ensure that the routers and switches have been erased and have no startup configurations.

Required Resources

- 1 ASA 5505 (OS version 9.2(3) and ASDM version 7.4(1) and Base license or comparable)

- 3 routers (Cisco 1941 with Cisco IOS Release 15.4(3)M2 image with a Security Technology package license)

- 3 switches (Cisco 2960 or comparable) (not required)
- 3 PCs (Windows 7 or Windows 8.1, with SSH Client software installed)
- Serial and Ethernet cables, as shown in the topology
- Console cables to configure Cisco networking devices

Part 1: Basic Router/Switch/PC Configuration

In Part 1, you will set up the network topology and configure basic settings on the routers, such as interface IP addresses and static routing.

Note: Do not configure any ASA settings at this time.

Step 1: Cable the network and clear previous device settings.

Attach the devices shown in the topology diagram and cable as necessary. Ensure that the routers and switches have been erased and have no startup configurations.

Step 2: Configure R1 using the CLI script.

In this step, you will use the following CLI script to configure basic settings on R1. Copy and paste the basic configuration script commands listed below. Observe the messages as the commands are applied to ensure that there are no warnings or errors.

Note: Depending on the router model, interfaces might be numbered differently than those listed. You might need to alter the designations accordingly.

Note: Passwords in this task are set to a minimum of 10 characters and are relatively simple for the purposes of performing the lab. More complex passwords are recommended in a production network.

```
hostname R1
security passwords min-length 10
enable algorithm-type scrypt secret cisco12345
username admin01 algorithm-type scrypt secret admin01pass
ip domain name ccnasecurity.com
line con 0
 login local
 exec-timeout 5 0
 logging synchronous
exit
line vty 0 4
 login local
 transport input ssh
 exec-timeout 5 0
 logging synchronous
exit
interface gigabitethernet 0/0
 ip address 209.165.200.225 255.255.255.248
 no shut
exit
```

```
int serial 0/0/0
 ip address 10.1.1.1 255.255.255.252
 clock rate 2000000
 no shut
exit
ip route 0.0.0.0 0.0.0.0 Serial0/0/0
crypto key generate rsa general-keys modulus 1024
```

Step 3: Configure R2 using the CLI script.

In this step, you will use the following CLI script to configure basic settings on R2. Copy and paste the basic configuration script commands listed below. Observe the messages as the commands are applied to ensure that there are no warnings or errors.

```
hostname R2
security passwords min-length 10
enable algorithm-type scrypt secret cisco12345
username admin01 algorithm-type scrypt secret admin01pass
ip domain name ccnasecurity.com
line con 0
 login local
 exec-timeout 5 0
 logging synchronous
exit
line vty 0 4
 login local
 transport input ssh
 exec-timeout 5 0
 logging synchronous
exit
interface serial 0/0/0
 ip address 10.1.1.2 255.255.255.252
 no shut
exit
interface serial 0/0/1
 ip address 10.2.2.2 255.255.255.252
 clock rate 2000000
 no shut
exit
ip route 209.165.200.224 255.255.255.248 Serial0/0/0
ip route 172.16.3.0 255.255.255.0 Serial0/0/1
crypto key generate rsa general-keys modulus 1024
```

Step 4: Configure R3 using the CLI script.

In this step, you will use the following CLI script to configure basic settings on R3. Copy and paste the basic configuration script commands listed below. Observe the messages as the commands are applied to ensure that there are no warnings or errors.

```
hostname R3
security passwords min-length 10
enable algorithm-type scrypt secret cisco12345
username admin01 algorithm-type scrypt secret admin01pass
ip domain name ccnasecurity.com
line con 0
 login local
 exec-timeout 5 0
 logging synchronous
exit
line vty 0 4
 login local
 transport input ssh
 exec-timeout 5 0
 logging synchronous
exit
interface gigabitethernet 0/1
 ip address 172.16.3.1 255.255.255.0
 no shut
exit
int serial 0/0/1
 ip address 10.2.2.1 255.255.255.252
 no shut
exit
ip route 0.0.0.0 0.0.0.0 Serial0/0/1
crypto key generate rsa general-keys modulus 1024
```

Step 5: Configure PC host IP settings.

Configure a static IP address, subnet mask, and default gateway for PC-A, PC-B, and PC-C as shown in the IP Addressing table.

Step 6: Verify connectivity.

Because the ASA is the focal point for the network zones, and it has not yet been configured, there will be no connectivity between devices that are connected to it. However, PC-C should be able to ping the R1 interface G0/0. From PC-C, ping the R1 G0/0 IP address (**209.165.200.225**). If these pings are unsuccessful, troubleshoot the basic device configurations before continuing.

Note: If you can ping from PC-C to R1 G0/0 and S0/0/0, you have demonstrated that static routing is configured and functioning correctly.

Save the **running configuration** for each router.

Part 2: Accessing the ASA Console and ASDM

Step 1: Clear the previous ASA configuration settings.

a. Use the **write erase** command to remove the **startup-config** file from flash memory.

   Note: The **erase startup-config** IOS command is not supported on the ASA.

b. Use the **reload** command to restart the ASA. This causes the ASA to display in CLI Setup mode. If you see the **System config has been modified. Save? [Y]es/[N]o:** message, type **n**, and press **Enter**.

Step 2: Bypass Setup mode.

When the ASA completes the reload process, it should detect that the startup configuration file is missing and go into Setup mode. If it does go into Setup mode, repeat Step 2.

a. When prompted to preconfigure the firewall through interactive prompts (Setup mode), respond with **no**.

b. Enter privileged EXEC mode with the **enable** command. The password should be kept blank (no password).

Step 3: Configure the ASA by using the CLI script.

In this step, you will use a CLI script to configure basic settings, the firewall, and the DMZ.

a. Use the **show run** command to confirm that there is no previous configuration in the ASA other than the defaults that the ASA automatically inserts.

b. Enter global configuration mode. When prompted to enable anonymous call-home reporting, respond **no**.

c. Copy and paste the Pre-VPN Configuration Script commands listed below at the ASA global configuration mode prompt to start configuring the SSL VPNs.

d. Observe the messages as the commands are applied to ensure that there are no warnings or errors. If prompted to replace the RSA key pair, respond **yes**.

```
hostname CCNAS-ASA
domain-name ccnasecurity.com
enable password cisco12345
!
interface Ethernet0/0
 switchport access vlan 2
 no shut
!
interface Ethernet0/1
 switchport access vlan 1
 no shut
!
interface Ethernet0/2
 switchport access vlan 3
 no shut
!
interface Vlan1
 nameif inside
```

```
 security-level 100
 ip address 192.168.1.1 255.255.255.0
!
interface Vlan2
 nameif outside
 security-level 0
 ip address 209.165.200.226 255.255.255.248
!
interface Vlan3
 no forward interface Vlan1
 nameif dmz
 security-level 70
 ip address 192.168.2.1 255.255.255.0
!
object network inside-net
 subnet 192.168.1.0 255.255.255.0
!
object network dmz-server
 host 192.168.2.3
!
access-list OUTSIDE-DMZ extended permit ip any host 192.168.2.3
!
object network inside-net
 nat (inside,outside) dynamic interface
!
object network dmz-server
 nat (dmz,outside) static 209.165.200.227
!
access-group OUTSIDE-DMZ in interface outside
!
route outside 0.0.0.0 0.0.0.0 209.165.200.225 1
!
username admin01 password admin01pass
!
aaa authentication ssh console LOCAL
aaa authentication http console LOCAL
!
http server enable
http 192.168.1.0 255.255.255.0 inside
ssh 192.168.1.0 255.255.255.0 inside
ssh timeout 10
!
class-map inspection_default
 match default-inspection-traffic
```

```
policy-map global_policy
 class inspection_default
    inspect icmp
!
crypto key generate rsa modulus 1024
```

e. At the privileged EXEC mode prompt, issue the **write mem** (or **copy run start**) command to save the running configuration to the startup configuration and the RSA keys to non-volatile memory.

Part 3: Configuring the ISR as a Site-to-Site IPsec VPN Endpoint Using the CLI

In Part 3 of this lab, you will configure R3 as an IPsec VPN endpoint for the tunnel between R3 and the ASA. R1 and R2 are unaware of the tunnel.

Step 1: Verify connectivity from the R3 LAN to the ASA.

In this step, you will verify that PC-C on the R3 LAN can ping the ASA outside interface.

Ping the ASA IP address of **209.165.200.226** from PC-C.

```
PC-C:\> ping 209.165.200.226
```

If the pings are unsuccessful, troubleshoot the basic device configurations before continuing.

Step 2: Enable IKE policies on R3.

IPsec is an open framework that allows for the exchange of security protocols as new technologies and encryption algorithms are developed.

There are two central configuration elements in the implementation of an IPsec VPN:

*   Implement Internet Key Exchange (IKE) parameters.

*   Implement IPsec parameters.

a. Verify that IKE is supported and enabled.

IKE Phase 1 defines the key exchange method used to pass and validate IKE policies between peers. In IKE Phase 2, the peers exchange and match IPsec policies for the authentication and encryption of data traffic.

IKE must be enabled for IPsec to function. IKE is enabled, by default, on IOS images with cryptographic feature sets. If it is disabled, you can enable it with the **crypto isakmp enable** command. Use this command to verify that the router IOS supports IKE and that it is enabled.

```
R3(config)# crypto isakmp enable
```

Note: If you cannot execute this command on the router, you must upgrade to the IOS image that includes the Cisco cryptographic services.

b. Establish an ISAKMP policy and view the available options.

To allow IKE Phase 1 negotiation, you must create an ISAKMP policy and configure a peer association involving that ISAKMP policy. An ISAKMP policy defines the authentication and encryption algorithms, and the hash function used to send control traffic between the two VPN endpoints. When an ISAKMP security association has been accepted by the IKE peers, IKE Phase 1 has been completed. IKE Phase 2 parameters will be configured later.

Issue the **crypto isakmp** *policy number* global configuration mode command on R1 for policy 10.

```
R1(config)# crypto isakmp policy 10
```

c. View the various IKE parameters available using Cisco IOS help by typing a question mark (**?**).

```
R1(config-isakmp)# ?
ISAKMP commands:
  authentication  Set authentication method for protection suite
  default         Set a command to its defaults
  encryption      Set encryption algorithm for protection suite
  exit            Exit from ISAKMP protection suite configuration mode
  group           Set the Diffie-Hellman group
  hash            Set hash algorithm for protection suite
  lifetime        Set lifetime for ISAKMP security association
  no              Negate a command or set its defaults
```

Step 3: Configure ISAKMP policy parameters on R3.

The encryption algorithm determines how confidential the control channel between the endpoints is. The hash algorithm controls data integrity, which ensures that the data received from a peer has not been tampered with in transit. The authentication type ensures that the packet was sent and signed by the remote peer. The Diffie-Hellman group is used to create a secret key shared by the peers that has not been sent across the network.

a. Configure an ISAKMP policy with a priority of **10**. Use **pre-shared key** as the authentication type,.**3des** for the encryption algorithm, **sha** as the hash algorithm, and the Diffie-Hellman group **2** key exchange.

Note: Older versions of Cisco IOS do not support AES 256 encryption and SHA as a hash algorithm. Substitute whatever encryption and hashing algorithm your router supports. Ensure that the same changes are made on R3 in order to be in sync.

```
R3(config)# crypto isakmp policy 10
R3(config-isakmp)# authentication pre-share
R3(config-isakmp)# encryption 3des
R3(config-isakmp)# hash sha
R3(config-isakmp)# group 2
R3(config-isakmp)# end
```

b. Verify the IKE policy with the **show crypto isakmp policy** command.

```
R3# show crypto isakmp policy

Global IKE policy
Protection suite of priority 10
        encryption algorithm:   Three key triple DES
        hash algorithm:         Secure Hash Standard
        authentication method:  Pre-Shared Key
        Diffie-Hellman group:   #2 (1024 bit)
        lifetime:            3600 seconds, no volume limit
```

Step 4: Configure pre-shared keys.

Because pre-shared keys are used as the authentication method in the IKE policy, a key must be configured on each router that points to the other VPN endpoint. These keys must match for authentication to be successful. The global configuration mode **crypto isakmp key** *key-string* **address** *ip-address* command is used to enter a pre-shared key. Use the IP address of the remote peer. The IP address is the remote interface that the peer would use to route traffic to the local router.

Which IP address should you use to configure the IKE peer, given the topology diagram and IP addressing table?

_____

_____

_____

a. Each IP address that is used to configure the IKE peers is also referred to as the IP address of the remote VPN endpoint. Configure the pre-shared key of **SECRET-KEY** on R3. Production networks should use a complex key. This command points to the remote ASA outside IP address.

```
R3(config)# crypto isakmp key SECRET-KEY address 209.165.200.226
```

Step 5: Configure the IPsec transform set and lifetime.

a. The IPsec transform set is another crypto configuration parameter that routers negotiate to form a security association. It is configured using the **crypto ipsec transform-set** *tag* global configuration command. Configure the transform set with the tag **ESP-TUNNEL**. Use **?** to see which parameters are available.

```
R3(config)# crypto ipsec transform-set ESP-TUNNEL ?
  ah-md5-hmac       AH-HMAC-MD5 transform
  ah-sha-hmac       AH-HMAC-SHA transform
  ah-sha256-hmac    AH-HMAC-SHA256 transform on R3
  ah-sha384-hmac    AH-HMAC-SHA384 transform
  ah-sha512-hmac    AH-HMAC-SHA512 transform
  comp-lzs          IP Compression using the LZS compression algorithm
  esp-3des          ESP transform using 3DES(EDE) cipher (168 bits)
  esp-aes           ESP transform using AES cipher
  esp-des           ESP transform using DES cipher (56 bits)
  esp-gcm           ESP transform using GCM cipher
  esp-gmac          ESP transform using GMAC cipher
  esp-md5-hmac      ESP transform using HMAC-MD5 auth
  esp-null          ESP transform w/o cipher
  esp-seal          ESP transform using SEAL cipher (160 bits)
  esp-sha-hmac      ESP transform using HMAC-SHA auth
  esp-sha256-hmac   ESP transform using HMAC-SHA256 auth
  esp-sha384-hmac   ESP transform using HMAC-SHA384 auth
  esp-sha512-hmac   ESP transform using HMAC-SHA512 auth
```

b. In our Site-to-site VPN with the ASA, we will use the two highlitghed parameters. Complete the command by entering the two highlighted parameters.

```
R3(config)# crypto ipsec transform-set ESP-TUNNEL esp-3des esp-sha-hmac
```

What is the function of the IPsec transform set?

_____

_____

_____

_____

Step 6: Define interesting traffic.

To make use of the IPsec encryption with the VPN, it is necessary to define extended access lists to tell the router which traffic to encrypt. A packet that is permitted by an access list used for defining IPsec traffic is encrypted if the IPsec session is configured correctly. A packet that is denied by one of these access lists is not dropped. The packet is sent unencrypted. Also, like any other access list, there is an implicit deny at the end, which means the default action is to not encrypt traffic. If there is no IPsec security association correctly configured, no traffic is encrypted and traffic is forwarded unencrypted.

In this scenario, from the perspective of R3, the traffic you want to encrypt is traffic going from R3's Ethernet LAN to the ASA inside LAN or vice versa from the perspective of the ASA.

a. Configure the IPsec VPN interesting traffic ACL on R3.

```
R3(config)# ip access-list extended VPN-ACL
R3(config-ext-nacl)# remark Link to the CCNAS-ASA
R3(config-ext-nacl)# permit ip 172.16.3.0 0.0.0.255 192.168.1.0 0.0.0.255
R3(config-ext-nacl)# exit
```

Does IPsec evaluate whether the access lists are mirrored as a requirement to negotiate its security association?

_____

_____

_____

Step 7: Create and apply a crypto map.

A crypto map associates traffic that matches an access list to a peer and various IKE and IPsec settings. After the crypto map is created, it can be applied to one or more interfaces. The interfaces that it is applied to should be the interfaces facing the IPsec peer.

To create a crypto map, use the **crypto map** *name sequence-num type* global configuration command to enter crypto map configuration mode for that sequence number. Multiple crypto map statements can belong to the same crypto map and are evaluated in ascending numerical order.

a. Create the crypto map on R3, name it **S2S-MAP**, and use **10** as the sequence number. Use a type of **ipsec-isakmp**, which means IKE is used to establish IPsec security associations. A message displays after the command is issued.

```
R3(config)# crypto map S2S-MAP 10 ipsec-isakmp
% NOTE: This new crypto map will remain disabled until a peer
        and a valid access list have been configured.
R3(config-crypto-map)#
```

b. Use the **match address** *access-list* command to specify which access list defines which traffic to encrypt.

```
R3(config-crypto-map)# match address VPN-ACL
```

   c.   Setting a peer IP or hostname is required. Set it to the ASA remote VPN endpoint interface using the following command.

```
R3(config-crypto-map)# set peer 209.165.200.226
```

   d.   Use the **set transform-set** *tag* command to hard code the transform set to be used with this peer.

```
R3(config-crypto-map)# set transform-set ESP-TUNNEL
R3(config-crypto-map)# exit
```

   e.   Apply the crypto map to interfaces.

      Note: The SAs are not established until the crypto map has been activated by interesting traffic. The router generates a notification that crypto is now on.

      Apply the crypto maps to the R3 Serial 0/0/1 interface.

```
R3(config)# interface Serial0/0/1
R3(config-if)# crypto map S2S-MAP
R3(config-if)# end
R3#
*Mar  9 06:23:03.863: %CRYPTO-6-ISAKMP_ON_OFF: ISAKMP is ON
R3#
```

Part 4: Configuring the ASA as a Site-to-Site IPsec VPN Endpoint Using ASDM

In Part 4 of this lab, you will configure the ASA as an IPsec VPN tunnel endpoint. The tunnel between the ASA and R3 passes through R1 and R2.

Step 1: Access ASDM.

   a.   Open a browser on PC-B and test the HTTPS access to the ASA by entering https://192.168.1.1. After entering the https://192.168.1.1 URL, you should see a security warning about the website security certificate. Click **Continue to this website**. Click **Yes** for any other security warnings.

      Note: Specify the HTTPS protocol in the URL.

b. At the ASDM welcome page, click **Run ASDM**. The ASDM-IDM Launcher will display.

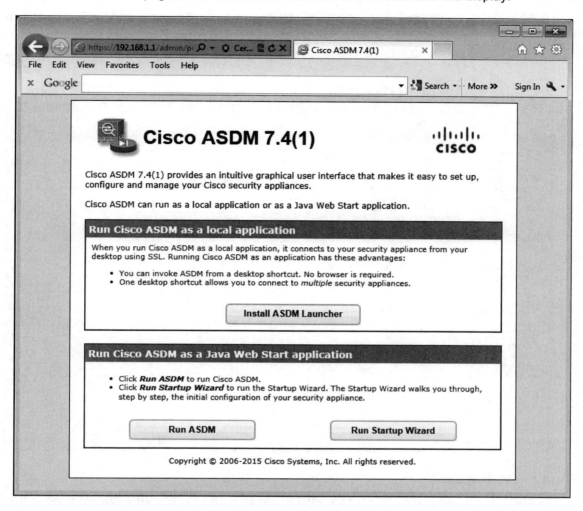

c. Log in as user **admin01** with the password **admin01pass**.

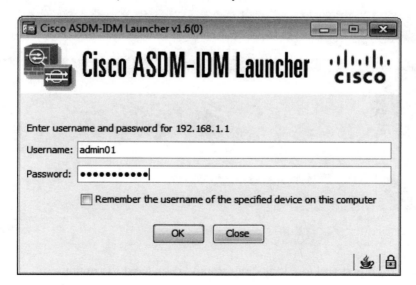

Step 2: Review the ASDM Home screen.

The Home screen displays and shows the current ASA device configuration and traffic flow statistics. Note the inside, outside, and dmz interfaces that were configured in Part 2 of this lab.

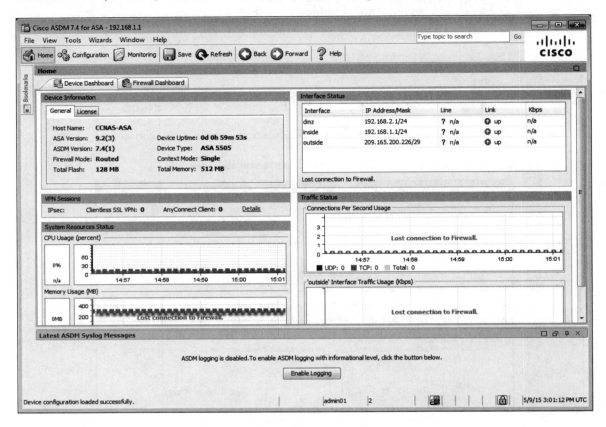

Step 3: Start the VPN wizard.

a. On the ASDM main menu, click **Wizards** > **VPN Wizards** > **Site-to-Site VPN Wizard** to open the Site-to-Site VPN Connection Setup Wizard Introduction window.

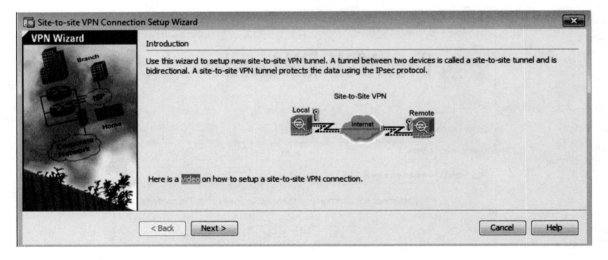

b. Review the on-screen text and topology diagram and click **Next** to continue.

Step 4: Configure peer device identification.

In the Peer Device Identification window, enter the IP address of the R3 Serial0/0/1 interface (**10.2.2.1**) as the Peer IP Address. Leave the default VPN Access Interface set to **outside**. The VPN tunnel will be between R3 S0/0/1 and the ASA outside interface (VLAN 2 E0/0). Click **Next** to continue.

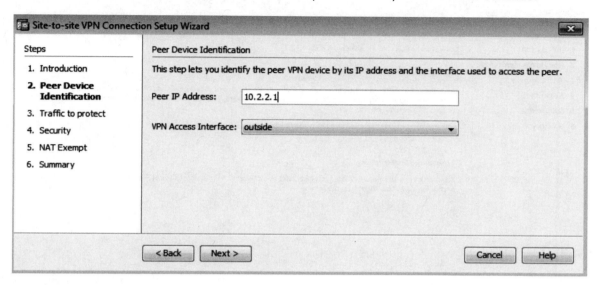

Step 5: Specify the traffic to protect.

In the Traffic to protect window, enter **inside-network/24** (192.168.1.0/24) as the Local Network and type **172.16.3.0/24** to add the R3 LAN as the Remote Network. Click **Next** to continue. A message may display stating that the certificate information is being retrieved.

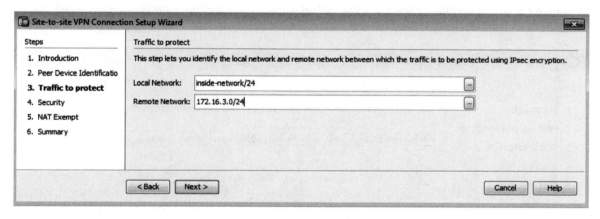

Note: If the ASA does not respond, you may need to close the window and continue to the next step. If prompted to authenticate, log in again as **admin01** with the password **admin01pass**.

Step 6: Configure authentication.

On the Security window, enter a pre-shared key of **SECRET-KEY**. You will not be using a device certificate. Click **Next** to continue.

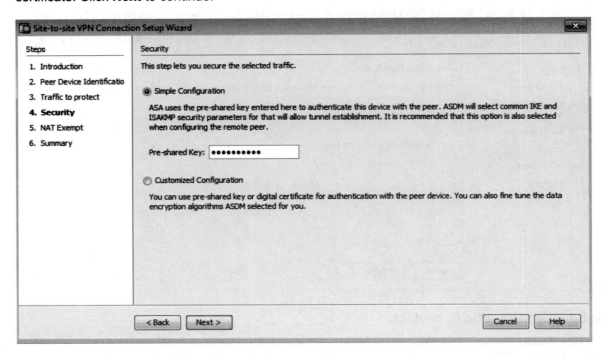

Step 7: Configure miscellaneous settings.

In the NAT Exempt window, click the **Exempt ASA** check box for the **inside** interface. Click **Next** to continue.

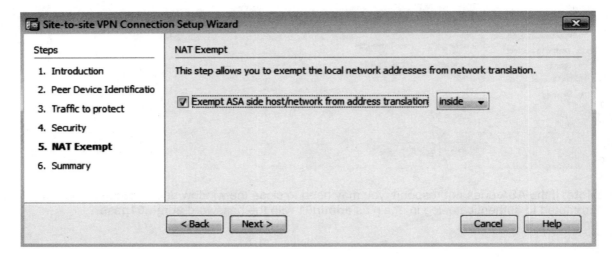

Step 8: Review the configuration summary and deliver the commands to the ASA.

The Summary page is displayed next. Verify that the information configured is correct. You can click **Back** to make changes, or click **Cancel** and restart the VPN wizard (recommended). Click **Finish** to complete the process and deliver the commands to the ASA.

Note: If prompted to authenticate, log in again as **admin01** with the password **admin01pass**.

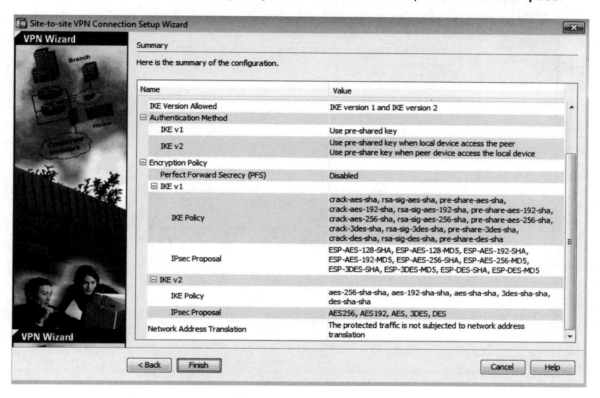

Step 9: Verify the ASDM VPN connection profile.

The ASDM **Configurations** > **Site-to-Site VPN** > **Connection Profiles** screen displays the settings you configured. From this window, the VPN configuration can be verified and edited.

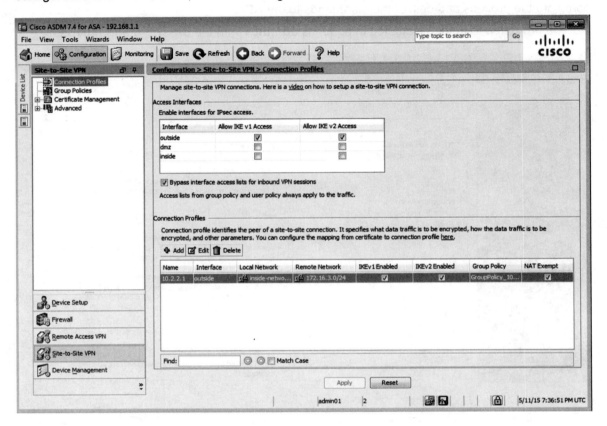

Step 10: Use ASDM monitoring to verify the tunnel.

On the ASDM menu bar, click **Monitoring** > **VPN** from the panels at the lower left of the screen. Click **VPN Statistics** > **Sessions**. Notice how there is no active session. This is because the VPN tunnel has not been established.

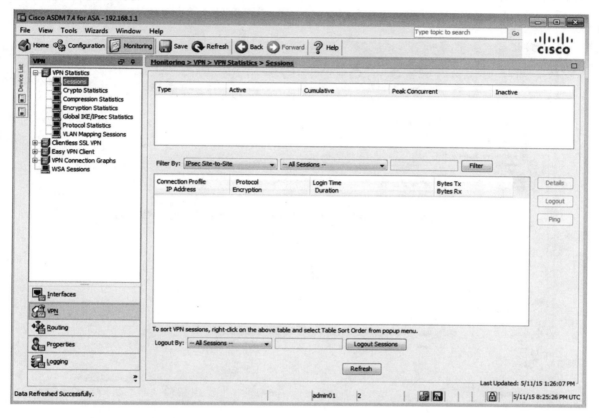

Step 11: Test the VPN configuration from PC-B.

a. To establish the VPN tunnel, interesting traffic must be generated. From PC-B, ping PC-C.

```
C:\Windows\system32\cmd.exe

Microsoft Windows [Version 6.1.7601]
Copyright (c) 2009 Microsoft Corporation.   All rights reserved.

C:\Users\NetAcad>ping 172.16.3.3

Pinging 172.16.3.3 with 32 bytes of data:
Request timed out.
Request timed out.
Reply from 172.16.3.3: bytes=32 time=40ms TTL=127
Reply from 172.16.3.3: bytes=32 time=41ms TTL=127

Ping statistics for 172.16.3.3:
    Packets: Sent = 4, Received = 2, Lost = 2 (50% loss),
Approximate round trip times in milli-seconds:
    Minimum = 40ms, Maximum = 41ms, Average = 40ms

C:\Users\NetAcad>
```

b. This generates interesting traffic. Notice how two pings failed before being successful. This is because the tunnel first had to be negotiated and established before the ICMP packets could be successful.

c. The VPN information is now being displayed on the ASDM **Monitoring** > **VPN** > **VPN Statistics** > **Sessions** page.

   Note: You may need to click **Refresh** before the statistics will display.

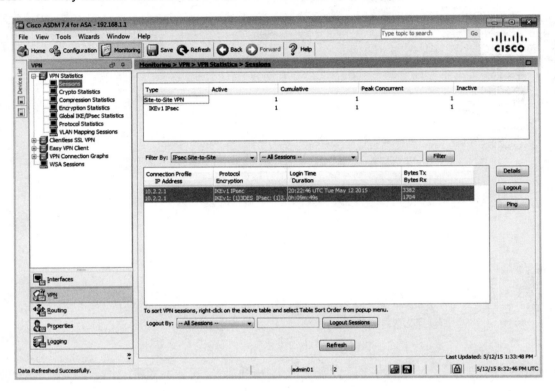

d. Click **Encryption Statistics**. You should see one or more sessions using the 3DES encryption algorithm.

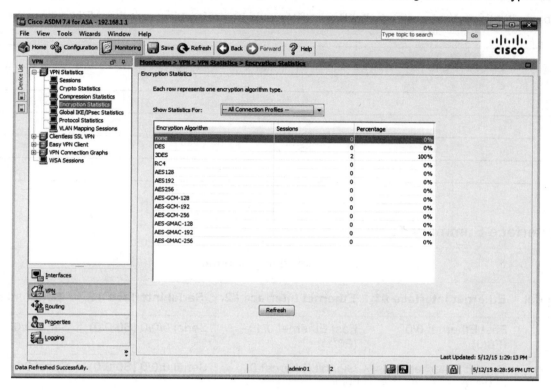

e. Click **Crypto Statistics**. You should see values for the number of packets encrypted and decrypted, security association (SA) requests, etc.

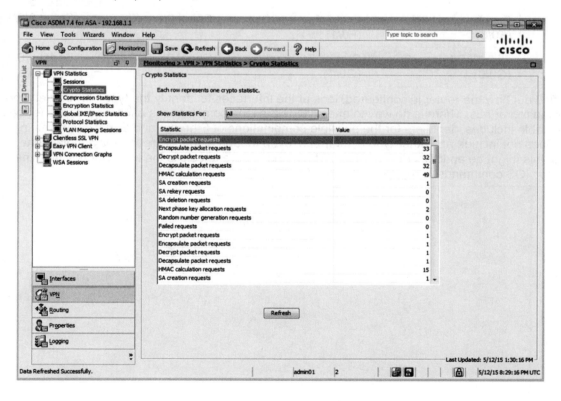

Reflection

Describe a situation where a site-to-site IPsec VPN would be preferable over other VPN options.

_____

_____

_____

_____

_____

_____

_____

Router Interface Summary Table

Router Interface Summary				
Router Model	Ethernet Interface #1	Ethernet Interface #2	Serial Interface #1	Serial Interface #2
1800	Fast Ethernet 0/0 (F0/0)	Fast Ethernet 0/1 (F0/1)	Serial 0/0/0 (S0/0/0)	Serial 0/0/1 (S0/0/1)
1900	Gigabit Ethernet 0/0 (G0/0)	Gigabit Ethernet 0/1 (G0/1)	Serial 0/0/0 (S0/0/0)	Serial 0/0/1 (S0/0/1)
2801	Fast Ethernet 0/0 (F0/0)	Fast Ethernet 0/1 (F0/1)	Serial 0/1/0 (S0/1/0)	Serial 0/1/1 (S0/1/1)
2811	Fast Ethernet 0/0 (F0/0)	Fast Ethernet 0/1 (F0/1)	Serial 0/0/0 (S0/0/0)	Serial 0/0/1 (S0/0/1)
2900	Gigabit Ethernet 0/0 (G0/0)	Gigabit Ethernet 0/1 (G0/1)	Serial 0/0/0 (S0/0/0)	Serial 0/0/1 (S0/0/1)

Note: To find out how the router is configured, look at the interfaces to identify the type of router and how many interfaces the router has. There is no way to effectively list all the combinations of configurations for each router class. This table includes identifiers for the possible combinations of Ethernet and Serial interfaces in the device. The table does not include any other type of interface, even though a specific router may contain one. An example of this might be an ISDN BRI interface. The string in parenthesis is the legal abbreviation that can be used in Cisco IOS commands to represent the interface.

Lab C 10.3.1.1 - Configure Clientless Remote Access SSL VPNs Using ASDM

Topology

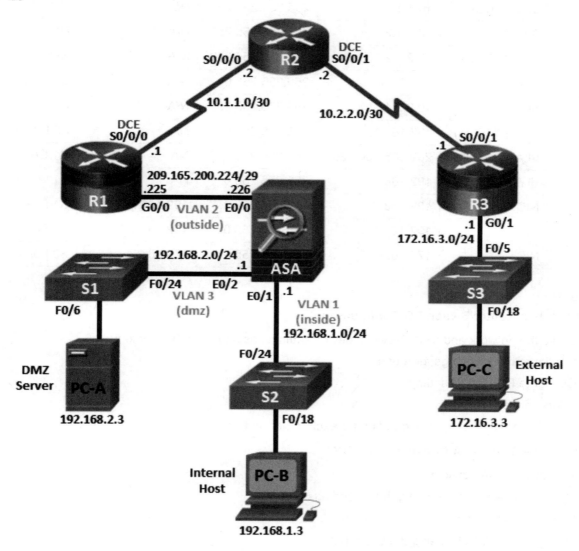

Note: ISR G1 devices use FastEthernet interfaces instead of GigabitEthernet Interfaces.

IP Addressing Table

Device	Interface	IP Address	Subnet Mask	Default Gateway	Switch Port
R1	G0/0	209.165.200.225	255.255.255.248	N/A	ASA E0/0
	S0/0/0 (DCE)	10.1.1.1	255.255.255.252	N/A	N/A
R2	S0/0/0	10.1.1.2	255.255.255.252	N/A	N/A
	S0/0/1 (DCE)	10.2.2.2	255.255.255.252	N/A	N/A
R3	G0/1	172.16.3.1	255.255.255.0	N/A	S3 F0/5
	S0/0/1	10.2.2.1	255.255.255.252	N/A	N/A
ASA	VLAN 1 (E0/1)	192.168.1.1	255.255.255.0	NA	S2 F0/24
	VLAN 2 (E0/0)	209.165.200.226	255.255.255.248	NA	R1 G0/0
	VLAN 3 (E0/2)	192.168.2.1	255.255.255.0	NA	S1 F0/24
PC-A	NIC	192.168.2.3	255.255.255.0	192.168.2.1	S1 F0/6
PC-B	NIC	192.168.1.3	255.255.255.0	192.168.1.1	S2 F0/18
PC-C	NIC	172.16.3.3	255.255.255.0	172.16.3.1	S3 F0/18

Objectives

Part 1: Basic Router/Switch/PC Configuration

- Cable the network and clear previous device settings, as shown in the topology.
- Configure basic settings for routers.
- Configure PC host IP settings.
- Verify connectivity.
- Save the basic running configuration for each router and switch.

Part 2: Access the ASA Console and ASDM

- Access the ASA console.
- Clear the previous ASA configuration settings.
- Bypass Setup mode.
- Configure the ASA by using the CLI script.
- Access ASDM.

Part 3: Configuring Clientless SSL VPN Remote Access Using ASDM

- Start the VPN wizard.
- Configure the SSL VPN user interface.
- Configure AAA user authentication.
- Configure the VPN group policy.
- Configure a bookmark list (clientless connections only).
- Review the configuration summary and deliver the commands to the ASA.

- Verify the ASDM SSL VPN connection profile.
- Verify VPN access from the remote host.
- Access the web portal page.
- View the clientless remote user session using the ASDM Monitor.

Background / Scenario

In addition to stateful firewall and other security features, the ASA can provide both site-to-site and remote access VPN functionality. The ASA provides two main deployment modes that are found in Cisco SSL remote access VPN solutions:

- **Clientless SSL VPN**—Clientless, browser-based VPN that lets users establish a secure, remote-access VPN tunnel to the ASA using a web browser and built-in SSL to protect VPN traffic. After authentication, users are presented with a portal page and can access specific, predefined internal resources from the portal.

- **Client-Based SSL VPN**—Provides full-tunnel SSL VPN connection, but requires a VPN client application to be installed on the remote host. After authentication, users can access any internal resource as if they were physically on the local network. The ASA supports both SSL and IPsec client-based VPNs.

In Part 1 of this lab, you will configure the topology and non-ASA devices. In Part 2, you will prepare the ASA for ASDM access. In Part 3, you will use the ASDM VPN wizard to configure a clientless SSL remote access VPN and verify access using a remote PC with a browser.

Your company has two locations connected to an ISP. Router R1 represents a CPE device managed by the ISP. Router R2 represents an intermediate Internet router. Router R3 connects users at the remote branch office to the ISP. The ASA is an edge security device that connects the internal corporate network and DMZ to the ISP while providing NAT services to inside hosts.

Management has asked you to provide VPN access, using the ASA as a VPN concentrator, to teleworkers. They want you to test the clientless access model, using SSL and a browser for client access.

Note: The router commands and output in this lab are from a Cisco 1941 router with Cisco IOS Release 15.4(3)M2 (with a Security Technology Package license). Other routers and Cisco IOS versions can be used. See the Router Interface Summary Table at the end of the lab to determine which interface identifiers to use based on the equipment in the lab. Depending on the router model and Cisco IOS version, the commands available and output produced might vary from what is shown in this lab.

The ASA used with this lab is a Cisco model 5505 with an 8-port integrated switch, running OS version 9.2(3) and ASDM version 7.4(1) and comes with a Base license that allows a maximum of three VLANs.

Note: Before beginning, ensure that the routers and switches have been erased and have no startup configurations.

Required Resources

- 1 ASA 5505 (OS version 9.2(3) and ASDM version 7.4(1) and Base license or comparable)
- 3 routers (Cisco 1941 with Cisco IOS Release 15.4(3)M2 image with a Security Technology package license)
- 3 switches (Cisco 2960 or comparable) (not required)
- 3 PCs (Windows 7 or Windows 8.1, with SSH Client software installed)
- Serial and Ethernet cables, as shown in the topology
- Console cables to configure Cisco networking devices

Part 1: Basic Router/Switch/PC Configuration

In Part 1, you will set up the network topology and configure basic settings on the routers such as interface IP addresses and static routing.

Note: Do not configure any ASA settings at this time.

Step 1: Cable the network and clear previous device settings.

Attach the devices shown in the topology diagram and cable as necessary. Ensure that the routers and switches have been erased and have no startup configurations.

Step 2: Configure R1 using the CLI script.

a. In this step, you will use the following CLI script to configure basic settings on R1. Copy and paste the basic configuration script commands listed below. Observe the messages as the commands are applied to ensure that there are no warnings or errors.

Note: Depending on the router model, interfaces might be numbered differently than those listed. You might need to alter the designations accordingly.

Note: Passwords in this task are set to a minimum of 10 characters but are relatively simple for the benefit of performing the lab. More complex passwords are recommended in a production network.

```
hostname R1
security passwords min-length 10
enable algorithm-type scrypt secret cisco12345
username admin01 algorithm-type scrypt secret admin01pass
ip domain name ccnasecurity.com
line con 0
 login local
 exec-timeout 5 0
 logging synchronous
exit
line vty 0 4
 login local
 transport input ssh
 exec-timeout 5 0
 logging synchronous
exit
interface gigabitethernet 0/0
 ip address 209.165.200.225 255.255.255.248
 no shut
exit
int serial 0/0/0
 ip address 10.1.1.1 255.255.255.252
 clock rate 2000000
 no shut
exit
ip route 0.0.0.0 0.0.0.0 Serial0/0/0
```

```
crypto key generate rsa general-keys modulus 1024
```

Step 3: Configure R2 using the CLI script.

a. In this step, you will use the following CLI script to configure basic settings on R2. Copy and paste the basic configuration script commands listed below. Observe the messages as the commands are applied to ensure that there are no warnings or errors.

```
hostname R2
security passwords min-length 10
enable algorithm-type scrypt secret cisco12345
username admin01 algorithm-type scrypt secret admin01pass
ip domain name ccnasecurity.com
line con 0
 login local
 exec-timeout 5 0
 logging synchronous
exit
line vty 0 4
 login local
 transport input ssh
 exec-timeout 5 0
 logging synchronous
exit
interface serial 0/0/0
 ip address 10.1.1.2 255.255.255.252
 no shut
exit
interface serial 0/0/1
 ip address 10.2.2.2 255.255.255.252
 clock rate 2000000
 no shut
exit
ip route 209.165.200.224 255.255.255.248 Serial0/0/0
ip route 172.16.3.0 255.255.255.0 Serial0/0/1
crypto key generate rsa general-keys modulus 1024
```

Step 4: Configure R3 using the CLI script.

a. In this step, you will use the following CLI script to configure basic settings on R3. Copy and paste the basic configuration script commands listed below. Observe the messages as the commands are applied to ensure that there are no warnings or errors.

```
hostname R3
security passwords min-length 10
```

```
enable algorithm-type scrypt secret cisco12345
username admin01 algorithm-type scrypt secret admin01pass
ip domain name ccnasecurity.com
line con 0
 login local
 exec-timeout 5 0
 logging synchronous
exit
line vty 0 4
 login local
 transport input
 exec-timeout 5 0
 logging synchronous
exit
interface gigabitethernet 0/1
 ip address 172.16.3.1 255.255.255.0
 no shut
exit
int serial 0/0/1
 ip address 10.2.2.1 255.255.255.252
 no shut
exit
ip route 0.0.0.0 0.0.0.0 Serial0/0/1
crypto key generate rsa general-keys modulus 1024
```

Step 5: Configure PC host IP settings.

Configure a static IP address, subnet mask, and default gateway for PC-A, PC-B, and PC-C as shown in the IP Addressing table.

Step 6: Verify connectivity.

Because the ASA is the focal point for the network zones and it has not yet been configured, there will be no connectivity between devices that are connected to it. However, PC-C should be able to ping the R1 interface G0/0. From PC-C, ping the R1 G0/0 IP address (**209.165.200.225**). If these pings are unsuccessful, troubleshoot the basic device configurations before continuing.

Note: If you can ping from PC-C to R1 G0/0 and S0/0/0, you have demonstrated that static routing is configured and functioning correctly.

Step 7: Save the basic running configuration for each router and switch.

Part 2: Accessing the ASA Console and ASDM

Step 1: Clear the previous ASA configuration settings.

a. Use the **write erase** command to remove the **startup-config** file from flash memory.

   Note: The **erase startup-config** IOS command is not supported on the ASA.

b. Use the **reload** command to restart the ASA. This causes the ASA to display in CLI Setup mode. If you
    see the `System config has been modified. Save? [Y]es/[N]o:` message, type **n**, and press
    Enter.

Step 2: Bypass Setup mode.

When the ASA completes the reload process, it should detect that the startup configuration file is missing and
go into Setup mode. If it does not come up in this mode, repeat Step 2.

a. When prompted to preconfigure the firewall through interactive prompts (Setup mode), respond with **no**.

b. Enter privileged EXEC mode with the **enable** command. The password should be kept blank (no
    password).

Step 3: Configure the ASA by using the CLI script.

In this step, you will use a CLI script to configure basic settings, the firewall and DMZ.

a. Other than the defaults that the ASA automatically inserts use the **show run** command to confirm that
    there is no previous configuration in the ASA.

b. Enter global configuration mode. When prompted to enable anonymous call-home reporting, respond **no**.

c. Copy and paste the Pre-VPN Configuration Script commands listed below at the ASA global configuration
    mode prompt to start configuring the SSL VPNs.

    Observe the messages as the commands are applied to ensure that there are no warnings or errors. If
    prompted to replace the RSA key pair, respond **yes**.

```
hostname CCNAS-ASA
domain-name ccnasecurity.com
enable password cisco12345
!
interface Ethernet0/0
 switchport access vlan 2
 no shut
!
interface Ethernet0/1
 switchport access vlan 1
 no shut
!
interface Ethernet0/2
 switchport access vlan 3
 no shut
!
interface Vlan1
 nameif inside
 security-level 100
 ip address 192.168.1.1 255.255.255.0
!
interface Vlan2
 nameif outside
```

```
 security-level 0
 ip address 209.165.200.226 255.255.255.248
!
interface Vlan3
 no forward interface Vlan1
 nameif dmz
 security-level 70
 ip address 192.168.2.1 255.255.255.0
!
object network inside-net
 subnet 192.168.1.0 255.255.255.0
!
object network dmz-server
 host 192.168.2.3
!
access-list OUTSIDE-DMZ extended permit ip any host 192.168.2.3
!
object network inside-net
 nat (inside,outside) dynamic interface
!
object network dmz-server
 nat (dmz,outside) static 209.165.200.227
!
access-group OUTSIDE-DMZ in interface outside
!
route outside 0.0.0.0 0.0.0.0 209.165.200.225 1
!
username admin01 password admin01pass
!
aaa authentication telnet console LOCAL
aaa authentication ssh console LOCAL
aaa authentication http console LOCAL
!
http server enable
http 192.168.1.0 255.255.255.0 inside
ssh 192.168.1.0 255.255.255.0 inside
telnet 192.168.1.0 255.255.255.0 inside
telnet timeout 10
ssh timeout 10
!
class-map inspection_default
 match default-inspection-traffic
policy-map global_policy
 class inspection_default
```

```
    inspect icmp
!
crypto key generate rsa modulus 1024
```

d. At the privileged EXEC mode prompt, issue the **write mem** (or **copy run start**) command to save the running configuration to the startup configuration and the RSA keys to non-volatile memory.

Step 4: Access ASDM.

a. Open a browser on PC-B and test the HTTPS access to the ASA by entering **https://192.168.1.1**. After entering the https://192.168.1.1 URL, you should see a security warning about the website security certificate. Click **Continue to this website**. Click **Yes** for any other security warnings.

Note: Specify the HTTPS protocol in the URL.

b. At the ASDM welcome page, click **Run ASDM**. The ASDM-IDM Launcher will display.

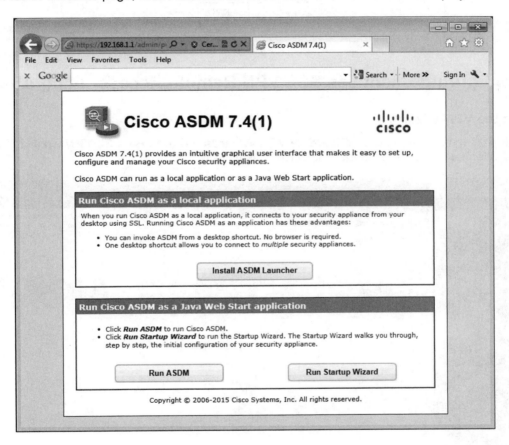

c.   Log in as user **admin01** with password **admin01pass**.

Part 3: Configuring Clientless SSL VPN Remote Access Using ASDM

Step 1: Start the VPN wizard.

a.   On the ASDM main menu, click **Wizards** > **VPN Wizards** > **Clientless SSL VPN wizard**. The SSL VPN wizard Clientless SSL VPN Connection screen displays.

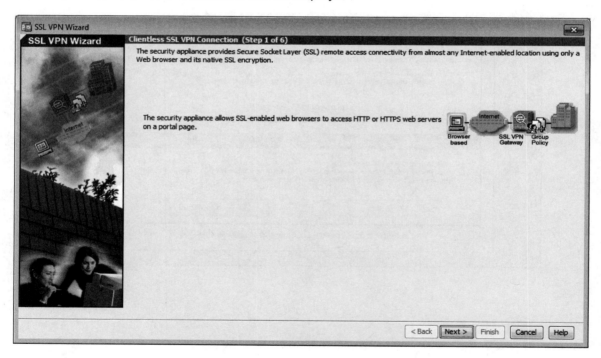

b.   Review the on-screen text and topology diagram, and then click **Next** to continue.

Step 2: Configure the SSL VPN user interface.

a. On the SSL VPN Interface screen, configure **SSL-VPN** as the Connection Profile Name, and specify **outside** as the interface to which outside users will connect.

Note: By default, the ASA uses a self-signed certificate to send to the client for authentication. Optionally, the ASA may be configured to use a third-party certificate that is purchased from a well-known certificate authority, such as VeriSign, to connect clients. In the event that a certificate is purchased, it may be selected in the Digital Certificate drop-down menu.

The SSL VPN Interface screen provides links in the Information section. These links identify the URLs that need to be used for the SSL VPN service access (log in) and for Cisco ASDM access (to access the Cisco ASDM software).

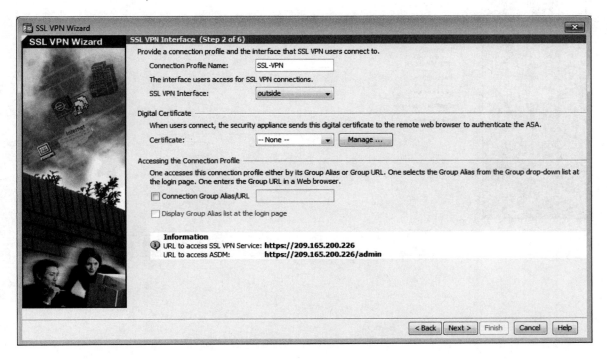

b. Click **Next** to continue.

Step 3: Configure AAA user authentication.

a. On the User Authentication screen, click **Authenticate using the local user database**.

b. Enter the user name **SSL-VPN-USER** with password **cisco12345**.

c. Click **Add** to create the new user and click **Next** to continue.

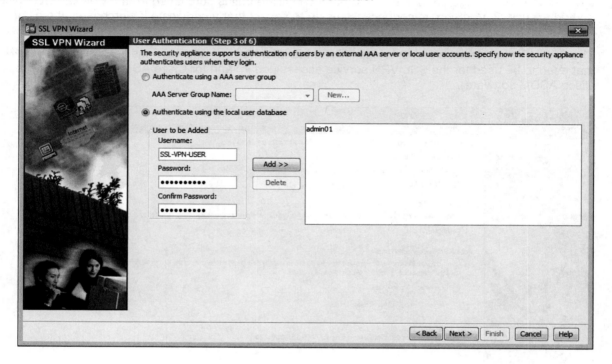

Step 4: Configure the VPN group policy.

a. On the Group Policy screen, create a new group policy named **SSL-VPN-POLICY**. (When configuring a new policy, the policy name cannot contain any spaces.)

Note: By default, the created user group policy inherits its settings from the DfltGrpPolicy. These settings may be modified after the wizard has been completed by navigating to the **Configuration** > **Remote Access VPN** > **Clientless SSL VPN Access** > **Group Policies** submenu.

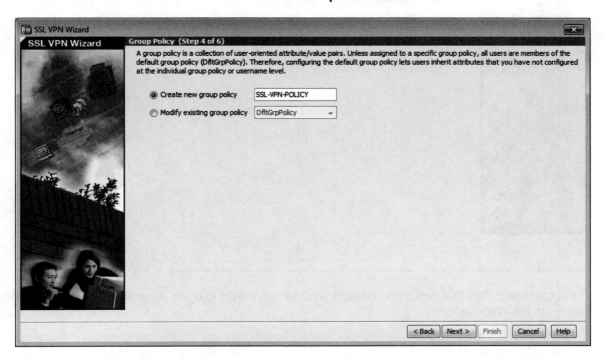

b. Click **Next** to continue.

Step 5: Configure the bookmark list (clientless connections only).

A bookmark list is a set of URLs configured to be used in the clientless SSL VPN web portal. If there are bookmarks already listed, use the **Bookmark List** drop-down list, select the bookmark of choice, and click **Next** to continue with the SSL VPN wizard.

Note: There are no configured bookmark lists by default and, therefore, they must be configured by the network administrator.

a. On the Clientless Connections Only – Bookmark List screen, click **Manage** to create an HTTP server bookmark in the bookmark list.

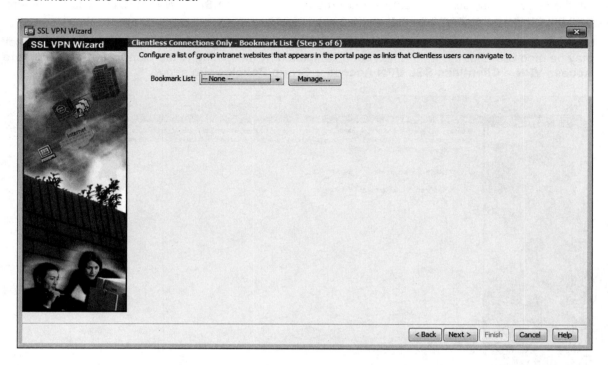

b. In the Configure GUI Customization Objects window, click **Add** to open the Add Bookmark List window. Name the list **Web-Server**.

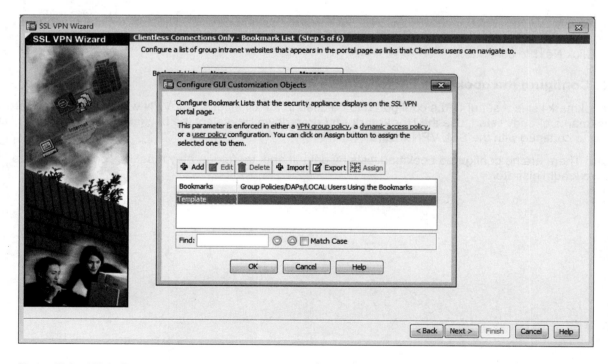

Note: If the Web-Server bookmark list is shown as available from a previous configuration, you can delete it in ASDM and re-create it.

c.   In the Add Bookmark List window, click **Add** to open the Select Bookmark Type window.

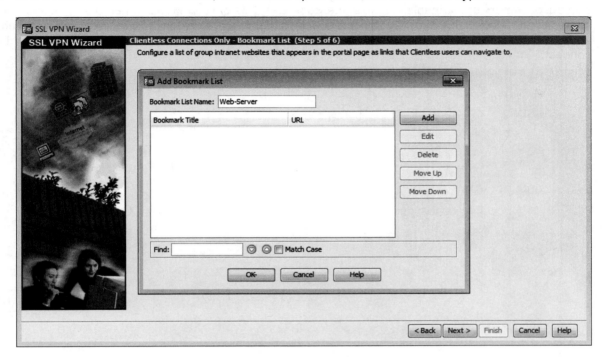

d.   As shown in the figure, the ASDM can create three types of bookmarks. Select the URL with GET or POST method, click **OK.**

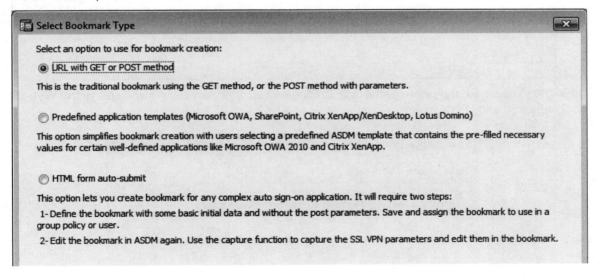

e. Enter the bookmark title and enter the server destination IP address or hostname as the URL to be used with the bookmark entry. In this example, the Bookmark Title of **Web-Mail** is entered and an internal IP address of **192.168.2.3** (the DMZ server) is specified. If this server has HTTP web services with web mail installed and functional, the outside users are able to access the server from the ASA portal when they connect.

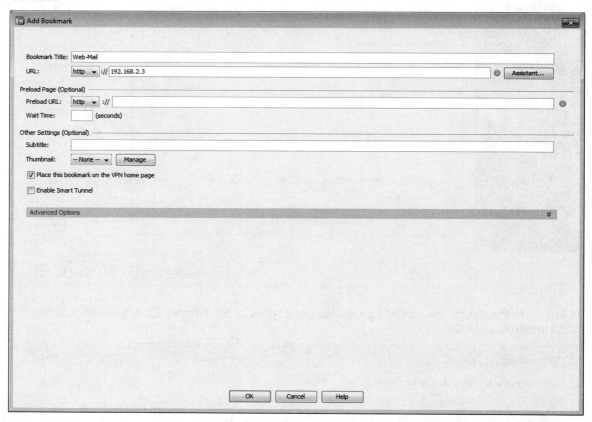

f. Click **OK** to continue and return to the Add Bookmark List window which now displays the Web-Server bookmark title and URL.

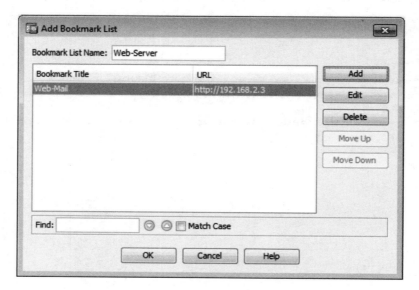

g. Click **OK** to continue and return to the Configure GUI Customization Objects window which now displays the Web-Server bookmark.

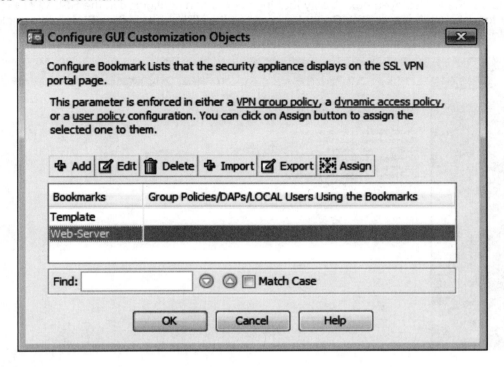

h. Click **OK** to continue and return to the Bookmark List window and click **Next** to continue.

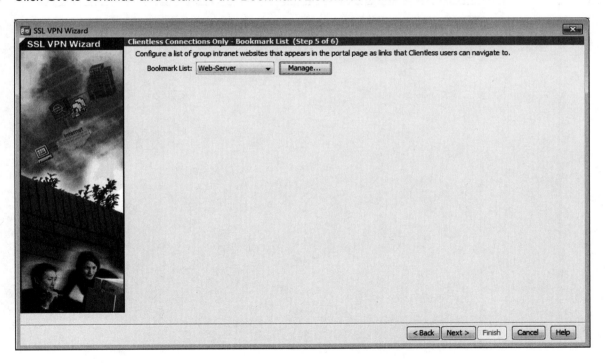

Step 6: Review the configuration summary and deliver the commands to the ASA.

The Summary page is displayed next. Verify that the information configured in the SSL VPN wizard is correct. Click **Back** to make changes, or click **Cancel** and restart the VPN wizard. Click **Finish** to complete the process and deliver the commands to the ASA.

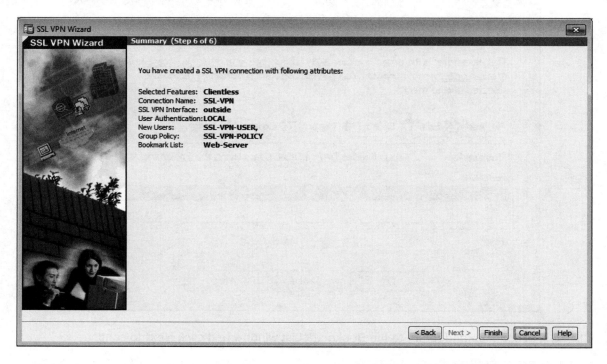

Step 7: Verify the ASDM SSL VPN connection profile.

In ASDM, click **Configuration** > **Remote Access VPN** > **Clientless SSL VPN Access** > **Connection Profiles**. In this window, the VPN configuration can be verified and edited.

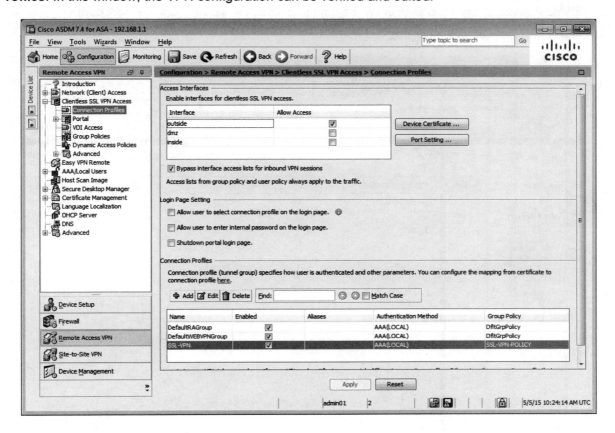

Step 8: Verify VPN access from the remote host.

a. Open the browser on PC-C and enter the login URL for the SSL VPN into the address field (**https://209.165.200.226**). Use secure HTTP (HTTPS) because SSL is required to connect to the ASA.

b. The Logon window should display. Enter the previously configured username **SSL-VPN-USER** and password **cisco12345,** and click **Logon** to continue.

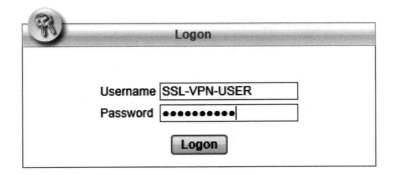

Step 9: Access the web portal window.

After the user authenticates, the ASA SSL web portal page lists the various bookmarks previously assigned to the profile. If the Bookmark points to a valid server IP address or hostname that has HTTP web services installed and functional, the outside user will be able to access the server from the ASA portal.

Note: In this lab, the web mail server is not installed.

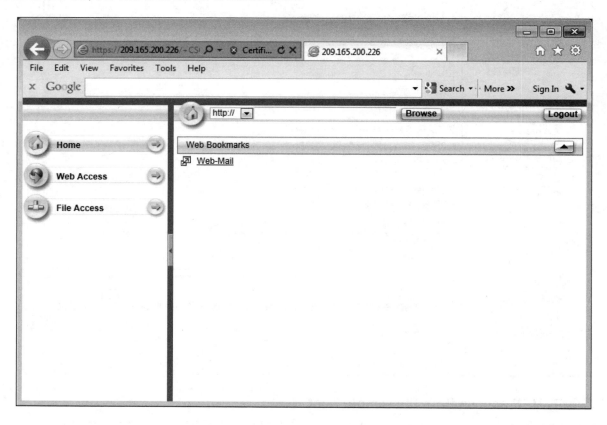

Step 10: View the clientless remote user session using the ASDM Monitor.

While the remote user at PC-C is still logged in and on the ASA portal page, you can view the session statistics using ASDM monitor.

From the ASDM menu bar on PC-B, click **Monitoring** and then select **VPN** > **VPN Statistics** > **Sessions**. Click the **Filter By** pull-down list and select **Clientless SSL VPN**. You should see the SSL-VPN-USER session logged in from PC-C (172.16.3.3).

Note: You may need to click **Refresh** to display the remote user session.

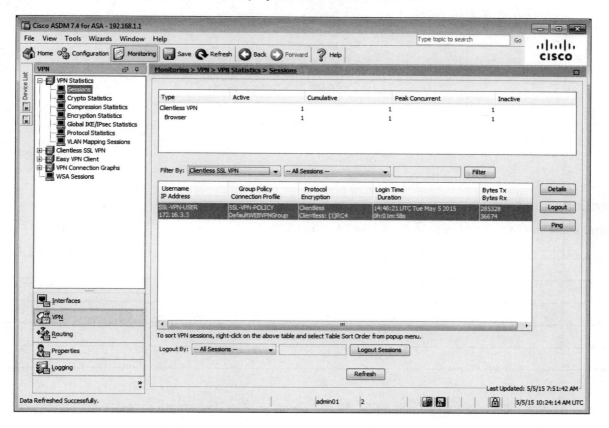

Step 11: Log out of the web portal page.

The user should log out of the web portal window on PC-C using the **Logout** button when done (See Step 10). However, the web portal will also time out if there is no activity. In either case a logout window will be displayed informing users that for additional security, they should clear the browser cache, delete the downloaded files, and close the browser window.

Reflection

1. What are some benefits of clientless vs. client-based VPNs?

   _____

   _____

   _____

   _____

   _____

   _____

2. What are some differences when using SSL as compared to IPsec for remote access tunnel encryption?

   _____

   _____

   _____

   _____

   _____

   _____

Router Interface Summary Table

Router Interface Summary				
Router Model	**Ethernet Interface #1**	**Ethernet Interface #2**	**Serial Interface #1**	**Serial Interface #2**
1800	Fast Ethernet 0/0 (F0/0)	Fast Ethernet 0/1 (F0/1)	Serial 0/0/0 (S0/0/0)	Serial 0/0/1 (S0/0/1)
1900	Gigabit Ethernet 0/0 (G0/0)	Gigabit Ethernet 0/1 (G0/1)	Serial 0/0/0 (S0/0/0)	Serial 0/0/1 (S0/0/1)
2801	Fast Ethernet 0/0 (F0/0)	Fast Ethernet 0/1 (F0/1)	Serial 0/1/0 (S0/1/0)	Serial 0/1/1 (S0/1/1)
2811	Fast Ethernet 0/0 (F0/0)	Fast Ethernet 0/1 (F0/1)	Serial 0/0/0 (S0/0/0)	Serial 0/0/1 (S0/0/1)
2900	Gigabit Ethernet 0/0 (G0/0)	Gigabit Ethernet 0/1 (G0/1)	Serial 0/0/0 (S0/0/0)	Serial 0/0/1 (S0/0/1)

Note: To find out how the router is configured, look at the interfaces to identify the type of router and how many interfaces the router has. There is no way to effectively list all the combinations of configurations for each router class. This table includes identifiers for the possible combinations of Ethernet and Serial interfaces in the device. The table does not include any other type of interface, even though a specific router may contain one. An example of this might be an ISDN BRI interface. The string in parenthesis is the legal abbreviation that can be used in Cisco IOS commands to represent the interface.

Lab D 10.3.1.2 – Configure AnyConnect Remote Access SSL VPN Using ASDM

Topology

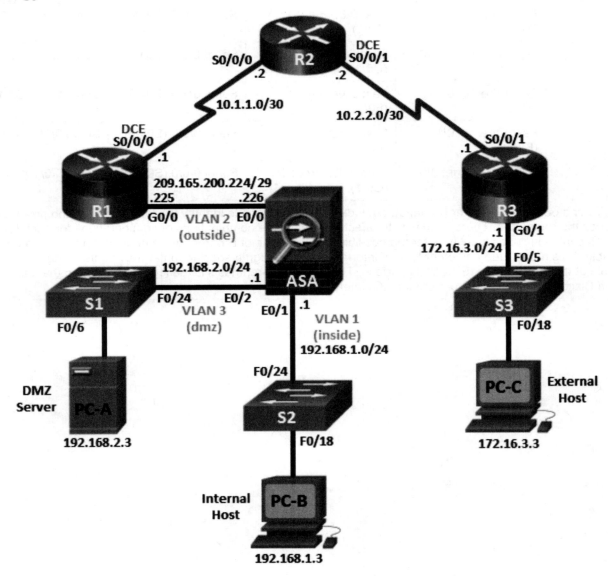

Note: ISR G1 devices use FastEthernet interfaces instead of GigabitEthernet interfaces.

IP Addressing Table

Device	Interface	IP Address	Subnet Mask	Default Gateway	Switch Port
R1	G0/0	209.165.200.225	255.255.255.248	N/A	ASA E0/0
	S0/0/0 (DCE)	10.1.1.1	255.255.255.252	N/A	N/A
R2	S0/0/0	10.1.1.2	255.255.255.252	N/A	N/A
	S0/0/1 (DCE)	10.2.2.2	255.255.255.252	N/A	N/A
R3	G0/1	172.16.3.1	255.255.255.0	N/A	S3 F0/5
	S0/0/1	10.2.2.1	255.255.255.252	N/A	N/A
ASA	VLAN 1 (E0/1)	192.168.1.1	255.255.255.0	NA	S2 F0/24
	VLAN 2 (E0/0)	209.165.200.226	255.255.255.248	NA	R1 G0/0
	VLAN 3 (E0/2)	192.168.2.1	255.255.255.0	NA	S1 F0/24
PC-A	NIC	192.168.2.3	255.255.255.0	192.168.2.1	S1 F0/6
PC-B	NIC	192.168.1.3	255.255.255.0	192.168.1.1	S2 F0/18
PC-C	NIC	172.16.3.3	255.255.255.0	172.16.3.1	S3 F0/18

Objectives

Part 1: Basic Router/Switch/PC Configuration

- Cable the network and clear previous device settings, as shown in the topology.
- Configure basic settings for routers.
- Configure PC host IP settings.
- Verify connectivity.
- Save the basic running configuration for each router and switch.

Part 2: Access the ASA Console and ASDM

- Access the ASA console.
- Clear the previous ASA configuration settings.
- Bypass Setup mode.
- Configure the ASA by using the CLI script.
- Access ASDM.

Part 3: Configuring AnyConnect Client SSL VPN Remote Access Using ASDM

- Start the VPN wizard.
- Specify the VPN encryption protocol.
- Specify the client image to upload to AnyConnect users.
- Configure AAA local authentication.
- Configure the client address assignment.

- Configure the network name resolution.
- Exempt address translation for VPN traffic.
- Review the AnyConnect client deployment details.
- Review the Summary screen and apply the configuration to the ASA.

Part 4: Connecting to an AnyConnect SSL VPN

- Verify the AnyConnect client profile.
- Log in from the remote host.
- Perform platform detection (if required).
- Perform an automatic installation of the AnyConnect VPN Client (if required).
- Manually install the AnyConnect VPN Client (if required).
- Confirm VPN connectivity.

Background/Scenario

In addition to stateful firewall and other security features, the ASA can provide both site-to-site and remote access VPN functionality. The ASA provides two main deployment modes that are found in Cisco SSL remote access VPN solutions:

- **Clientless SSL VPN -** A clientless, browser-based VPN that lets users establish a secure, remote-access VPN tunnel to the ASA and use a web browser and built-in SSL to protect VPN traffic. After authentication, users are presented with a portal page and can access specific, predefined internal resources from the portal.

- **Client-Based SSL VPN -** A client-based VPN that provides full-tunnel SSL VPN connection, but requires a VPN client application to be installed on the remote host. After authentication, users can access any internal resource as if they were physically on the local network. The ASA supports both SSL and IPsec client-based VPNs.

In Part 1 of this lab, you will configure the topology and non-ASA devices. In Part 2, you will prepare the ASA for ASDM access. In Part 3, you will use the ASDM VPN wizard to configure an AnyConnect client-based SSL remote access VPN. In Part 4 you will establish a connection and verify connectivity.

Your company has two locations connected to an ISP. R1 represents a CPE device managed by the ISP. R2 represents an intermediate Internet router. R3 connects users at the remote branch office to the ISP. The ASA is an edge security device that connects the internal corporate network and DMZ to the ISP while providing NAT services to inside hosts.

Management has asked you to provide VPN access to teleworkers using the ASA as a VPN concentrator. They want you to test the client-based model using SSL and the Cisco AnyConnect client.

Note: The router commands and output in this lab are from a Cisco 1941 router with Cisco IOS Release 15.4(3)M2 (with a Security Technology Package license). Other routers and Cisco IOS versions can be used. See the Router Interface Summary Table at the end of the lab to determine which interface identifiers to use based on the equipment in the lab. Depending on the router model and Cisco IOS version, the commands available and the output produced might vary from what is shown in this lab.

The ASA used with this lab is a Cisco model 5505 with an 8-port integrated switch, running OS version 9.2(3) and ASDM version 7.4(1) and comes with a Base license that allows a maximum of three VLANs.

Note: Before beginning, ensure that the routers and switches have been erased and have no startup configurations.

Required Resources

- 1 ASA 5505 (OS version 9.2(3) and ASDM version 7.4(1) and Base license or comparable)
- 3 routers (Cisco 1941 with Cisco IOS Release 15.4(3)M2 image with a Security Technology package license)
- 3 switches (Cisco 2960 or comparable) (not required)
- 3 PCs (Windows 7 or Windows 8.1, with SSH client software installed)
- Serial and Ethernet cables, as shown in the topology
- Console cables to configure Cisco networking devices

Part 1: Basic Router/Switch/PC Configuration

In Part 1, you will set up the network topology and configure basic settings on the routers such as interface IP addresses and static routing.

Note: Do not configure any ASA settings at this time.

Step 1: Cable the network and clear previous device settings.

Attach the devices shown in the topology diagram and cable as necessary. Ensure that the routers and switches have been erased and have no startup configurations.

Step 2: Configure R1 using the CLI script.

In this step, you will use the following CLI script to configure basic settings on R1. Copy and paste the basic configuration script commands listed below. Observe the messages as the commands are applied to ensure that there are no warnings or errors.

Note: Depending on the router model, interfaces might be numbered differently than those listed. You might need to alter the designations accordingly.

Note: Passwords in this task are set to a minimum of 10 characters and are relatively simple for the purposes of performing the lab. More complex passwords are recommended in a production network.

```
hostname R1
security passwords min-length 10
enable algorithm-type scrypt secret cisco12345
username admin01 algorithm-type scrypt secret admin01pass
ip domain name ccnasecurity.com
line con 0
 login local
 exec-timeout 5 0
 logging synchronous
exit
line vty 0 4
 login local
 transport input ssh
 exec-timeout 5 0
 logging synchronous
exit
```

```
interface gigabitethernet 0/0
 ip address 209.165.200.225 255.255.255.248
 no shut
exit
int serial 0/0/0
 ip address 10.1.1.1 255.255.255.252
 clock rate 2000000
 no shut
exit
ip route 0.0.0.0 0.0.0.0 Serial0/0/0
crypto key generate rsa general-keys modulus 1024
```

Step 3: Configure R2 using the CLI script.

In this step, you will use the following CLI script to configure basic settings on R2. Copy and paste the basic configuration script commands listed below. Observe the messages as the commands are applied to ensure that there are no warnings or errors.

```
hostname R2
security passwords min-length 10
enable algorithm-type scrypt secret cisco12345
username admin01 algorithm-type scrypt secret admin01pass
ip domain name ccnasecurity.com
line con 0
 login local
 exec-timeout 5 0
 logging synchronous
exit
line vty 0 4
 login local
 transport input ssh
 exec-timeout 5 0
 logging synchronous
exit
interface serial 0/0/0
 ip address 10.1.1.2 255.255.255.252
 no shut
exit
interface serial 0/0/1
 ip address 10.2.2.2 255.255.255.252
 clock rate 2000000
 no shut
exit
ip route 209.165.200.224 255.255.255.248 Serial0/0/0
ip route 172.16.3.0 255.255.255.0 Serial0/0/1
```

```
crypto key generate rsa general-keys modulus 1024
```

Step 4: Configure R3 using the CLI script.

In this step, you will use the following CLI script to configure basic settings on R3. Copy and paste the basic configuration script commands listed below. Observe the messages as the commands are applied to ensure that there are no warnings or errors.

```
hostname R3
security passwords min-length 10
enable algorithm-type scrypt secret cisco12345
username admin01 algorithm-type scrypt secret admin01pass
ip domain name ccnasecurity.com
line con 0
 login local
 exec-timeout 5 0
 logging synchronous
exit
line vty 0 4
 login local
 transport input ssh
 exec-timeout 5 0
 logging synchronous
exit
interface gigabitethernet 0/1
 ip address 172.16.3.1 255.255.255.0
 no shut
exit
int serial 0/0/1
 ip address 10.2.2.1 255.255.255.252
 no shut
exit
ip route 0.0.0.0 0.0.0.0 Serial0/0/1
crypto key generate rsa general-keys modulus 1024
```

Step 5: Configure PC host IP settings.

Configure a static IP address, subnet mask, and default gateway for PC-A, PC-B, and PC-C as shown in the IP Addressing table.

Step 6: Verify connectivity.

The ASA is the focal point for the network zones, and it has not yet been configured. Therefore, there will be no connectivity between devices that are connected to it. However, PC-C should be able to ping the R1 interface G0/0. From PC-C, ping the R1 G0/0 IP address (**209.165.200.225**). If these pings are unsuccessful, troubleshoot the basic device configurations before continuing.

Note: If you can ping from PC-C to R1 G0/0 and S0/0/0, you have demonstrated that static routing is configured and functioning correctly.

Step 7: Save the basic running configuration for each router and switch.

Part 2: Accessing the ASA Console and ASDM

Step 1: Clear the previous ASA configuration settings.

   a.   Use the **write erase** command to remove the **startup-config** file from flash memory.

       Note: The **erase startup-config** IOS command is not supported on the ASA.

   b.   Use the **reload** command to restart the ASA. This causes the ASA to display in CLI Setup mode. If you see the **System config has been modified. Save? [Y]es/[N]o:** message, type **n**, and press **Enter**.

Step 2: Bypass Setup mode.

When the ASA completes the reload process, it should detect that the startup configuration file is missing and go into Setup mode. If it does not go into Setup mode, repeat Step 2.

   a.   When prompted to preconfigure the firewall through interactive prompts (Setup mode), respond with **no**.

   b.   Enter privileged EXEC mode with the **enable** command. The password should be kept blank (no password).

Step 3: Configure the ASA by using the CLI script.

In this step, you will use a CLI script to configure basic settings, the firewall, and the DMZ.

   a.   Use the **show run** command to confirm that there is no previous configuration in the ASA other than the defaults that the ASA automatically inserts.

   b.   Enter global configuration mode. When prompted to enable anonymous call-home reporting, respond **no**.

   c.   Copy and paste the Pre-VPN Configuration Script commands listed below at the ASA global configuration mode prompt to start configuring the SSL VPNs.

       Observe the messages as the commands are applied to ensure that there are no warnings or errors. If prompted to replace the RSA key pair, respond **yes**.

```
hostname CCNAS-ASA
domain-name ccnasecurity.com
enable password cisco12345
!
interface Ethernet0/0
 switchport access vlan 2
 no shut
!
interface Ethernet0/1
 switchport access vlan 1
 no shut
!
interface Ethernet0/2
 switchport access vlan 3
```

```
 no shut
!
interface Vlan1
 nameif inside
 security-level 100
 ip address 192.168.1.1 255.255.255.0
!
interface Vlan2
 nameif outside
 security-level 0
 ip address 209.165.200.226 255.255.255.248
!
interface Vlan3
 no forward interface Vlan1
 nameif dmz
 security-level 70
 ip address 192.168.2.1 255.255.255.0
!
object network inside-net
 subnet 192.168.1.0 255.255.255.0
!
object network dmz-server
 host 192.168.2.3
!
access-list OUTSIDE-DMZ extended permit ip any host 192.168.2.3
!
object network inside-net
 nat (inside,outside) dynamic interface
!
object network dmz-server
 nat (dmz,outside) static 209.165.200.227
!
access-group OUTSIDE-DMZ in interface outside
!
route outside 0.0.0.0 0.0.0.0 209.165.200.225 1
!
username admin01 password admin01pass
!
aaa authentication telnet console LOCAL
aaa authentication ssh console LOCAL
aaa authentication http console LOCAL
!
http server enable
http 192.168.1.0 255.255.255.0 inside
```

```
ssh 192.168.1.0 255.255.255.0 inside
telnet 192.168.1.0 255.255.255.0 inside
telnet timeout 10
ssh timeout 10
!
class-map inspection_default
 match default-inspection-traffic
policy-map global_policy
 class inspection_default
    inspect icmp
!
crypto key generate rsa modulus 1024
```

d. At the privileged EXEC mode prompt, issue the **write mem** (or **copy run start**) command to save the running configuration to the startup configuration and the RSA keys to non-volatile memory.

Step 4: Access ASDM.

a. Open a browser on PC-B and test the HTTPS access to the ASA by entering **https://192.168.1.1**. After entering the https://192.168.1.1 URL, you should see a security warning about the website security certificate. Click **Continue to this website**. Click **Yes** for any other security warnings.

Note: Specify the HTTPS protocol in the URL.

b. At the ASDM welcome page, click **Run ASDM**. The ASDM-IDM Launcher will display.

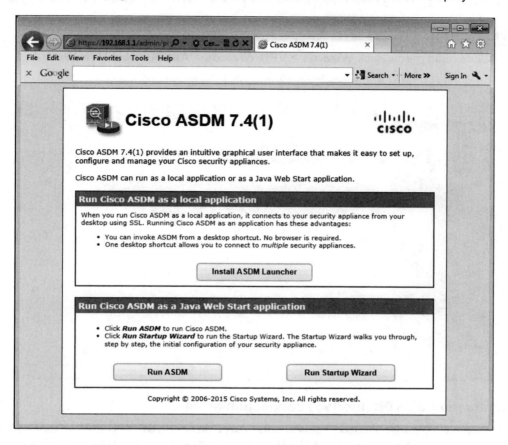

c. Log in as user **admin01** with the password **admin01pass**.

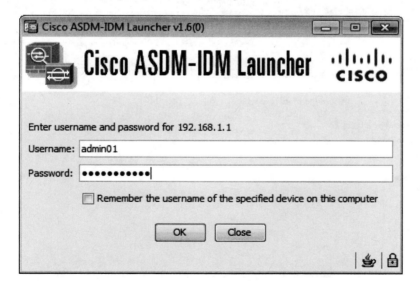

Part 3: Configuring AnyConnect SSL VPN Remote Access Using ASDM

Step 1: Start the VPN wizard.

a. On the ASDM main menu, click **Wizards** > **VPN Wizards** > **AnyConnect VPN Wizard**.

b. Review the on-screen text and topology diagram. Click **Next** to continue.

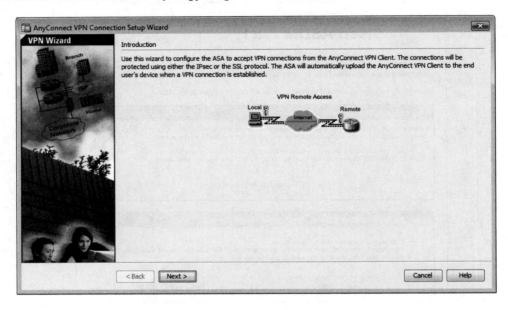

Step 2: Configure the SSL VPN interface connection profile.

On the Connection Profile Identification screen, enter **AnyConnect-SSL-VPN** as the Connection Profile Name and specify the **outside** interface as the VPN Access Interface. Click **Next** to continue.

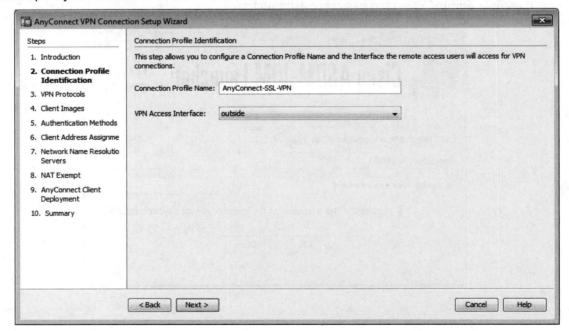

Step 3: Specify the VPN encryption protocol.

On the VPN Protocols screen, uncheck the **IPsec** check box and leave the **SSL** check box checked. Do not specify a device certificate. Click **Next** to continue.

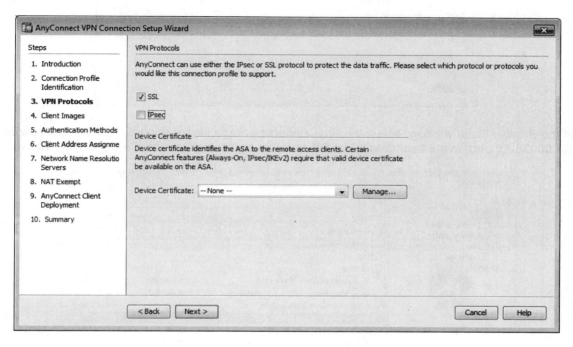

Step 4: Specify the client image to upload to AnyConnect users.

a.   On the Client Images screen, click **Add** to specify the AnyConnect client image filename.

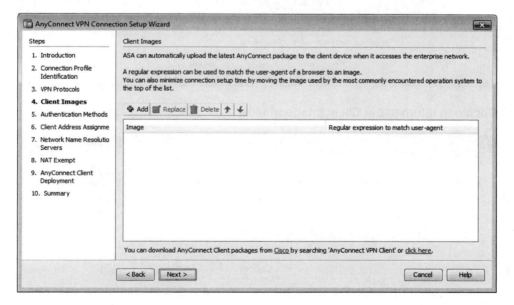

b. In the Add AnyConnect Client Image window, click **Browse Flash**.

c. In the Browse Flash window, select the AnyConnect package file for Windows (**anyconnect-win-4.1.00028-k9.pkg**, in the example). Click **OK** to return to the AnyConnect Client Image window.

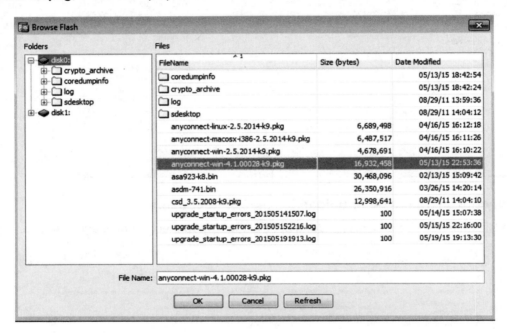

d. Click **OK** again to return to the Client Image window.

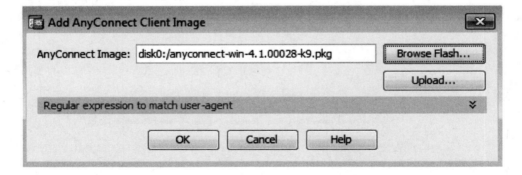

e. The selected image is now displayed on the Client Image window. Click **Next** to continue.

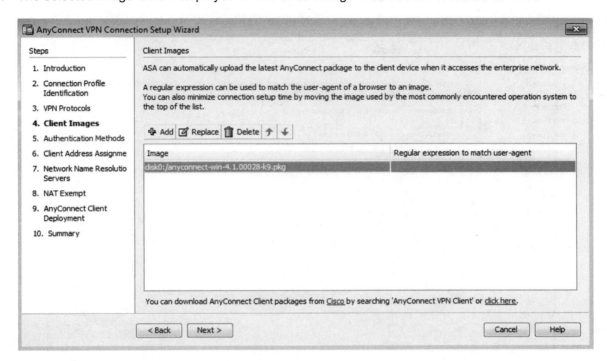

Step 5: Configure AAA local authentication.

a. On the Authentication Methods screen, ensure that the AAA Server Group is specified as **LOCAL**.

b. Enter a new user named **REMOTE-USER** with the password **cisco12345**. Click **Add**.

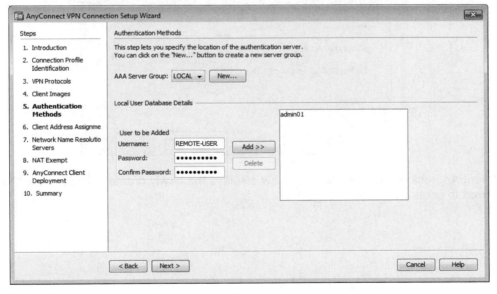

c. Click **Next** to continue.

Step 6: Configure the client address assignment.

a. In the Client Address Assignment window, click **New** to create an IPv4 address pool.

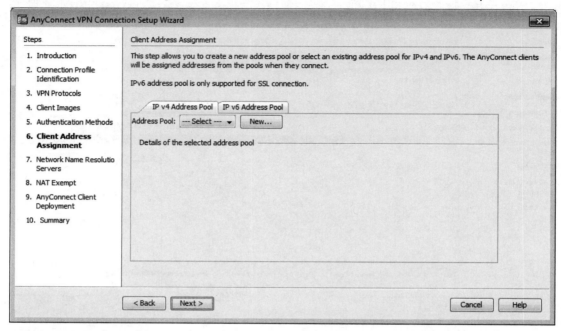

b. In the Add IPv4 Pool window, name the pool **Remote-Pool** with a starting IP address of **192.168.1.100**, an ending IP address of **192.168.1.125**, and a subnet mask of **255.255.255.0**. Click **OK** to return to the Client Address Assignment window, which now displays the newly created remote user IP address pool.

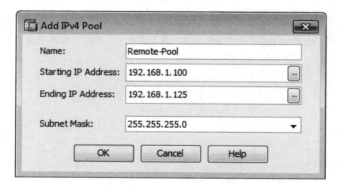

c. The Client Address Assignment window now displays the newly created remote user IP address pool. Click **Next** to continue.

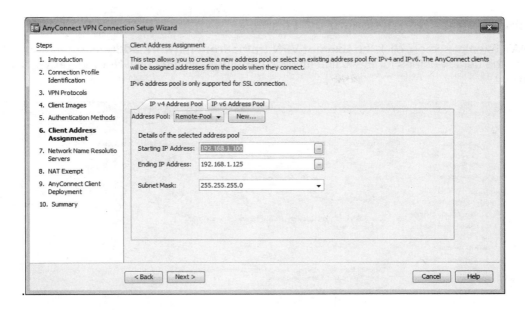

Step 7: Configure the network name resolution.

On the Network Name Resolution Servers screen, enter the IP address of a DNS server (**192.168.2.3**). Leave the current domain name as **ccnasecurity.com**. Click **Next** to continue.

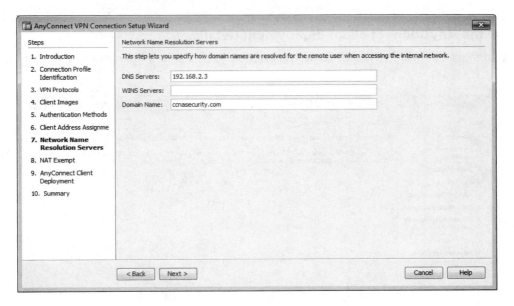

Step 8: Exempt address translation for VPN traffic.

On the NAT Exempt screen, click the **Exempt VPN traffic from network address translation** check box. Do not change the default entries for the Inside Interface (**inside**) and the Local Network (**any4**). Click **Next** to continue.

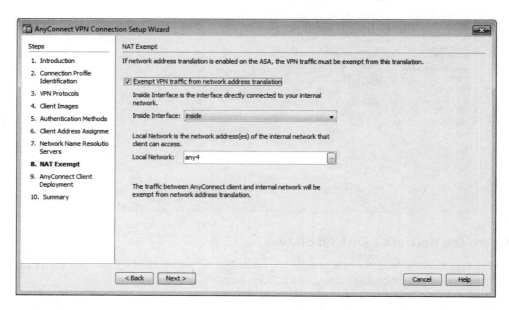

Step 9: Review the AnyConnect client deployment details.

On the AnyConnect Client Deployment screen, read the text describing the options, and then click **Next** to continue.

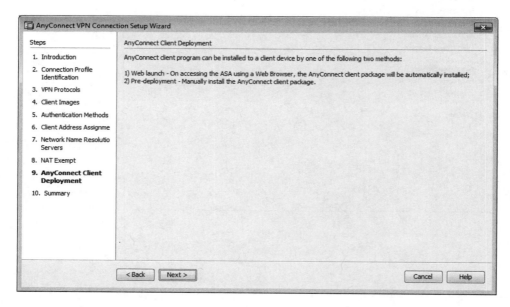

Step 10: Review the Summary screen and apply the configuration to the ASA.

On the Summary screen, review the configuration description and then click **Finish**.

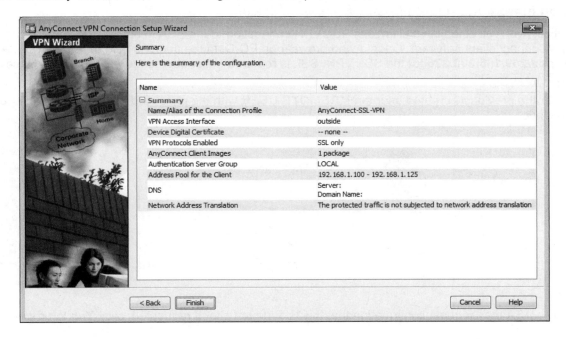

Step 11: Verify the AnyConnect client profile.

After the configuration is delivered to the ASA, the AnyConnect Connection Profiles screen displays.

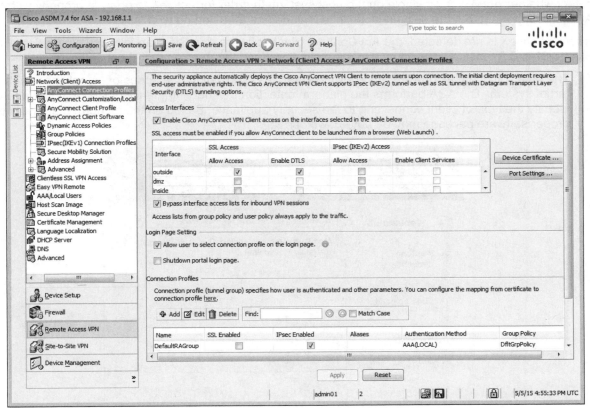

Part 4: Connecting to an AnyConnect SSL VPN

Step 1: Log in from the remote host.

a. Initially, you will establish a clientless SSL VPN connection to the ASA in order to download the AnyConnect client software. Open a web browser on PC-C. In the address field of the browser, enter **https://209.165.200.226** for the SSL VPN. SSL is required to connect to the ASA, therefore, use secure HTTP (HTTPS).

b. Enter the previously created username **REMOTE-USER** with the password **cisco12345**. Click **Logon** to continue.

Note: The ASA may request confirmation that this is a trusted site. If requested, click **Yes** to proceed.

Step 2: Perform platform detection (if required).

If the AnyConnect client must be downloaded, a security warning will display on the remote host. The ASA will detect whether ActiveX is available on the host system. In order for ActiveX to operate properly with the Cisco ASA, it is important that the security appliance is added as a trusted network site.

Note: If ActiveX is not detected, the AnyConnect client software must be manually downloaded and installed. Skip to **Step 3** for instructions on how to manually download the AnyConnect client software.

a. The ASA will begin a software auto-download process consisting of a series of compliance checks for the target system. The ASA performs the platform detection by querying the client system in an attempt to identify the type of client connecting to the security appliance. Based on the platform that is identified, the proper software package may be auto-downloaded.

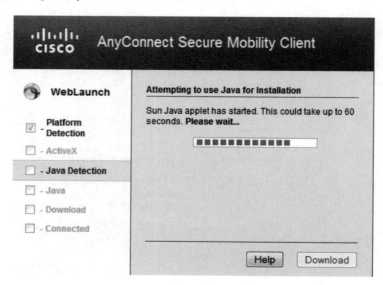

b. If you are presented with the AnyConnect Downloader window that indicates the 209.165.200.226
    AnyConnect server could not be verified, click the **Change Setting** button.

c. The AnyConnect Downloader will present a verification window to change the setting that blocks
    untrusted connections. Click **Apply Change**.

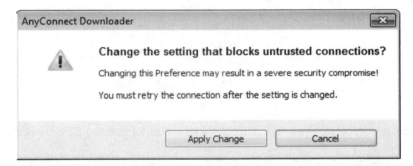

d. If you receive the Security Waning: Untrusted Server Certificate message, Click **Connect Anyway**.

e. The AnyConnect Secure Mobility Client Downloader window counts down the download time.

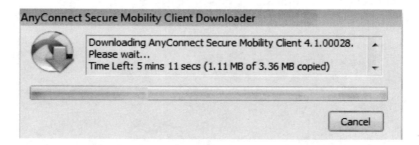

f. After the download is complete, the software will automatically start to install. Click **Yes** when asked to allow the program to make changes to the computer.

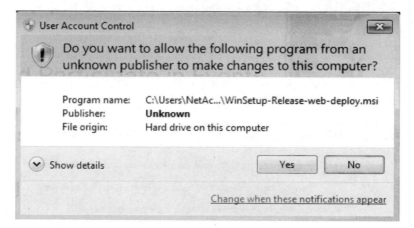

g. When installation is complete, the AnyConnect client will establish the SSL VPN connection.

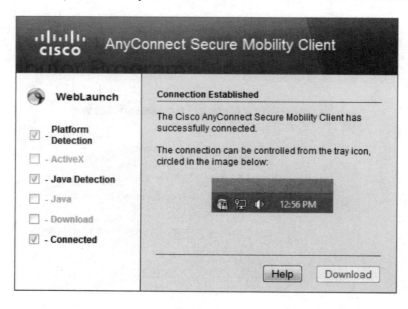

h. If the Connected option in the panel on the left is checked, skip to **Step 5**. If the Connect option is not checked, continue to **Step 3**.

Step 3: Install the AnyConnect VPN Client (if required).

If ActiveX is not detected, the AnyConnect client software must be manually downloaded and installed.

a. On the Manual Installation screen, click **Windows 7/Vista/64/XP**.

b. Click **Run** to install the AnyConnect VPN client.

c. After the download is complete, the Cisco AnyConnect VPN Client Setup starts. Click **Next** to continue.

d. Read the End-User License Agreement. Select **I accept the terms in the License Agreement** and click **Next** to continue.

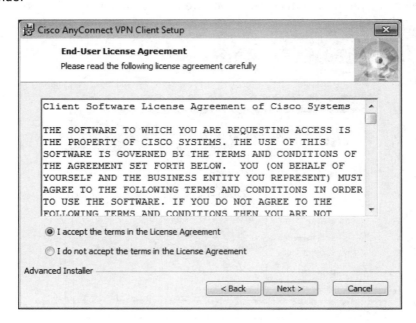

e. The Ready to Install window is displayed. Click **Install** to continue.

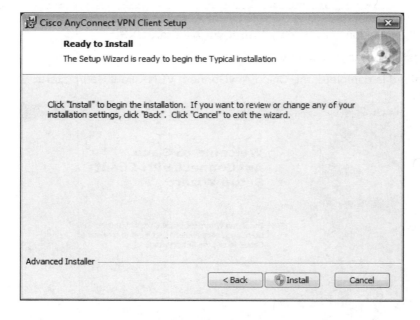

Note: If a security warning is displayed, click **Yes** to continue.

f. Click **Finish** to complete the installation.

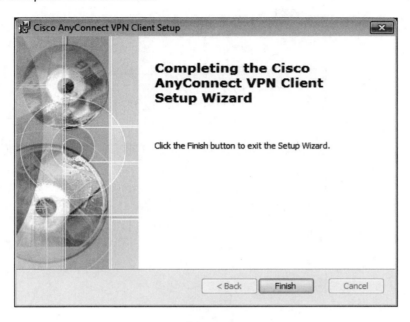

Step 4: Establish an AnyConnect SSL VPN Connection.

a. When the AnyConnect VPN client has been installed, manually start the program by clicking **Start** > **Cisco AnyConnect VPN Client**.

b. When prompted to enter the secure gateway address, enter **209.165.200.226** in the Connect to field, and click **Select**.

Note: If a security warning is displayed, click **Yes** to proceed.

c. When prompted, enter **REMOTE-USER** for the username and **cisco12345** as the password.

Step 5: Confirm VPN connectivity.

When the full tunnel SSL VPN connection is established, an icon will appear in the system tray that signifies that the client has successfully connected to the SSL VPN network.

a. Display connection statistics and information by double-clicking the **AnyConnect** icon in the system tray. You will be able to disconnect the SSN VPN session from here. **Do Not** click **Disconnect** at this time. Click the **gear icon** at the bottom left corner of the Cisco AnyConnect Secure Mobility client window.

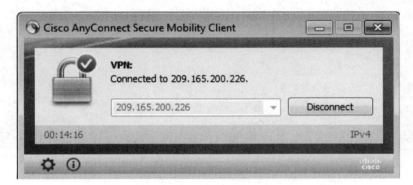

b. Use the scroll bar on the right side of the Virtual Private Network (VPN) – Statistics tab for additional connection information.

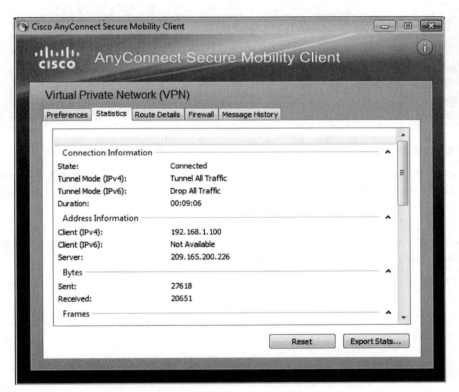

Note: The inside IP address that is assigned to the client from the VPN pool is 192.168.1.100-125.

c. From a command prompt on the remote host PC-C, verify the IP addressing by using the **ipconfig** command. Notice that there are two IP addresses listed. One is for the PC-C remote host local IP address (172.16.3.3) and the other is the IP address assigned to the SSL VPN tunnel (192.168.1.100).

```
C:\Windows\system32\cmd.exe

C:\Users\NetAcad>ipconfig

Windows IP Configuration

Ethernet adapter Local Area Connection 3:

   Connection-specific DNS Suffix   . : ccnasecurity.com
   IPv4 Address. . . . . . . . . . . : 192.168.1.100
   Subnet Mask . . . . . . . . . . . : 255.255.255.0
   Default Gateway . . . . . . . . . : 192.168.1.1

Ethernet adapter Local Area Connection:

   Connection-specific DNS Suffix   . :
   Link-local IPv6 Address . . . . . : fe80::70f5:f35c:59de:53a7%11
   IPv4 Address. . . . . . . . . . . : 172.16.3.3
   Subnet Mask . . . . . . . . . . . : 255.255.255.0
   Default Gateway . . . . . . . . . : 172.16.3.1

C:\Users\NetAcad>
```

d. From remote host PC-C, ping PC-B (**192.168.1.3**) to verify connectivity.

```
C:\Windows\system32\cmd.exe

C:\Users\NetAcad>ping 192.168.1.3

Pinging 192.168.1.3 with 32 bytes of data:
Reply from 192.168.1.3: bytes=32 time=4ms TTL=128
Reply from 192.168.1.3: bytes=32 time=4ms TTL=128
Reply from 192.168.1.3: bytes=32 time=9ms TTL=128
Reply from 192.168.1.3: bytes=32 time=4ms TTL=128

Ping statistics for 192.168.1.3:
    Packets: Sent = 4, Received = 4, Lost = 0 (0% loss),
Approximate round trip times in milli-seconds:
    Minimum = 4ms, Maximum = 9ms, Average = 5ms

C:\Users\NetAcad>
```

Step 6: Use the ASDM Monitor to view the AnyConnect remote user session.

Note: Future SSL VPN sessions can be launched through the web portal or through the installed Cisco AnyConnect SSL VPN client. While the remote user at PC-C is still logged in using the AnyConnect client, you can view the session statistics by using the ASDM monitor.

On the ASDM menu bar, click **Monitoring** and then select **VPN** > **VPN Statistics** > **Sessions**. Click the **Filter By** pull-down list and select **AnyConnect Client**. You should see the **VPN-User** session logged in from PC-C, which has been assigned an inside network IP address of 192.168.1.100 by the ASA.

Note: You may need to click **Refresh** to display the remote user session.

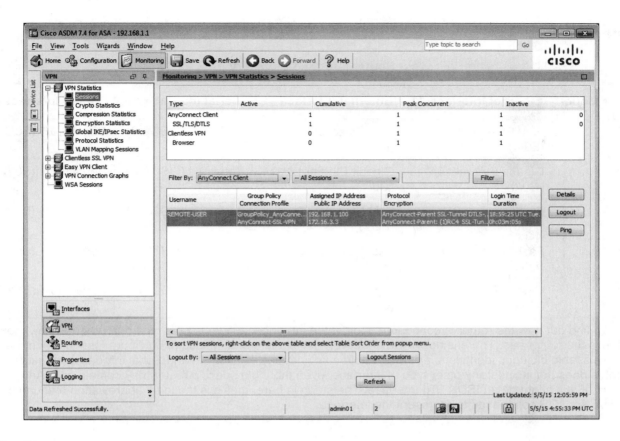

Reflection

1. Describe at least two benefits of client–based vs. clientless VPNs?

_____

_____

_____

_____

_____

2. Describe at least one difference between using SSL compared to IPsec for remote access tunnel encryption?

_____

_____

_____

_____

Router Interface Summary Table

Router Interface Summary				
Router Model	Ethernet Interface #1	Ethernet Interface #2	Serial Interface #1	Serial Interface #2
1800	Fast Ethernet 0/0 (F0/0)	Fast Ethernet 0/1 (Fa0/1)	Serial 0/0/0 (S0/0/0)	Serial 0/0/1 (S0/0/1)
1900	Gigabit Ethernet 0/0 (G0/0)	Gigabit Ethernet 0/1 (G0/1)	Serial 0/0/0 (S0/0/0)	Serial 0/0/1 (S0/0/1)
2801	Fast Ethernet 0/0 (F0/0)	Fast Ethernet 0/1 (F0/1)	Serial 0/1/0 (S0/1/0)	Serial 0/1/1 (S0/1/1)
2811	Fast Ethernet 0/0 (F0/0)	Fast Ethernet 0/1 (F0/1)	Serial 0/0/0 (S0/0/0)	Serial 0/0/1 (S0/0/1)
2900	Gigabit Ethernet 0/0 (G0/0)	Gigabit Ethernet 0/1 (G0/1)	Serial 0/0/0 (S0/0/0)	Serial 0/0/1 (S0/0/1)

Note: To find out how the router is configured, look at the interfaces to identify the type of router and how many interfaces the router has. There is no way to effectively list all the combinations of configurations for each router class. This table includes identifiers for the possible combinations of Ethernet and Serial interfaces in the device. The table does not include any other type of interface, even though a specific router may contain one. An example of this might be an ISDN BRI interface. The string in parenthesis is the legal abbreviation that can be used in Cisco IOS commands to represent the interface.

Chapter 11: Managing a Secure Network

Lab 11.3.1.2 – CCNA Security Comprehensive Lab

Topology

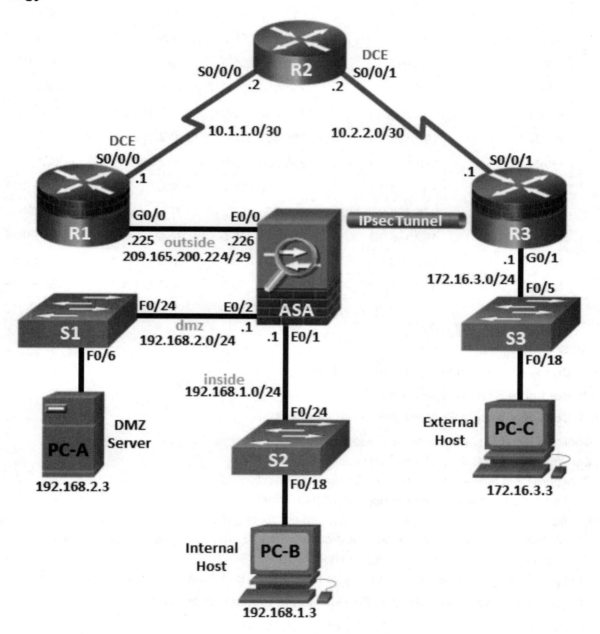

IP Addressing Table

Device	Interface	IP Address	Subnet Mask	Default Gateway	Switch Port
R1	G0/0	209.165.200.225	255.255.255.248	N/A	ASA E0/0
	S0/0/0 (DCE)	10.1.1.1	255.255.255.252	N/A	N/A
	Loopback 1	172.20.1.1	255.255.255.0	N/A	N/A
R2	S0/0/0	10.1.1.2	255.255.255.252	N/A	N/A
	S0/0/1 (DCE)	10.2.2.2	255.255.255.252	N/A	N/A
R3	G0/1	172.16.3.1	255.255.255.0	N/A	S3 F0/5
	S0/0/1	10.2.2.1	255.255.255.252	N/A	N/A
S1	VLAN 1	192.168.2.11	255.255.255.0	192.168.2.1	N/A
S2	VLAN 1	192.168.1.11	255.255.255.0	192.168.1.1	N/A
S3	VLAN 1	172.16.1.11	255.255.255.0	172.30.3.1	N/A
ASA	VLAN 1 (E0/1)	192.168.1.1	255.255.255.0	N/A	S2 F0/24
	VLAN 2 (E0/0)	209.165.200.226	255.255.255.248	N/A	R1 G0/0
	VLAN 2 (E0/2)	192.168.2.1	255.255.255.0	N/A	S1 F0/24
PC-A	NIC	192.168.2.3	255.255.255.0	192.168.2.1	S1 F0/6
PC-B	NIC	192.168.1.3	255.255.255.0	192.168.1.1	S2 F0/18
PC-C	NIC	172.16.3.3	255.255.255.0	172.16.3.1	S3 F0/18

Objectives

Part 1: Create a Basic Technical Security Policy

Part 2: Configure Basic Device Settings

Part 3: Configure Secure Router Administrative Access

- Configure encrypted passwords and a login banner.
- Configure the EXEC timeout value on console and VTY lines.
- Configure login failure rates and VTY login enhancements.
- Configure Secure Shell (SSH) access and disable Telnet.
- Configure local authentication, authorization, and accounting (AAA) user authentication.
- Secure the router against login attacks, and secure the IOS image and the configuration file.
- Configure a router NTP server and router NTP clients.
- Configure router syslog reporting and a syslog server on a local host.

Part 4: Configure a Zone-Based Policy Firewall and Intrusion Prevention System

- Configure a Zone-Based Policy Firewall (ZPF) on an ISR using the CLI.
- Configure an intrusion prevention system (IPS) on an ISR using the CLI.

Part 5: Secure Network Switches

- Configure passwords and a login banner.
- Configure management VLAN access.
- Secure access ports.
- Protect against Spanning Tree Protocol (STP) attacks.
- Configure port security and disable unused ports.

Part 6: Configure ASA Basic Settings and Firewall

- Configure basic settings, passwords, date, and time.
- Configure the inside and outside VLAN interfaces.
- Configure port address translation (PAT) for the inside network.
- Configure a Dynamic Host Configuration Protocol (DHCP) server for the inside network.
- Configure administrative access via Telnet and SSH.
- Configure a static default route for the Adaptive Security Appliance (ASA).
- Configure Local AAA user authentication.
- Configure a DMZ with a static NAT and ACL.
- Verify address translation and firewall functionality.

Part 7 Configure a DMZ, Static NAT, and ACLs on an ASA

Part 8: Configure ASA Clientless SSL VPN Remote Access Using ASDM

- Configure a remote access SSL VPN using the Cisco Adaptive Security Device Manager (ASDM).
- Verify SSL VPN access to the portal.

Part 9: Configure a Site-to-Site VPN between the ASA and ISR

- Configure an IPsec site-to-site VPN between the ASA and R3 using ASDM and the CLI.
- Activate and verify the IPsec site-to-site VPN tunnel between the ASA and R3.

Background/Scenario

This comprehensive lab is divided into nine parts. The parts should be completed sequentially. In Part 1, you will create a basic technical security policy. In Part 2, you will configure the basic device settings. In Part 3, you will secure a network router using the command-line interface (CLI) to configure IOS features, including AAA and SSH. In Part 4, you will configure a ZPF and IPS on an ISR. In Part 5, you will configure a network switch using the CLI. In Parts 7 and 8, you will configure the ASA firewall functionality and clientless SSL VPN remote access. In Part 9, you will configure a site-to-site VPN between the ASA and R3.

Note: The router commands and output in this lab are from a Cisco 1941 router with Cisco IOS Release 15.4(3)M2 (with a Security Technology Package license). The switch commands and output are from Cisco WS-C2960-24TT-L switches with Cisco IOS Release 15.0(2)SE4 (C2960-LANBASEK9-M image). Other routers, switches, and Cisco IOS versions can be used. See the Router Interface Summary Table at the end of the lab to determine which interface identifiers to use based on the equipment in the lab. Depending on the router, or switch model and Cisco IOS version, the commands available and the output produced might vary from what is shown in this lab.

The ASA used with this lab is a Cisco model 5505 with an 8-port integrated switch, running OS version 9.2(3) and the Adaptive Security Device Manager (ASDM) version 7.4(1) and comes with a Base license that allows a maximum of three VLANs.

Note: Before beginning, ensure that the routers and switches have been erased and have no startup configurations.

Required Resources

- 1 ASA 5505 (OS version 9.2(3) and ASDM version 7.4(1) and Base license or comparable)
- 3 routers (Cisco 1941 with Cisco IOS Release 15.4(3)M2 image with a Security Technology package license)
- 3 switches (Cisco 2960 or comparable) (not required)
- 3 PCs (Windows 7 or Windows 8.1, SSH Client, and WinRadius)
- Serial and Ethernet cables, as shown in the topology
- Console cables to configure Cisco networking devices

Part 1: Create a Basic Technical Security Policy (Chapters 1 and 11)

In Part 1, you will create a Network Device Security Guidelines document that can serve as part of a comprehensive network security policy. This document addresses specific router and switch security measures and describes the security requirements to be implemented on the infrastructure equipment.

Task 1: Identify Potential Sections of a Basic Network Security Policy.

A network security policy should include several key sections that can address potential issues for users, network access, device access, and other areas. List some key sections you think could be part of a basic security policy.

_____

_____

_____

_____

Task 2: Create a "Network Equipment Security Guidelines" Document As a Supplement to a Basic Security Policy

Step 1: Review the objectives from previous CCNA Security labs.

a. Open each of the labs completed from chapters 1 to 9, and review the objectives listed for each one.

b. Copy the objectives to a separate document and use it as a starting point. Focus on the objectives that involve security practices and device configuration.

Step 2: Create a "Network Device Security Guidelines" document for router and switch security.

Create a high-level list of tasks to include for network access and device security. This document should reinforce and supplement the information presented in a basic security policy. It is based on the content of previous CCNA Security labs and on the networking devices present in the course lab topology.

Note: The "Network Device Security Guidelines" document should be no more than two pages, and will be the basis for the equipment configuration in the remaining parts of the lab.

Step 3: Submit the "Network Device Security Guidelines" to your instructor.

Provide the "Network Device Security Guidelines" document to your instructor for review before starting Part 2 of this lab. You can send the document as an e-mail attachment or put it on removable storage media, such as a flash drive.

Part 2: Configure Basic Device Settings (Chapters 2 and 6)

Step 1: Cable the network as shown in the topology.

Attach the devices, as shown in the topology diagram, and cable as necessary.

Step 2: Configure basic settings for all routers.

a.   Configure hostnames, as shown in the topology.

b.   Configure the interface IP addresses, as shown in the IP addressing table.

c.   Configure a serial interface DCE clock rate of **128000** for the routers, if using routers other than those specified with this lab.

d.   Disable DNS lookup on each router.

Step 3: Configure static default routes on R1 and R3.

a.   Configure a static default route from R1 to R2 and from R3 to R2.

b.   Configure static routes from R2 to the R1 simulated LAN (Loopback 1), the R1 Fa0/0-to-ASA subnet, and the R3 LAN.

Step 4: Configure basic settings for each switch.

a.   Configure hostnames, as shown in the topology.

b.   Configure the VLAN 1 management address on each switch, as shown in the IP Addressing table.

c.   Configure the IP default gateway for each of the three switches.

d.   Disable DNS lookup on each switch.

Step 5: Configure PC host IP settings.

Configure a static IP address, subnet mask, and default gateway for each PC, as shown in the IP Addressing table.

Step 6: Verify connectivity between PC-C and R1 G0/0.

Step 7: Save the basic running configuration for each router and switch.

Part 3: Configure Secure Router Administrative Access (Chapters 2 and 3)

You will use the CLI to configure passwords and device access restrictions.

Task 1: Configure Settings for R1 and R3

Step 1: Configure a minimum password length of 10 characters.

Step 2: Encrypt plaintext passwords.

Step 3: Configure a login warning banner.

Configure a warning to unauthorized users with a message-of-the-day (MOTD) banner that says: **Unauthorized access strictly prohibited and prosecuted to the full extent of the law!**.

Step 4: Configure the enable secret password.

Use **cisco12345** as the **enable secret** password. Use the strongest encryption type available.

Step 5: Configure the local user database.

Create a local user account of **Admin01** with a secret password of **Admin01pa55** and a privilege level of **15**. Use the strongest encryption type available.

Step 6: Enable AAA services.

Step 7: Implement AAA services using the local database.

Create the default login authentication method list. Use case-sensitive local authentication as the first option and the enable password as the backup option to be used if an error occurs in relation to local authentication.

Step 8: Configure the console line.

Configure the console line for privilege level 15 access on login. Set the **exec-timeout** value to log out after 15 minutes of inactivity. Prevent console messages from interrupting command entry.

Step 9: Configure the VTY lines.

Configure the VTY lines for privilege level 15 access on login. Set the **exec-timeout** value to log out a session after **15** minutes of inactivity. Allow for remote access using SSH only.

Step 10: Configure the router to log login activity.

a. Configure the router to generate system logging messages for successful and failed login attempts. Configure the router to log every successful login. Configure the router to log every second failed login attempt.

b. Issue the **show login** command. What additional information is displayed?

_____

_____

Step 11: Enable HTTP access.

a. Enable the HTTP server on R1 to simulate an Internet target for later testing.

b. Configure HTTP authentication to use the local user database on R1.

Task 2: Configure the SSH Server on R1 and R3

Step 1: Configure the domain name.

Configure a domain name of **ccnasecurity.com**.

Step 2: Generate the RSA encryption key pair.

Configure the RSA keys with **1024** as the number of modulus bits.

Step 3: Configure the SSH version.

Specify that the router accept only **SSH version 2** connections.

Step 4: Configure SSH timeouts and authentication parameters.

The default SSH timeouts and authentication parameters can be altered to be more restrictive. Configure SSH timeout to **90** seconds and the number of authentication attempts to **2**.

Step 5: Verify SSH connectivity to R1 from PC-C.

a. Launch the SSH client on PC-C, enter the R1 S0/0/0 IP address (**10.1.1.1**), and log in as **Admin01** with the password **Admin01pa55**. If prompted by the SSH client with a security alert regarding the server's host key, click **Yes**.

b. Issue the **show run** command from the SSH session on PC-C. The configuration for R1 should be displayed.

Task 3: Secure against Login Attacks and Secure the IOS and Configuration File on R1

Step 1: Configure enhanced login security.

If a user experiences two failed login attempts within a **30**-second time span, disable logins for **1** minute. Log all failed login attempts.

Step 2: Secure the Cisco IOS image and archive a copy of the running configuration.

a. The **secure boot-image** command enables Cisco IOS image resilience, which hides the file from the **dir** and **show** commands. The file cannot be viewed, copied, modified, or removed using EXEC mode commands. (It can be viewed in ROMMON mode.)

b. The **secure boot-config** command takes a snapshot of the router running configuration and securely archives it in persistent storage (flash).

Step 3: Verify that your image and configuration are secured.

a. You can use only the **show secure bootset** command to display the archived filename. Display the status of configuration resilience and the primary bootset filename.

What is the name of the archived running config file and on what is the name based?

_____

_____

b. Save the running configuration to the startup configuration from the privileged EXEC mode prompt.

Step 4: Restore the IOS and configuration files back to the default setting.

You have verified the Secure IOS and configuration file settings. Now, use the **no secure boot-image** and **no secure boot config** commands to restore the default settings for these files.

Task 4: Configure a Synchronized Time Source Using NTP

R2 will be the master NTP clock source for R1 and R3.

Step 1: Set up the NTP master using Cisco IOS commands.

R2 is the master NTP server in this lab. All other routers and switches learn the time from it, either directly or indirectly. For this reason, you must ensure that R2 has the correct UTC set.

a. Use the **show clock** command to display the current time set on the router.

b. Use the **clock set** *time* command to set the time on the router.

c. Configure NTP authentication by defining the authentication key number **1** with **md5** hashing, and a password of **NTPpassword**. The password is case sensitive.

d. Configure the trusted key that will be used for authentication on R2.

e. Enable the NTP authentication feature on R2.

f. Configure R2 as the NTP master using the **ntp master** *stratum-number* command in global configuration mode. The stratum number indicates the distance from the original source. For this lab, use a stratum number of **3** on R2. When a device learns the time from an NTP source, its stratum number becomes one greater than the stratum number of its source.

Step 2: Configure R1 and R3 as NTP clients using the CLI.

a. Configure NTP authentication by defining the authentication key number **1** with **md5** hashing, and a password of **NTPpassword**.

b. Configure the trusted key that will be used for authentication. This command provides protection against accidentally synchronizing the device with a time source that is not trusted.

c. Enable the NTP authentication feature.

d. R1 and R3 will become NTP clients of R2. Use the **ntp server** *hostname* global configuration mode command. Use R2's serial IP address for the hostname. Issue the **ntp update-calendar** command on R1 and R3 to periodically update the calendar with the NTP time.

e. Use the **show ntp associations** command to verify that R1 has made an association with R2. You can also use the more verbose version of the command by adding the *detail* argument. It might take some time for the NTP association to form.

f. Verify the time on R1 and R3 after they have made NTP associations with R2.

Task 5: Configure Syslog Support on R3 and PC-C

Step 1: Install the syslog server on PC-C.

a. The Tftpd32 software from jounin.net is free to download and install, and it includes a TFTP server, TFTP client, and a syslog server and viewer. If not already installed, download Tftpd32 at http://tftpd32.jounin.net and install it on PC-C.

b. Run the **Tftpd32.exe** file, click **Settings**, and ensure that the **syslog serve**r check box is checked. In the **SYSLOG** tab, you can configure a file for saving syslog messages. Close the settings and in the main Tftpd32 interface window, note the server interface IP address and select the **Syslog server** tab to bring it to the foreground.

Step 2: Configure R3 to log messages to the syslog server using the CLI.

a. Verify that you have connectivity between R3 and PC-C by pinging the R3 G0/1 interface IP address **172.16.3.1**. If it is unsuccessful, troubleshoot as necessary before continuing.

b. NTP was configured in Task 2 to synchronize the time on the network. Displaying the correct time and date in syslog messages is vital when using syslog to monitor a network. If the correct time and date of a message is not known, it can be difficult to determine what network event caused the message.

Verify that the timestamp service for logging is enabled on the router by using the **show run** command. Use the **service timestamps log datetime msec** command if the timestamp service is not enabled.

c. Configure the syslog service on the router to send syslog messages to the syslog server.

Step 3: Configure the logging severity level on R3.

Logging traps can be set to support the logging function. A trap is a threshold that triggers a log message. The level of logging messages can be adjusted to allow the administrator to determine what kinds of messages are sent to the syslog server. Routers support different levels of logging. The eight levels range from 0 (emergencies), which indicates that the system is unstable, to 7 (debugging), which sends messages that include router information.

Note: The default level for syslog is 6 (informational logging). The default for console and monitor logging is 7 (debugging).

a.   Use the **logging trap** command to set the severity level for R3 to level 4 (**warnings**).

b.   Use the **show logging** command to see the type and level of logging enabled.

Part 4: Configure a Zone-Based Policy Firewall and Intrusion Prevention System (Chapters 4 and 5)

In Part 4, you will configure a ZPF and IPS on R3 using the CLI.

Task 1: Configure a ZPF on R3 using the CLI

Step 1: Creating the security zones.

a.   Create the **INSIDE** and **OUTSIDE** security zones.

b.   Create an inspect class-map to match the traffic to be allowed from the **INSIDE** zone to the **OUTSIDE** zone. Because we trust the **INSIDE** zone, we allow all the main protocols. Use the **match-any** keyword to instruct the router that the following **match** protocol statements will qualify as a successful match. This results in a policy being applied. Match for **TCP**, **UDP**, or **ICMP** packets.

c.   Create an inspect policy-map named **INSIDE-TO-OUTSIDE**. Bind the **INSIDE-PROTOCOLS** class-map to the policy-map. All packets matched by the **INSIDE-PROTOCOLS** class-map will be inspected.

d.   Create a zone-pair called **INSIDE-TO-OUTSIDE** that allows traffic initiated from the internal network to the external network but does not allow traffic originating from the external network to reach the internal network.

e.   Apply the policy-map to the zone-pair.

f.   Assign R3's G0/1 interface to the **INSIDE** security zone and the S0/0/1 interface to the **OUTSIDE** security zone.

g.   Verify your ZPF configuration by using the **show zone-pair security**, **show policy-map type inspect zone-pair,** and **show zone security** commands.

Task 2: Configure IPS on R3 using the CLI.

Step 1: Prepare router R3 and the TFTP server.

To configure Cisco IOS IPS 5.x, the IOS IPS signature package file and public crypto key files must be available on the PC with the TFTP server installed. R3 uses PC-C as the TFTP server. Ask your instructor if these files are not on the PC.

a.   Verify that the **IOS-Sxxx-CLI.pkg** signature package file is in the default TFTP folder. The *xxx* is the version number and varies depending on which file was downloaded from Cisco.com.

b.   Verify that the **realm-cisco.pub.key.txt** file is available and note its location on PC-C. This is the public crypto key used by Cisco IOS IPS.

c. Verify or create the IPS directory (**ipsdir**) in router flash on R3. From the R3 CLI, display the content of flash memory and check to see if the **ipsdir** directory exists.

d. If the **ipsdir** directory is not listed, create it in privileged EXEC mode, using the **mkdir** command.

Note: If the IPSDIR directory is listed and there are files in it, contact your instructor. This directory must be empty before configuring IPS. If there are no files in it, you may proceed to configure IPS.

Step 2: Verify the IOS IPS signature package location and TFTP server setup.

a. Use the **ping** command to verify connectivity between R3, PC-C, and the TFTP server.

b. Start Tftpd32 (or another TFTP server) and set the default directory to the one with the IPS signature package in it. Note the filename for use in the next step.

Step 3: Copy and paste the crypto key file into R3's configuration.

In global configuration mode, select and copy the crypto key file named **realm-cisco.pub.key.txt**. Paste the copied crypto key content at the global configuration mode prompt.

Note: The contents of the realm-cisco.pub.key.txt file have been provided below:

```
crypto key pubkey-chain rsa
 named-key realm-cisco.pub signature
  key-string
   30820122 300D0609 2A864886 F70D0101 01050003 82010F00 3082010A 02820101
   00C19E93 A8AF124A D6CC7A24 5097A975 206BE3A2 06FBA13F 6F12CB5B 4E441F16
   17E630D5 C02AC252 912BE27F 37FDD9C8 11FC7AF7 DCDD81D9 43CDABC3 6007D128
   B199ABCB D34ED0F9 085FADC1 359C189E F30AF10A C0EFB624 7E0764BF 3E53053E
   5B2146A9 D7A5EDE3 0298AF03 DED7A5B8 9479039D 20F30663 9AC64B93 C0112A35
   FE3F0C87 89BCB7BB 994AE74C FA9E481D F65875D6 85EAF974 6D9CC8E3 F0B08B85
   50437722 FFBE85B9 5E4189FF CC189CB9 69C46F9C A84DFBA5 7A0AF99E AD768C36
   006CF498 079F88F8 A3B3FB1F 9FB7B3CB 5539E1D1 9693CCBB 551F78D2 892356AE
   2F56D826 8918EF3C 80CA4F4D 87BFCA3B BFF668E9 689782A5 CF31CB6E B4B094D3
   F3020301 0001
  quit
```

Step 4: Configure the IPS settings on R3 from the CLI.

a. Create an IPS rule, and name the rule **IOSIPS**.

b. Set the IPS Signature storage location to the **IPSDIR** directory you created in flash in step 1d.

c. Enable HTTP server and IPS SDEE event notification.

d. Configure IOS IPS to use one of the pre-defined signature categories.

Note: When configuring IOS IPS, it is required to first retire all the signatures in the "all" category and then unretire selected signature categories.

After you have retired all signatures in the **all** category, unretire the **ios_ips basic** category.

e. Apply the IPS rule to inbound traffic to R3's S0/0/1 interface.

Step 5: Start the TFTP server on PC-C and verify the IPS file directory.

Verify that PC-C has the IPS Signature package file in a directory on the TFTP server. This file is typically named IOS-S*xxx*-CLI.pkg. The *xxx* is the signature file version.

Note: If this file is not present, contact your instructor before continuing.

Step 6: Copy the signature package from the TFTP server to R3.

a. Use the **copy tftp** command to retrieve the signature file and load it into the Intrusion Detection Configuration. Use the **idconf** keyword at the end of the **copy** command.

   Note: Signature compiling begins immediately after the signature package is loaded to the router. You can see the messages on the router with logging level 6 or above enabled.

b. Use the **dir flash** command to see the contents of the **IPSDIR** directory you created earlier in this lab. There should be six files, as shown here.

c. Use the **show ip ips signature count** command to see the counts for the compiled signature package.

```
R3# show ip ips signature count
```

   Note: You may see an error message during signature compilation, such as "%IPS-3-INVALID_DIGITAL_SIGNATURE: Invalid Digital Signature found (key not found)". The message means the public crypto key is invalid. Refer to Task 3, Configure the IPS Crypto Key, to reconfigure the public crypto key.

d. Use the **show ip ips all** command to view the IPS configuration status summary.

Part 5: Secure Network Switches (Chapter 6)

Note: Not all security features in this part of the lab will be configured on all switches. However, in a production network all security features would be configured on all switches.

Step 1: Configure basic security settings on S1

a. HTTP access to the switch is enabled by default. Prevent HTTP access by disabling the HTTP server and HTTP secure server.

   Use an enable secret password of **cisco12345**. Use the strongest encryption available.

b. Encrypt plaintext passwords.

c. Configure a warning to unauthorized users with an MOTD banner that says **"Unauthorized access strictly prohibited!"**.

Step 2: Configure SSH server settings on S1.

a. Configure a domain name.

b. Configure username **Admin01** in the local database with a password of **Admin01pa55**. Configure this user to have the highest possible privilege level. The strongest encryption method available should be used for the password.

c. Configure the RSA keys with 1024 modulus bits.

d. Enable SSH version 2.

e. Set the SSH time-out to **90** seconds and the number of authentication retries to **2**.

Step 3: Configure the console and VTY lines.

a. Configure a console to use the local database for login. If the user has the highest privileges, then automatically enable privilege exec mode upon login. Set the **exec-timeout** value to log out after five minutes of inactivity. Prevent console messages from interrupting command entry.

b. Configure VTY lines to use the local database for login. If the user has the highest privileges, then automatically enable privilege exec mode upon login. Set the **exec-timeout** value to log out after five minutes of inactivity. Allow remote SSH access to all VTY lines

Step 4: Configure Port Security and Disable Unused Ports

Note: Configuration changes made in step 4 to interface F0/6 in a NETLAB+ environment may have an adverse effect on lab results because of a hidden control switch between S1 and PC-A. If you are performing this lab on a NETLAB+ pod, it is recommended that you perform configuration changes to F0/7 (an inactive port) instead of F0/6 for this step only.

a. Disable trunking on port F0/6.

b. Enable PortFast on F0/6.

c. Enable BPDU guard on F0/6.

d. Apply basic default port security on F0/6. This sets the maximum MAC addresses to 1 and the violation action to shut down. Use the sticky option to allow the secure MAC address that is dynamically learned on a port to the switch running configuration.

e. Disable unused ports on S1.

Step 5: Set loop guard as the default for all non-designated ports on S1.

Step 6: Save the running configuration to the startup configuration for each switch.

Part 6: Configure ASA Basic Settings and Firewall (Chapter 9)

Task 1: Prepare the ASA for ASDM Access

Step 1: Clear the previous ASA configuration settings.

a. Use the **write erase** command to remove the **startup-config** file from flash memory.

b. Use the **reload** command to restart the ASA.

Step 2: Bypass Setup Mode and configure the ASDM VLAN interfaces using the CLI.

a. When prompted to preconfigure the firewall through interactive prompts (Setup mode), respond with **no**.

b. Enter privileged EXEC mode. The password should be blank (no password) at this point.

c. Enter global configuration mode. Respond with **no** to the prompt to enable anonymous reporting.

d. The VLAN 1 logical interface will be used by PC-B to access ASDM on ASA physical interface E0/1. Configure interface **VLAN 1** and name it **inside**. The Security Level should be automatically set to the highest level of 100. Specify IP address **192.168.1.1** and subnet mask **255.255.255.0**.

e. Enable physical interface **E0/1**.

f. Preconfigure interface **VLAN 2**, name it **outside**, assign IP address **209.165.200.226**, and the subnet mask **255.255.255.248**. Notice that the VLAN is automatically assigned a 0 as the security level.

g. Assign **VLAN 2** to the physical interface **E0/0** and enable the interface.

h. Configure VLAN 3, which is where the public access web server will reside. Assign it IP address **192.168.2.1/24**, name it **dmz**, and assign it a security level of **70**.

Note: If you are working with the ASA 5505 base license, you will see the error message shown in the output below. The ASA 5505 Base license allows for the creation of up to three named VLAN interfaces. However, you must disable communication between the third interface and one of the other interfaces using the **no forward** command. This is not an issue if the ASA has a Security Plus license, which allows 20 named VLANs.

Because the server does not need to initiate communication with the inside users, disable forwarding to interface VLAN 1.

i. Assign **VLAN 3** to the interface **E0/2** and enable the interface.

j. Display the status of all ASA interfaces by using the **show interface ip brief** command.

k. Display the information for the Layer 3 VLAN interfaces by using the **show ip address** command.

l. Display the VLANs and port assignments on the ASA by using the **show switch vlan** command.

Step 3: Configure and verify access to the ASA from the inside network.

a. From PC-B, ping the ASA's inside interface (192.168.1.1). Pings should be successful.

b. Use the **http** command to configure the ASA to accept HTTPS connections and to allow access to ASDM from any host on the inside network (192.168.1.0/24).

c. Open a browser on PC-B and test the HTTPS access to the ASA by entering **https://192.168.1.1**.

d. From the ASDM Welcome page, click **Run ASDM**. When prompted for a username and password, leave them blank and click **OK**.

Task 2: Configure Basic ASA Settings Using the ASDM Startup Wizard

Step 1: Access the Configuration menu and launch the Startup wizard.

At the top left of the screen, click **Configuration** > **Launch Startup wizard**.

Step 2: Configure the hostname, domain name, and the enable password.

a. On the first Startup wizard screen, select the **Modify Existing Configuration** option.

b. On the Startup Wizard Step 2 screen, configure the ASA hostname **CCNAS-ASA** and domain name **ccnasecurity.com**. Change the enable mode password from blank (no password) to **cisco12345**.

Step 3: Verify the VLAN and interface settings.

a. On the Startup Wizard Step 3 screen, do not change the current settings; these were previously defined using the CLI.

b. On the Startup Wizard Step 4 screen, verify that port **Ethernet 0/1** is allocated to inside VLAN 1 and that port **Ethernet 0/0** is allocated to Outside VLAN 2.

c. On the Startup Wizard Step 5 screen verify the Outside and Inside IP address settings are correct. Click **Next**.

Step 4: Configure DHCP, address translation, and administrative access.

a. On the Startup Wizard Step 6 screen – DHCP Server, select **Enable DHCP server on the Inside Interface** and specify a starting IP address of **192.168.1.5** and an ending IP address of **192.168.1.30**. Enter the DNS Server 1 address of **10.3.3.3** and enter **ccnasecurity.com** for the domain name. Do **NOT** check the box to enable auto-configuration from interface.

b. On the Startup Wizard Step 7 screen – Address Translation (NAT/PAT), configure the ASA to **Use Port Address Translation (PAT)** and select the **Use the IP address of the outside interface** option.

c. On the Startup Wizard Step 8 screen – Administrative Access, HTTPS/ASDM access is currently configured for hosts on the inside network (192.168.1.0/24). Add **SSH** access to the ASA for the **inside** network (**192.168.1.0**) with a subnet mask of **255.255.255.0**.

d. Finish the wizard and deliver the commands to the ASA.

Note: When prompted to log in again, leave the **Username** field blank and enter **cisco12345** as the password.

Task 3: Configuring ASA Settings from the ASDM Configuration Menu

Step 1: Set the ASA date and time.

At the **Configuration** > **Device Setup** screen, click **System Time** > **Clock.** Set the time zone, current date and time, and apply the commands to the ASA.

Step 2: Configure a static default route for the ASA.

a. At the **Configuration** > **Device Setup** screen, click **Routing** > **Static Routes**. Click the **IPv4 only** button and then add a static route for the **outside** interface. Specify **any4** for the Network and a Gateway IP of **209.165.200.225** (R1 G0/0). **Apply** the static route to the ASA.

b. On the ASDM **Tools** menu, select **Ping** and enter the IP address of router R1 S0/0/0 (**10.1.1.1**). The ping should succeed.

Step 3: Test access to an external website from PC-B.

Open a browser on PC-B and enter the IP address of the R1 S0/0/0 interface (**10.1.1.1**) to simulate access to an external website. The R1 HTTP server was enabled in Part 2 of this lab. You should be prompted with a user authentication login dialog box from the R1 GUI device manger. Exit the browser.

Note: You will be unable to ping from PC-B to R1 S0/0/0 because the default ASA application inspection policy does not permit ICMP from the internal network.

Step 4: Configure AAA for SSH client access.

a. At the **Configuration** > **Device Management** screen, click **Users/AAA** > **User Accounts** > **Add**. Create a new user named **Admin01** with a password of **Admin01pa55**. Allow this user **Full access** (ASDM, SSH, Telnet, and console) and set the privilege level to **15**. Apply the command to the ASA.

b. At the **Configuration** > **Device Management** screen, click **Users/AAA** > **AAA Access**. On the Authentication tab, require authentication for **HTTP/ASDM** and **SSH** connections and specify the **LOCAL** server group for each connection type. Click **Apply** to send the commands to the ASA.

Note: The next action you attempt within ASDM will require that you log in as **Admin01** with the password **Admin01pa55**.

c. From PC-B, open an SSH client and attempt to access the ASA inside interface at **192.168.1.1**. You should be able to establish the connection. When prompted to log in, enter username **Admin01** and the password **Admin01pa55**.

d. After logging in to the ASA using SSH, enter the **enable** command and provide the password **cisco12345**. Issue the **show run** command in order to display the current configuration you have created using ASDM. Close the SSH session.

Task 4: Modify the Default Modular Policy Framework using ASDM.

Step 1: Modify the MPF application inspection policy.

The default global inspection policy does not inspect ICMP. To enable hosts on the internal network to ping external hosts and receive replies, ICMP traffic must be inspected.

a.   From PC-B, select the ASDM **Configuration** screen > **Firewall** menu. Click **Service Policy Rules**.

b.   Select the **inspection_default** policy and click **Edit** to modify the default inspection rules. In the Edit Service Policy Rule window, click the **Rule Actions** tab and select the **ICMP** check box. Do not change the other default protocols that are checked. Click **OK** > **Apply** to send the commands to the ASA.

   Note: If prompted, log in as **Admin01** with the password **Admin01pa55**.

Step 2: Verify that returning ICMP traffic is allowed.

From PC-B, attempt to ping the R1 G0/0 interface at IP address **209.165.200.225**. The pings should be successful because ICMP traffic is now being inspected.

Part 7: Configuring a DMZ, Static NAT, and ACLs (Chapter 10)

In Part 6 of this lab, you configured address translation using PAT for the inside network using ASDM. In this part, you will use ASDM to configure the DMZ, Static NAT, and ACLs on the ASA.

To accommodate the addition of a DMZ and a web server, you will use another address from the ISP range assigned (209.165.200.224/29). R1 G0/0 and the ASA outside interface already use 209.165.200.225 and .226. You will use public address **209.165.200.227** and static NAT to provide address translation access to the server.

Step 1: Configure static NAT to the DMZ server using a network object.

a.   From PC-B, select the ASDM **Configuration** screen > **Firewall** menu. Click the **Public Servers** option and click **Add** to define the DMZ server and services offered. In the Add Public Server dialog box, specify the Private Interface as **dmz**, the Public Interface as **outside**, and the Public IP address as **209.165.200.227**.

b.   Click the ellipsis button to the right of Private IP Address. In the Browse Private IP Address window, click **Add** to define the server as a **Network Object**. Enter the name **DMZ-SERVER**, select **Host** for the Type, enter the Private IP Address of **192.168.2.3**, and a Description of **PC-A.**

c.   From the Browse Private IP Address window, verify that the DMZ-Server appears in the Selected Private IP Address field and click **OK**. You will return to the Add Public Server dialog box.

d.   In the Add Public Server dialog, click the ellipsis button to the right of Private Service. In the Browse Private Service window, double-click to select the following services: **tcp/ftp**, **tcp/http** and **icmp/echo** (scroll down to see all services). Click **OK** to continue and return to the **Add Public Server** dialog.

e.   Click **OK** to add the server. Click **Apply** at the Public Servers screen to send the commands to the ASA

Step 2: View the DMZ Access Rule (ACL) generated by ASDM.

With the creation of the DMZ server object and selection of services, ASDM automatically generates an Access Rule (ACL) to permit the appropriate access to the server and applies it to the outside interface in the incoming direction.

View this Access Rule in ASDM by clicking **Configuration** > **Firewall** > **Access Rules**. It appears as an outside incoming rule. You can select the rule and use the horizontal scroll bar to see all of the components.

Step 3: Test access to the DMZ server from the outside network.

a. From PC-C, ping the IP address of the static NAT public server address (**209.165.200.227**). The pings should be successful.

b. You can also access the DMZ server from a host on the inside network because the ASA inside interface (VLAN 1) is set to security level 100 (the highest) and the DMZ interface (VLAN 3) is set to 70. The ASA acts like a router between the two networks. Ping the DMZ server (PC-A) internal address (**192.168.2.3**) from PC-B. The pings should be successful due to the interface security level and the fact that ICMP is being inspected on the inside interface by the global inspection policy.

c. The DMZ server cannot ping PC-B because the DMZ interface VLAN 3 has a lower security level and because it was necessary to specify the **no forward** command when the VLAN 3 interface was created. Try to ping from the DMZ server PC-A to PC-B. The pings should not be successful.

Part 8: Configure ASA Clientless SSL VPN Remote Access (Chapter 10)

In Part 8 of this lab, you will use ASDM's Clientless SSL VPN wizard to configure the ASA to support clientless SSL VPN remote access. You will verify your configuration by using a browser from PC-C.

Step 1: Start the VPN wizard.

Using ASDM on PC-B, click **Wizards** > **VPN Wizards** > **Clientless SSL VPN wizard**. The SSL VPN wizard Clientless SSL VPN Connection screen displays.

Step 2: Configure the SSL VPN user interface.

On the SSL VPN Interface screen, configure **VPN-PROFILE** as the Connection Profile Name and specify **outside** as the interface to which outside users will connect.

Step 3: Configure AAA user authentication.

On the User Authentication screen, click **Authenticate Using the Local User Database** and enter the username **VPNuser** with a password of **Remotepa55**. Click **Add** to create the new user.

Step 4: Configure the VPN group policy.

On the Group Policy screen, create a new group policy named **VPN-GROUP**.

Step 5: Configure the bookmark list.

a. From the Clientless Connections Only – Bookmark List screen, click **Manage** to create an HTTP server bookmark in the bookmark list. In the Configure GUI Customization Objects window, click **Add** to open the Add Bookmark List window. Name the list **WebServer**.

b. Add a new bookmark with **Web Mail** as the Bookmark Title. Enter the server destination IP address of **192.168.1.3** (PC-B is simulating an internal web server) as the URL.

c. Click OK to complete the wizard and **Apply** to the ASA

Step 6: Verify VPN access from the remote host.

a. Open the browser on PC-C and enter the login URL for the SSL VPN into the address field (**https://209.165.200.226**). Use secure HTTP (HTTPS) because SSL is required to connect to the ASA.

Note: Accept security notification warnings.

b. The Login window should display. Enter the previously configured username **VPNuser**, enter the password **Remotepa55**, and click **Logon** to continue.

Step 7: Access the web portal window.

After the user authenticates, the ASA SSL web portal webpage will be displayed. This webpage lists the bookmarks previously assigned to the profile. If the bookmark points to a valid server IP address or hostname that has HTTP web services installed and functional, the outside user can access the server from the ASA portal.

Note: In this lab, the web mail server is not installed on PC-B.

Part 9: Configure a Site-to-Site IPsec VPN between R3 and the ASA. (Chapters 8 & 10)

In Part 9 of this lab, you will use the CLI to configure an IPsec VPN tunnel on R3 and use ASDM's Site-to-Site Wizard to configure the other side of the IPsec tunnel on the ASA.

Task 1: Configure the Site-to-Site IPsec VPN Tunnel on R3

Step 1: Enable IKE and configure the ISAKMP policy parameters.

a. Verify that IKE is supported and enabled.

b. Create an ISAKMP policy with a priority number of **1**. Use **pre-shared key** as the authentication type, **3des** for the encryption algorithm, **sha** as the hash algorithm, and the Diffie-Helman group **2** key exchange.

c. Configure the pre-shared key of **Site2SiteKEY1** and point it to the ASA's outside interface IP address.

d. Verify the IKE policy with the **show crypto isakmp policy** command.

Step 2: Configure the IPsec transform set and lifetime.

Create a transform set with tag **TRNSFRM-SET** and use an ESP transform with an AES 256 cipher with ESP and the SHA hash function.

Step 3: Define interesting traffic.

Configure the IPsec VPN interesting traffic ACL. Use extended access list number **101**. The source network should be R3's LAN (172.16.3.0/24), and the destination network should be the ASA's LAN (192.168.1.0/24).

Step 4: Create and apply a crypto map.

a. Create the crypto map on R3, name it **CMAP**, and use **1** as the sequence number.

b. Use the **match address <access-list>** command to specify which access list defines which traffic to encrypt.

c. Set the peer address to the ASA's remote VPN endpoint interface IP address (**209.165.200.226**).

d. Set the transform set to **TRNSFRM-SET**.

e. Apply the crypto map to R3's S0/0/1 interface.

Step 5: Verify IPsec configuration on R3.

Use the **show crypto map** and **show crypto ipsec sa** commands to verify R3's IPsec VPN configuration.

Task 2: Configure Site-to-Site VPN on ASA using ASDM

Step 1: Use a browser on PC-B to establish an ASDM session to the ASA.

a. After the ASDM is established, use the **Site-to-Site VPN Wizard** to configure the ASA for IPsec site-to-site VPN.

b. Set the Peer IP Address to R3's S0/0/1 IP address (**10.2.2.1**). Verify that **outside** is selected for the VPN Access Interface.

c. Identify the traffic to protect. Set the Local Network to **inside-network/24** and the Remote Network to **172.16.3.0/24**.

d. Configure the pre-shared key. Enter the Pre-shared Key of **Site2SiteKEY1**.

e. Enable NAT exemption. Check the **Exempt ASA side host/network from address translation** box and verify that the **inside** interface is selected.

Step 2: Apply IPsec configuration to the ASA.

Click **Finish** to apply the site-to-site configuration to the ASA.

Task 3: Test the Site-to-Site IPsec VPN Connection between the ASA and R3

Step 1: From PC-B, ping R3's LAN interface.

This should access the IPsec Site-to-site VPN connection between the ASA and R3.

Step 2: Verify the IPsec Site-to-Site VPN session is active.

a. From ASDM on PC-B, click the **Monitoring>VPN** menu. A connection profile IP address of 10.2.2.1 should be displayed in the middle of the screen. Click the **Details** button to see IKE and IPsec session details.

b. Issue the **show crypto isakmp sa** command to verify that an IKE security association (SA) is active.

c. From PC-C, issue the command **tracert 192.168.1.3**. If the site-to-site VPN tunnel is working correctly, you will not see traffic being routed through R2 (10.2.2.2).

d. Issue the **show crypto ipsec sa** command on R3 to view the number of packets that have been encapsulated and decapsulated. Verify that there are no failed packet attempts or send and receive errors.

Router Interface Summary Table

Router Interface Summary				
Router Model	**Ethernet Interface #1**	**Ethernet Interface #2**	**Serial Interface #1**	**Serial Interface #2**
1700	Fast Ethernet 0 (F0)	Fast Ethernet 1 (F1)	Serial 0 (S0)	Serial 1 (S1)
1800	Fast Ethernet 0/0 (F0/0)	Fast Ethernet 0/1 (F0/1)	Serial 0/0/0 (S0/0/0)	Serial 0/0/1 (S0/0/1)
1900	Gigabit Ethernet 0/0 (G0/0)	Gigabit Ethernet 0/1 (G0/1)	Serial 0/0/0 (S0/0/0)	Serial 0/0/1 (S0/0/1)
2801	Fast Ethernet 0/0 (F0/0)	Fast Ethernet 0/1 (F0/1)	Serial 0/1/0 (S0/1/0)	Serial 0/1/1 (S0/1/1)
2811	Fast Ethernet 0/0 (F0/0)	Fast Ethernet 0/1 (F0/1)	Serial 0/0/0 (S0/0/0)	Serial 0/0/1 (S0/0/1)
2900	Gigabit Ethernet 0/0 (G0/0)	Gigabit Ethernet 0/1 (G0/1)	Serial 0/0/0 (S0/0/0)	Serial 0/0/1 (S0/0/1)

Note: To find out how the router is configured, look at the interfaces to identify the type of router and how many interfaces the router has. There is no way to effectively list all the combinations of configurations for each router class. This table includes identifiers for the possible combinations of Ethernet and Serial interfaces in the device. The table does not include any other type of interface, even though a specific router may contain one. An example of this might be an ISDN BRI interface. The string in parenthesis is the legal abbreviation that can be used in Cisco IOS commands to represent the interface.